**Handbook of Publicity
and Public Relations
for the Nonprofit Organization**

Handbook of Publicity and Public Relations for the Nonprofit Organization

ROBERT H. RUFFNER

Prentice-Hall, Inc.
Englewood Cliffs, New Jersey

Prentice-Hall International, Inc., *London*
Prentice-Hall of Australia, Pty. Ltd., *Sydney*
Prentice-Hall Canada Inc., *Toronto*
Prentice-Hall of India Private Ltd., *New Delhi*
Prentice-Hall of Japan, Inc., *Tokyo*
Prentice-Hall of Southeast Asia Pte. Ltd., *Singapore*
Whitehall Books, Ltd., Wellington, *New Zealand*
Editora Prentice-Hall do Brasil, Ltda., *Rio de Janeiro*

Library of Congress Cataloging in Publication Data

Ruffner, Robert H.
  Handbook of publicity and public relations for the
nonprofit organization.

  Includes bibliographical references and index.
  1. Public relations—United States—Endowments.
2. Endowments—United States—Management. 3. Corporations,
Nonprofit—United States—Management. I. Title.
HV97.A3R83   1984   659.2′9361763′0973   84-3379

ISBN 0-13-380528-X

Printed in the United States of America

DEDICATION

To Margaret Call Sharood.

ACKNOWLEDGMENTS

My appreciation to the nonprofit organizations which are leading, educating, challenging, changing and enriching the lives of all Americans.

Through the battle, through defeat,
moving yet and never stopping,
Pioneers! O pioneers!

Walt Whitman

My gratitude to my colleagues in public and private nonprofits, to my students at The American University, and to friends who have contributed to my development and growth.

My particular thanks to my wife, who has made this book possible by her continued interest and support.

THE AUTHOR

Robert H. Ruffner is a community relations planner and writer nationally recognized for communications programs developed for the President's Committee on Employment of the Handicapped. He has advised and counseled national and international organizations including the Agency for International Development, the World Rehabilitation Fund, the Canadian Rehabilitation Council for the Disabled, and the International Council for Public Relations in Rehabilitation.

Photo by Billy Rose

FOREWORD: The Nonprofit and Its Publics

Nonprofit organizations are the vital vanguard of American society. Creative, innovative, contentious, their roles range from guardian of the past to instigator of social, economic, and political change.

Nonprofits range from multimillion dollar health centers to world-renowned universities, from art museums to symphony orchestras to ballet groups, from churches to human service delivery agencies, from foundations to political parties, from trade and professional associations to think-tanks, from history clubs to private primary and secondary schools.

The nonprofit world is a big one. It is also a diverse and fluid one. An idea of the diversity can be seen from the Internal Revenue Service's Form 1040.

Examples of these organizations are:

- Churches, temples, synagogues, Salvation Army, Red Cross, CARE, Goodwill Industries, United Way, Boy Scouts, Girl Scouts, Boys Club of America, etc.
- Fraternal orders . . .
- Veterans' and certain cultural groups.
- Nonprofit schools, hospitals, and organizations whose purpose is to find a cure for, or help people who have arthritis, asthma, birth defects, cancer, cerebral palsy, cystic fibrosis, diabetes, heart disease, hemophilia, mental illness or retardation, multiple sclerosis, muscular dystrophy, tuberculosis, etc.
- Federal, State, and local governments if the gifts are solely for public purposes.

GOVERNMENT: THE SURPRISE NONPROFIT

The surprise entry on this Internal Revenue Service list of organizations that can receive tax-deductible contributions from citizens is the last one, "governments." Federal, state and local governments have long played an important role with private nonprofit organizations.

Exemptions from taxes, subsidization of postal service, loans, gifts of property, grants, legislation, are all long-standing established contributions to private nonprofits by all levels of government.

The past few decades, however, have seen a dramatic increase in government involvement with the nonprofit. New, quasi-private nonprofit organizations, the heart of the "public" nonprofits, have been established. These organizations include the National Public Radio and the Corporation for Public

Broadcasting. These new public nonprofits are joining a host of others that enjoy substantial government aid: the Red Cross, the U.S.O., the Smithsonian Institution.

Other public nonprofits include large art museums with lands and buildings owned by governments and with staffs supported by government funds. The Philadelphia Museum of Art and the Detroit Institute of Arts are two such examples.

Now, add to this list the hundreds of organizations that the government funds directly and that have depended entirely on these government funds for their existence. These organizations are found throughout the country, often providing human services. Because of their sole-source government funding in the past, these organizations have not actively sought alternative sources of funds and community support.

This situation has changed. Today these "public" nonprofits are actively competing with private nonprofits for government monies and community support. This community support embraces volunteers and funds and frequently takes the form of a "friends" group which attracts community support for a public nonprofit.

Many of yesterday's public nonprofits are becoming increasingly private in their actions. These public nonprofits constitute a strong competitor with the private nonprofit for community support.

TWO TIES THAT BIND

The first tie that binds together all nonprofits, public and private, is this community support. The community may be national, regional, urban, rural, or highly specific. The support sought includes funding, volunteers, members, consumers, public identity and opinion. Community support is fundamental to all nonprofits.

The second binding tie is the Internal Revenue Service (IRS). The IRS determines the tax-exempt status of the nonprofit, outlines the responsibilities of the nonprofit, establishes the rules and regulations under which a nonprofit operates if the tax-exempt status is to be maintained. All of this is done under Section 501 of the Internal Revenue Code of 1954. Additionally, the IRS determines, as seen in the above excerpt from Form 1040, which organizations may receive tax-deductible charitable contributions. It also determines which nonprofits may receive tax-deductible political or professional donations. The IRS is the determiner of the nonprofit and its findings are the nonprofit's life blood.

THE RISE OF THE NONPROFIT

Thousands of new nonprofits are formed each year. These organizations are joining the estimated 846,433 that qualified as private nonprofit organizations in 1980.[1] 165,614 of these organizations had at least one paid employee in 1977, a

---

[1]"Tax-Exemption Specialists Give and Take by the Rules," by Pete Earley, the *Washington Post*, January 27, 1982.

INTERNAL REVENUE SERVICE PUBLICATIONS
FORM 1040—1982
PUBLICATION 557, "TAX-EXEMPT STATUS FOR YOUR ORGANIZATION," 1982

payroll of 4.4 million people, and 1980 revenues exceeding $100 billion.[2] The non-profit is big business.

And it is a growing, vibrant big business. Individual concern is translated into national household recognition with amazing rapidity. Drunk driving, rights of victims of violence, bewildering new diseases are issues that rapidly rose into the nation's conscience and purse.

The ability to identify, respond to, and initiate action is the great strength of the nonprofit organization. The nonprofits are the eyes and ears of America, the conscience of society, the voice of the individual.

INDIVIDUALS: THE STRENGTH OF THE NONPROFIT

Jane Addams founded Hull House in Chicago in the late 19th Century. She also pioneered the profession of social work and instituted the nation's concern for people who needed help, and after receiving help, could help themselves. Jan Scruggs saw his one-man campaign to honor Vietnam veterans realized with the 1982 dedication of the Vietnam Memorial in Washington, D.C. These are individuals who provided leadership through nonprofit organizations.

The nonprofit's strength comes from the individual. It is the founders of the great foundations who wanted to contribute to their society. It is the man or woman calling the nation's attention and resources to a problem. It has been this individual concern that has generated the government's involvement with the nonprofit. This same individual will maintain government involvement and support for those nonprofits whose private resources cannot match the public need.

The individual, founder, supporter, contributor, is the backbone of the non-profit movement, yesterday, today, and tomorrow. Individual contributions to private nonprofits amounted to $39.9 billion in 1980.[3]

OTHER SUPPORTERS

Foundations and corporations contributed about $3 billion each to private nonprofit organizations last year, while the Federal Government alone provided $40.4 billion to service providing nonprofits in 1980.[4]

Government then is both provider and competitor. There are indications that the Federal Government has been providing a larger share of total revenues of private nonprofit organizations, other than religious ones, than all private giving combined (individual, foundation, corporation).

Government support of the private nonprofit is hard to track as it takes both direct and indirect form. In addition to tax-exempt status on the Federal level, there is tax exemption from property and sales taxes on the State and local levels. There are subsidies through lowered mail costs as well as direct grants and contracts.

---

[2]*The Federal Budget and the Nonprofit Sector,* by Lester M. Salamon & Alan J. Abramson. The Urban Institute Press, Washington DC. 1982.
[3]"The Challenge on Donations," by Kathleen Teltsch, the *New York Times*, November 4, 1981.
[4]*The Federal Budget and the Nonprofit Sector.*

Government at all levels is now, and will be, an important audience for the nonprofit. Fortunately for the private nonprofit, governments need them and depend upon them for services and other crucial functions. The private nonprofit is an effective competitor.

THE ALARM IS SOUNDED

A sampling of headlines sounds the alarm: "U.S. FUND CUTS FOUND TO PERIL SERVICE GROUPS." "RECESSION IMPACT HITS ARTS ORGANIZATIONS HARD, FORCING CUTBACKS AND LIMITING ANY INNOVATION." "THE DEATH OF A COLLEGE UNDERSCORES THE PLIGHT OF PRIVATE INSTITUTIONS." "AREA AGENCIES FACING CUTBACK IN THE MILLIONS." "THE MAILED FIST: NONPROFIT GROUPS HIT BY POSTAGE JUMP."[5]

The private nonprofit is responding to these headlines with a flurry of studies, conferences, and effective dialogues with government leaders. Some of these activities are having positive results and nonprofits are gaining skills and sophistication in dealing with hard times. It's too soon to tell, however, as indications are that there is more to come.

THE WORST OF TIMES

We are facing high unemployment, shrinking resources, the decline of America's industrial might. Mind-boggling expenditures on military, ever higher operating costs, new expenses for Social Security and employee benefits, rising costs of operating. Churches and charities have been forced to lay workers off, to freeze wages, to negotiate reductions with employees.

Rapid change is having a perplexing impact on the nonprofit. The impact of many of the changes is difficult to interpret: the apparent transition from an industrial to a "who knows" society; the working woman; the single parent; the migration from inner cities; the aging of the population; the decline in numbers of college-age people; public demand for accountability; public mistrust of government and other institutions; the falling-off of Americans affiliated with organized religions; the strength of the consumer movement; a growing self-help movement; the complexity and costs of medical care.

While the impact of these developments on the nonprofit may be hard to interpret, it seems clear that they will have a profound impact. How can the nonprofit deal effectively and surely in a rapidly changing country?

---

[5]"U.S. Fund Cuts Found to Peril Service Groups," by Joanne Omang, the *Washington Post*, September 2, 1982.

"Culture Crunch: Recession Impact Hits Arts Organizations Hard, Forcing Cutbacks and Limiting Any Innovation," by Cynthia Saltzman, the *Wall Street Journal*, December 7, 1982.

"Requiescat in Pace: The Death of a College Underscores the Plight of Private Institutions," by Anne Mackay-Smith, the *Wall Street Journal*, December 14, 1982.

"Area Agencies Facing Cutback in the Millions," by Peter Perl, the *Washington Post*, September 1982.

"The Mailed Fist: Nonprofit Groups Hit by Postage Jump," by Jane Seaberry, the *Washington Post*, January 7, 1982.

YOUR PUBLIC TO THE RESCUE

All nonprofits have their own publics. It may be a public reached in national fundraising campaigns; it may be a public of dues-paying members; it may be local, regional, or national. Publics are the source of the nonprofit's strength.

A particularly important public is the recipient: the season ticket holder, the member, the user, the consumer of the nonprofit's service. This public, potential, active and alumni, is the crucial one.

Other important publics include volunteers, staff, contributors. All of these publics will determine the nonprofit's future.

SUCCEEDING WITH YOUR PUBLIC

The importance of the nonprofit dictates the use of management techniques. Today's challenges and keen competition call for responses that professional management techniques can help to provide. Adapting and adopting these techniques are fundamental to the growth and success of the nonprofit organization.

Public relations is one of these management techniques that will greatly assist the nonprofit in succeeding with its public.

Robert H. Ruffner

What the *Handbook* Offers the Nonprofit Manager

Head in hands, today's nonprofit manager contemplates a bewildering complexity of trends and issues that appear to threaten the very existence of the organization.

The *Handbook of Publicity and Public Relations for the Nonprofit Organization* puts the manager's head and hands to far more constructive use. The Handbook identifies and examines the major trends and issues that are affecting the nonprofit manager, regardless of the nature of the organization. Whether the manager is guiding the destiny of a trade or professional association, a hospital, a college, a social service, a trade union, or a political organization, the Handbook offers a solid blueprint for success.

The Handbook is written for winners and it is lavishly illustrated with examples from today's successful nonprofits. It is designed for the manager who intends to lead the organization through today's complexities and into a successful future.

Problems are not minimized. Rather, the manager is shown by example how to overcome problems. The Handbook shows how to successfully meet fierce competition for member loyalty, for sources of income, for volunteers, for qualified personnel, for public support.

All nonprofit organizations, from art museums to human service delivery agencies, are affected by trends and issues. An example is the decline in student-age population. This decline threatens the existence of many nonprofit colleges. The Handbook shows how colleges are overcoming these smaller enrollments and are building a strong base for prosperity and future growth.

High unemployment causes members to drop affiliation with professional associations. The Handbook explores the ways in which associations are redesigning and retargeting their services to keep existing members and to attract new ones.

Reductions in government spending, coupled with high unemployment, have placed unprecedented demands on nonprofit social services. The Handbook examines how skillful and successful publicity increased public funding for these needed services.

The Handbook is able to answer so many of the nonprofit manager's concerns because it identifies public relations as an integral management function crucial to the organization in bad as well as in good times. Successful public relations is not an isolated function. Rather, it affects every aspect of the organization: service delivery, membership, funding, productive staff and volunteers, consumer/users.

Effective public relations builds a two-way street between the nonprofit and its publics. It also is instrumental in building a two-way street between nonprofit management, boards of trustees, staff, volunteers, and consumer/users. The Handbook breaks new ground in planning and executing effective two-way communications programs.

The Handbook leads the manager through the planning process essential to establishing a firm base for successful operations. It shows the manager, by examples, how to question, assess, evaluate and account for each program and expenditure. It uses case studies of successful nonprofits to illustrate step-by-step techniques for establishing or improving the organization's position in the community.

The Handbook outlines innovative ways to raise money, to recruit and retain volunteers, to make full use of the organization's natural allies and constituencies. It examines the value of user fees and shows how these fees can be augmented by cooperation with other organizations. It details methods of successfully approaching corporations for funding and other forms of assistance. It discusses the value of mergers.

The Handbook offers ways to get more out of the personnel dollar by training and using existing employees for broader community development work as well as improved services. It offers the manager ways to augment staff by selective use of experienced volunteers.

Publicity comes in many forms, and the Handbook illustrates ways of attracting positive public attention. It offers guidance on dealing with bad news and negative stories. It takes publicity beyond the press release or news conference and into the development of community support.

The successful nonprofit today is a consumer-conscious organization. The Handbook illustrates ways to attract and maintain consumer support while involving the consumer in building support for the organization's goals.

It shows the nonprofit manager how to attract community allies for developing needed political support without endangering the organization's tax status.

In his book *The Endangered Sector*, Waldemar A. Nielsen found that

> . . . the United States is on the verge of a period of great political innovation and creativity as it seeks to achieve its purposes of social justice, individual freedom, and responsible government in some fundamentally new combinations of private and public initiative and capabilities. If this is so, and there are many and increasing indications that it could well be, then the Third Sector (i.e., the nonprofit organization) and the values it embodies become crucially important both as a touchstone by which to judge new policy courses and as an instrumentality for their execution.[1]

---

[1]*The Endangered Sector*, by Waldemar A. Nielsen. (Columbia University Press, New York, 1979.) Page 251.

The *Handbook of Publicity and Public Relations for the Nonprofit Organization* identifies countless ways by which the nonprofit organization can insure its future and successfully respond to the national need for innovation in ideas, programs, services, and solutions through effective public relations management.

Robert H. Ruffner

Table of Contents

**Handbook of Publicity
and Public Relations
for the Nonprofit Organization**

CHAPTER 1

The Role of Public Relations in the Nonprofit Organization

A survey of 500 university presidents asked them to list in order of priority the 20 key issues for their institutions over the next decade. The top issue was "declining enrollment," the third was "changing mission and purpose of the institution," and the fourth was "government relations." "Public relations" was ranked 18th, and even then was cited by only 4 percent of the responding presidents.[1]

This low ranking of "public relations" by a group of nonprofit leaders is not surprising. Many nonprofit managers abhor "publicity stunts" and hold in contempt "p.r. types" who spend their days grinding out press releases and running errands.

Mistrust and misunderstanding of "business" techniques is not limited to public relations. Financial management, marketing, and other management techniques are also neglected by many nonprofit organizations.

Today's successful nonprofit needs professional public relations. As a management technique, afforded equal standing with budget and service-providing functions, public relations can assist universities in resolving the issues of "declining enrollment," "changing mission and purpose of the institution," and "government relations."

Professional public relations in today's nonprofit is integral to the growth and success of the organization. It should play a leading role in identifying publics, strengthening community support, encouraging long-range planning, estab-

---

[1] "Public Relations' Role in Strategic Planning for Higher Education," by John Higgins, *Public Relations Journal*, May 1983.

lishing goals, attracting political and financial resources, determining cost-effective and accountable programs. Effective public relations is an active participant in sound management.

TODAY'S PUBLIC RELATIONS IS AS CHANGED AS THE NONPROFIT'S SITUATION

The multimillion dollar nonprofit health complex bears little resemblance to the horse-and-buggy doctor. The same holds true for the nonprofit management technique of public relations. Successful nonprofit public relations maintains a two-way communication with the organization's publics and community. It contributes to planning, programming, accountability and cost effectiveness. It embodies marketing techniques, research capabilities, analytical and forecasting skills. It is contributing to strategies for success, today and tomorrow.

A TEAM EFFORT

Successful public relations is a team effort. It is not relegated to a single person or to a single office in the basement. As a management technique, it requires the collaboration of all areas of the nonprofit. While one person may orchestrate a nonprofit's public relations, that person requires the informed support of management, trustees, staff, volunteers, user/consumers. Team effort is crucial to meet the nonprofit demands of the 1980s.

Demand One: Change.

Change is one constant facing the nonprofit in the years ahead. The public is changing. Volunteers are changing. The identity of the nonprofit is changing. Public mistrust of institutions does not exclude the nonprofit. Women, the traditional strength of the volunteer movement, are going to work for money in ever-increasing numbers. National nonprofits such as the Girl Scouts, the Junior Leagues, the Young Men's Christian Association (YMCA), are responding to demands for clear identities through new programs. Many of the major nonprofits have embraced management techniques to strengthen their organizations and their position in the community.

Demand Two: Competition.

The sheer number—846,433—of nonprofits creates unprecedented competition for public attention and support. Add to this the growing aggressiveness of public (government) nonprofits competing for public support. Then there are the thousands of new nonprofits appearing each year.

"Friends" of government are on the rise. Associations of citizens are forming to support public schools, publicly owned parks and buildings, public transportation systems.

A bewildering array of new diseases is spurring new nonprofits: herpes, AIDs, Infant Death Syndrome, Agent Orange.

Changes in the law are generating new nonprofits. The "deinstitutionaliza-tion" of mental patients has generated hundreds of new organizations dealing with half-way houses, transitional living programs, job training, education and community centers.

Then there are the grass-roots movements: Mothers Against Drunk Driving (MADD) and citizens groups against nuclear waste dumps.

The women's movement has spawned a host of nontraditional nonprofits that are operating houses for battered women, rape crisis counseling centers, hotlines on venereal disease . . . a multitude of services.

There is a growing tendency to bypass nonprofit organizations. Increas-ingly, people are turning to the government for direct assistance, bypassing non-profits established to act as intermediaries for these people. Other nonprofits are being bypassed by minority leaders who are taking their case for jobs and train-ing directly to corporations.

The self-health movement could have a dramatic impact on hospitals as growing numbers of Americans are practicing preventive health measures and relying on themselves rather than on doctors and hospitals.

Competition for the cream is growing with the burgeoning for-profit move in the traditional nonprofit area: nursing homes, hospitals, schools, rehabilitation centers, job training, education. These for-profits are finding dollars and profita-bility in areas traditionally held to be sacredly nonprofit. These for-profits are also attracting those who may be the best prepared to pay for services as well as those with third-party funding.

A study of for-profits involved in the nonprofit interest area shows that there is no hesitation to use management techniques, including highly skilled public relations techniques.

Demand Three: Consumers.

The consumer movement is real. Surveys find a depth and breadth to the movement that far exceeds that identified a few years ago. This movement poses an opportunity and a challenge to nonprofits. Human service delivery agencies are going to have to involve their recipients in decision making and in all aspects of the operation of the organization . . . that is, if these organizations wish to continue. Cultural institutions have their problems with the stigma of "elite," universities with students, hospitals with patients, training programs with clients.

Demand Four: Costs.

Costs are up and public demands for accountability are growing. Cost effec-tiveness is more important than ever—and is indeed essential. National fundrais-ing organizations are spending millions more each year in postage and produc-tion costs to reach the same number of people. Energy costs are up. Rents, telephones, employee benefit costs, all are up with no sign of relief in sight. The state of the nation's economy has strained the resources of religious and human service agencies. As expenses climb, the public diverts its money away from non-profits and students are, for example, sent to state-supported schools in lieu of private nonprofit schools. People postpone operations and dental care.

Corporations are withdrawing their funding of cultural institutions and providing first-time funding to human service agencies because of the well-publicized need. Corporations are not immune from economic trouble, and poor sales and slim profit margins are curtailing contributions.

Yet the demands on the nonprofit are greater than ever. It must continue to attract students, patients, patrons, users, consumers. It has to spend more to compete for these consumers while its revenues from donations and fees are going down.

One very costly demand faced by universities and hospitals is the demand for the latest in technology. Many nonprofits find themselves having to invest heavily in high technology to remain competitive . . . this at the time of lowered incomes.

User fees are one answer to raising much needed income. Great care, however, must be used as user fees can also drive away the very supporters that the nonprofit needs.

FORWARD INTO THE FUTURE

These demands can be successfully met by the nonprofit. Effective public relations can help meet them by strengthening the nonprofit's identity, building community support, and planning a strong future. Some nonprofits will merge with others to insure their futures. Others will find new sources of funding and community support. Public relations can help in making these vital decisions.

THESE CAN BE THE BEST OF TIMES

The nonprofit organization can use these times to best advantage by evaluating, eliminating, strengthening. These four demands *can* be met. The nonprofit is too vital a force to be lost. The importance of the nonprofit's services and contributions must be aggressively shared with staff, donors, members, volunteers, consumers, alumni, patrons—all of the nonprofit's publics.

Management techniques, including professional public relations, can help the nonprofit to be an effective competitor, an efficient operator, an accountable, cost-effective contributor to its community.

CHAPTER 2

Blueprint for the Public Relations Program

Change, competition, consumers, costs: meeting these important demands requires planning. Planning is a strategy for successful management. A plan will generate questions—questions that must be answered as a strategy is developed.

PLANNING IS STRATEGY

All aspects of the nonprofit must be included in the planning—budget, staffing, volunteers, membership development, service delivery, fundraising, marketing, public relations. A plan is flexible and comprehensive: flexible to encompass change, comprehensive to meet known demands and to prepare for unknown ones.

WHO NEEDS THE NONPROFIT?

The fundamental basis for all planning: "Who needs the nonprofit?" Who benefits from the service that the nonprofit provides? Does only the consumer/ user benefit? Probably not, for if only the consumer/user benefited, there would be fewer nonprofits. Who else then, benefits? How? How does one track the benefits of the organization and demonstrate accountability of the funds that are raised and the cost effectiveness of the nonprofit's operations?

Is the service needed? Who is using it and can this need be substantiated? How can what is done today be used to improve finances and services/product tomorrow? A plan incorporates these concerns and identifies competition.

WHAT DOES THE NONPROFIT HAVE?

What's available to the nonprofit at the present time? What are its resources, its strengths, its weaknesses? In addition to staff and trustees, on whom can the nonprofit depend for continuing support? Where does the present money come from and what other sources of funding are being, or could be, developed? A plan addresses these issues, looks at costs.

PLANNING IS QUESTIONING

Planning is a series of questions—questions that are fluid and changing. Planning is designed to find the answers to existing questions and to identify new resources and directions. Planning is too important to depend on one person. It needs the benefit of the best thinking available to the nonprofit. Planning can be a start of consumer involvement. (See Figure 2–1.)

Professional Identity

Does the public know what your members really do?

Because a layman can't answer the "what's in it for me" question unless he knows what a profession or industry actually does, a lot of work is being done to create the association equivalent of corporate identity.

Some of the most skillful work in this area has been done by The Society of Chartered Property & Casualty Underwriters. To increase awareness of what a CPCU actually is, the Society sends out columns of technical insurance advice with identification in the byline.

There's an insatiable hunger among suburban newspaper editors for helpful columns of expert information, so the Q&A approach assures clippings, and it is simply good journalism to identify the source of this information.

Distinguished public service, without public knowledge of it, won't win public appreciation and support. So even the YMCA goes into the newspapers with a series on what it is and what it is doing.

The American Production And Inventory Control Society has a different problem—letting prospective members know about the group, and subtly notifying employers (who must approve or disapprove requests for membership expenses) about what's in it for them.

America's engineers, who are literally building a better world, need public understanding and support to do it. To win such support, both the American Society of Civil Engineers and the IEEE (Institute of Electrical and Electronics Engineers) send releases to newspapers in suburbia, where there is high interest in land use and environmental matters, on what the professionals are doing, and trying to do, for us.

FIGURE 2–1.   Courtesy of Ronald N. Levy, President, North American Precis Syndicate, Inc., 201 East 42nd Street, New York, New York 10017.

PLANNING IS ASSESSING

Planning takes into account the available resources, the background and history of the nonprofit, the staff performance, the quality and quantity of volunteers, the present objectives and future goals, the assessment of every phase of the nonprofit. Every phase of the nonprofit can be weighed and assessed and judged. Many criteria may be used but the end result is the same. The nonprofit can be found to be performing well, not performing well, or missing opportunities.

ASKING THE RIGHT QUESTIONS

A successful plan answers the right questions. It is fluid and adaptable. It maintains existing supporters, locates new ones, and successfully attracts community support in funding, legislation, volunteers, and visibility. It, as a minimum, incorporates the following steps:

Step One: Assessment.

Who needs the nonprofit?
What are the resources available to the nonprofit?
What works, what doesn't work, why?
What's the history?
What's the competition?
What does the community understand about the nonprofit?

Step Two: Basic Program Objectives.

What does the nonprofit really want to accomplish?
Is this feasible? Can it be made feasible?
Does the objective address consumers, change, competition, costs?

Step Three: Problem Identification.

What social changes impact on the nonprofit?
Is the nonprofit watching its language?
Are programs cost effective?
How to build on existing support?
Is there public accountability?
Is there poor public image?
How to meet costs?
What is the real "product" of the nonprofit?
Knowing the community.

Step Four: Specific Audiences.

Media representatives.
Legislators and officials.
Other nonprofits.
Individuals.
Patrons, consumers, donors, volunteers.
Staff.
Board of Trustees.

Step Five: Basic Ways to Go Public.

Marketing programs.
News conferences.
Radio and television news.
Speeches.

News releases.
Open Houses.
Ground-breaking ceremonies.
Photographs.
Job/volunteer fairs.
Radio-TV interviews and talk shows.
Book/author parties.
Radio/TV "nonprofit-a-thons" or "fundraising-thons."
Speakers' bureaus.
Dedications.
Community thank-yous.
Special newspaper sections.
Displays in libraries and malls.
Proclamations.
Dedications.
Demonstrations.
Follow-up on news stories.
Initiating story ideas.
   Letters to the Editor.
    Op-Ed articles.
   Columnists.
Newsletters.
Public service advertising.
Another's paid advertising.
Paid advertising.
Direct mail.

Step Six: Cost Effectiveness.

Use volunteers.
Universities.
For-profit services.
Radio/television stations.

Step Seven: Cooperation.

Cooperate. The community is full of resources to be shared.

A MODEL PLAN

The following model is designed to further public recognition of a non-profit's contributions to its service recipients. These recipients, the nonprofit's "consumers," have been identified by the organization as the focal point of this plan. (The assessment and questioning revealed to the nonprofit management several findings which prompted this particular plan.)

PROGRAM OBJECTIVES

This human-service-providing nonprofit determined on its model meeting the following objectives:

1. To increase public awareness and understanding of the service recipient;
2. To offset distortions about the capabilities of the service recipient generated through some fundraising efforts without damaging these vital efforts;
3. To change the nonprofit's identity from a professional provider of services to that of an ally of the consumer/recipient;
4. To meet consumer demands for respect and recognition;
5. To maintain leadership in providing services to consumers;
6. To maintain and broaden community contacts and to identify new funding sources;
7. To maintain importance as a service provider;
8. To establish validity for the nonprofit through past and present consumers.

The objectives provide for a new consumer-oriented and based approach designed to regain consumer support which had declined. The model is equally valid in developing an identity for a new organization or for gaining interest among specific members, volunteers, and interest groups. A cultural organization, for example, could adapt this model to reach new, selected audiences. A trade or professional organization could adapt it to reach potential members. Many target audiences can be reached by applying the model to several specific audiences at the same time. It is a model that thrives on elaboration and creative programming.

CONSUMER/RECIPIENTS OF SERVICES

The importance of the individual is the basis of this model plan (Figure 2–2). It is a plan dealing with people and aimed at people, not just consumers in need of services. The plan aims at raising money without denigrating the person in need. The plan's ambition is to attract consumers in need of services, the funds needed to service them, while recognizing that these consumers are contributing members of society, particularly so after they have received the agency's services. It is a bold plan and one that depends on intelligent execution. It is a plan that meets today's consumer consciousness and an educated public's demand for cost-effectiveness and accountability.

The plan goes beyond the immediate needs of the nonprofit. (The assessment showed that many of the former recipients of services were not finding opportunities in the community.) This plan addresses that need and is concerned with the larger issues of opportunity and participation in society.

Note that this plan encompasses change, competition, and consumers. Consumerism is on the rise. A Louis Harris and Associates study released in February 1983 followed up on data collected in a 1976 consumer study.[1] The new study's most significant finding was that the consumer movement in 1983 is stronger and deeper than ever, and that Americans are more concerned about a number of consumer problems than they were in 1976. The nonprofit organization is not immune from this growing consumer pressure. Symphony orchestras,

---

[1]"What's New in Consumer Research," Pamela G. Hollie. The *New York Times*. Sunday, March 27, 1983.

GOODWILL AT WORK
People and Projects for the Future

THE PEOPLE OF GOODWILL INDUSTRIES

National Goodwill Graduate of the Year—Larry Young, a 27 year old from Jacksonville, Florida was chosen by four judges from among 23 nominees. Larry was paralyzed from the waist down by a gunshot wound when he was only six years old. Four years later, his left leg was amputated as a result of another injury. He was unable to attend public school because of his hospitalizations for surgery and other ailments. Following evaluation and training at Goodwill Industries of North Florida, Larry interviewed for, and won, a job as clerk-dispatcher in the Central Control room of Jacksonville's International Airport.

National Goodwill Employer of the year, more than 300 employees: Fort Lewis/Madigan, Washington, made 15 trial placements, provided training sites and supervision for 32 disabled persons and conducted special programs to improve physical accommodations and accessibility.

National Goodwill Employer of the Year, less than 300 employees: Randall Plating, Inc., Butler, Wisconsin, nominated by Goodwill Industries, Milwaukee Area. A family-operated chrome plating business, the firm had

PHOTO BY CHAN BLISS

PHOTO BY MARY SWARTOUT

Larry Young, National Goodwill Graduate of the Year, and Mitchell M. Sowell, Jr., National Goodwill Achiever of the Year.

problems with high turnover of employees and hired a disabled person seven years ago. That person proved so reliable that now most of the firm's 15 employees are physically, emotionally or mentally handicapped.

National Goodwill Achiever of the Year—Mitchell M. Sowell, Jr., 22, Columbus, Georgia, was selected from 25 candidates by the three judges. Disabled by club feet, hip dislocation and mild mental retardation, Mitchell has been at Goodwill Industries of the Chattahoochee Valley since 1974 and is working now for his equivalency diploma. He performs in special olympics and has won numerous weight lifting contests. Mitchell was the leading achiever of five nominees from Region Three, comprised of 10 states.

VOLUNTEERS

The Goodwill Industries Volunteer Services (GIVS) is one of the nation's largest volunteer groups helping disabled persons. GIVS is more than 15,000 strong and is growing. These men and women, of all ages and walks of life, contribute and bring in substantial funding through community promotional programs. More than 4,500 volunteers serve as members of the local and national Goodwill Board of Directors providing leadership and professional advice, and strengthening Goodwill's ties with the local communities they serve and with businesses and industries throughout America.

Major goals of this volunteer corps include: interpreting Goodwill to the public, helping to raise money, promoting donations of household goods and contract work, and working directly with Goodwill's disabled people—often in the areas of recreation,

FIGURE 2–2.   Reprinted with permission from the 1981 Annual Report of Goodwill Industries of America, Inc., Bethesda, Maryland.

environmental groups, battered women's shelters, all are going to have to respond to their consumers positively and strongly. The women's movement has been actively concerned with language and nuances and has made considerable progress in replacing "girls" with "women," "office pranks" with "office harassment," "miss" with "ms." Language and the sensitivity of consumers are crucial concerns in the nonprofit area.

STEPPING UP TO AN EFFECTIVE PLAN

Step One: Examine Your Language.

Service recipients are people, not dehumanized abstractions such as "the handicapped," "the aged," "the poor." Be sensitive to language that accurately describes the people about whom you are talking: a deaf student, a group of elderly people, an unwed teenage mother, a low-income worker. It is not difficult to do and much more humane and comprehensive to the public. Avoid professional jargon and "in" terms that mean nothing to the general public. Translate the nonprofit's services into easily understood English.

Step Two: Consumers Should Represent Themselves.

Arrange to have recipients of services do the talking about the nonprofit in public appearances. Don't forget that the end result of the services you provide are people. Seek consumers willing to appear in fundraising activities. People who have used your services can be the best testimony to their effectiveness. Consumers should be sought for radio and television appearances, newspaper interviews, magazine feature stories, all communication with the general public.

Step Three: Consumers Are Not Superpeople.

Don't oversell, for you will only be emphasizing their dissimilarities.

Step Four: Know What Your Organization Offers.

You must know what it offers to consumers and to the general public. As an example, a small consumer group must identify the purpose for organizing. Can the group provide social outlets, job referral, information on the availability of other services within the community? Assess the strengths and weaknesses of the group, both real and potential. If you cannot provide information, don't claim that you can. If you don't have consumers actively participating in your organization, form an advisory council and recruit consumers as volunteers and employees. Know the program and services and people you want to include in your program. Recognize your limitations and potential before going public.

Step Five: Know the Facts about Your Community.

How many service consumers live in your community? How many people are served by government programs? What other types of programs are available in the community: housing, education, counseling, training? What other programs are available through nonprofit organizations or through for-profit firms?

By surveying the community, you have identified the competition, assessed the position of your nonprofit, and recognized the particular program you wish to stress and the audience to whom you are addressing it.

You have the facts about the community; now these facts must be used honestly. These facts include the basis for media contacts, legislative development, fundraising efforts, community support. In assessing the position of the nonprofit, you have made new contacts throughout the community.

SPECIFIC AUDIENCE APPROACHES

Media Representatives.

Editors, reporters and broadcasters who know you are better prepared to appreciate the stories, press releases, and ideas that you pass on to them. News people are like anybody else. They want to know their sources of information. So, get to know them. Call them up, drop by and see them, have lunch with them. As the people who write and broadcast the news may not know your consumers, it is crucial that these two groups be brought together by the nonprofit. Arrange interviews and talk show appearances for consumers. This means that the organization working with them must know them well, know their strengths and weaknesses, know who is an effective communicator, and then assist these consumer/communicators in contacts with the press, radio, and television.

Legislators and Officials.

Meetings, hearings, and informal contacts must be arranged to bring consumers into frequent and sustained contact with legislators and officials to expand knowledge and information about issues of concern to consumers and their organizations.

Other Nonprofits.

Don't limit your sights or your interests solely to those other organizations and agencies working with the same consumers. In your community (these should have been identified in your assessment) are a number of organizations working with other groups of people. Contact these organizations and suggest cooperative efforts. Working together, organizations can gain and realize fuller attention and support for their interests.

Individuals.

Identify a community personality who has a personal interest in your organization and efforts and who can help you realize your goals. A personality can be a community leader in politics, education, theater, television, publishing, any field.

Patrons, Consumers, Donors, Volunteers, and Other Friends.

Use awards to honor these friends for their contributions to the community through your organization. Honor employers and educators and city managers and housing authority officials and doctors who have helped to create opportunities for your consumers.

For every nonprofit organization, there is a host of special audiences that need to be addressed, persuaded, cajoled, and brought into, or kept in, contact with the nonprofit. There is a myriad of techniques to use, including adapting those for a general public to the needs and interests of specific audiences.

BASIC WAYS TO GO PUBLIC

News Releases.

Be absolutely sure that you have something to say and then say it clearly and simply. If you have done your assessment, you'll have something to say. Remember to type your release (double or triple spaced), and include your name and telephone number as the contact person at the top of the release and the name and address of the organization.

Get your information (the who, what, where, when, why and how) in the opening paragraph. Type only on one side of the sheet of paper. Never send sloppy work or carbon copies. Keep your release to the minimum (one page preferably) and remember you are not writing "the Great American Novel," you are writing a release.

Why send a release? To call attention to a specific happening or event. The most effective releases are those that attract an assignment editor's attention to a specific event or to a specific piece of information. If you want a newspaper, radio or TV station to interview someone, a release may not be the best way to handle it. A phone call generating interest in the interview is a first step. Then follow the media's directions on sending backup materials such as a brief biography of the person to be interviewed.

If you have never written a news release, adapt the examples shown in Figures 2–3 and 2–4, or seek advice from a media professional. See Figure 2–5, a release from the Detroit Institute of Arts, which illustrates how to incorporate detailed information in a release.

SAMPLE NEWS RELEASE: FORMAT #1

FROM   : NAME OF NONPROFIT ORGANIZATION, STREET ADDRESS, CITY,
             STATE, ZIP CODE
CONTACT : NONPROFIT PERSON
             TELEPHONE(S): OFFICE AND HOME
FOR IMMEDIATE RELEASE: (DATE RELEASE WAS SENT)
     /OR/FOR RELEASE : (DATE TO BE USED)
   FIRST PARAGRAPH. Simply state who did or will do what, where, when, how, and if space available, why.
   SECOND PARAGRAPH. What does the first paragraph mean to the media's audience? Use the names of local people involved in the event other than those already mentioned in the first paragraph. Use statistics on the community to bolster the significance of the event. Elaborate on the why and how.
   THIRD PARAGRAPH. What can the media's audience do in connection with this event? Opportunities to attend, volunteer, donate, participate.
   FOURTH PARAGRAPH. If the event is out of town, list local people attending. Add telephone number for further information.

FIGURE 2–3.

SAMPLE NEWS RELEASE FORMAT #2

EVENT ANNOUNCEMENT
FROM   :   NAME OF NONPROFIT, STREET ADDRESS, CITY, STATE, ZIP CODE
CONTACT :   NONPROFIT PERSON
                  TELEPHONE(S): OFFICE AND HOME
FOR IMMEDIATE RELEASE: (DATE RELEASE WAS SENT)
    /OR/FOR RELEASE   :   (DATE RELEASE TO BE USED)
    FIRST PARAGRAPH: The (name of nonprofit) plans an event (lunch,
seminar, dinner) on (day, date, time) at (place) to observe (Awareness Day, Week,
Month), the Chairman of the Board of Trustees (name) announced today.
    SECOND PARAGRAPH: "This (Awareness Day, Week, Month) is an
opportunity to thank the community for its support during the past year when
(name of nonprofit) raised more funds and provided more services than ever
before," the Chairman added. "The (name of guest speaker) will speak at the
(lunch, seminar, dinner) and awards will be given to (names of persons to be
honored)."
    THIRD PARAGRAPH: "Tickets for the event are available from (name,
address, phone number). (Price and allowable tax deduction.)"

FIGURE 2–4.

In marketing your news release, have a good media list that includes the names (current) of editors of daily papers, weekly newspapers, wire services (AP and UPI) in your community, magazine and corporate publication editors, editors at private and public agencies, editors of cooperating nonprofits, radio and television news or assignment desks, producers of talk shows (for interviews), public service directors at radio and television stations. Keep your list up to date (or buy one) and use names wherever possible. Send releases to the right person. If you have a release that is a news item, send it to the City Editor or the News Director. If your release is a feature, send it to the appropriate person.

Marketing the release is crucial. A nonprofit can send out hundreds of releases and have no impact whatsoever (other than an adverse one on the cost effectiveness of the agency) if the releases are not picked up by the media and used.

News Conferences.

Be certain that the conference is absolutely necessary and that it will generate news of interest to reporters and editors; be sure to let the media know in advance that the outcome will benefit them in their news gathering (if you can't explain satisfactorily in advance, forget your conference); give editors plenty of advance notice of the conference and suit the needs of the media you are inviting (evening TV news programs need their news in the morning, while morning newspapers need theirs in the afternoon or early evening); put together a kit of pertinent materials; brief the person holding the conference so that he or she knows exactly what is expected (you can act the role of reporter in doing this and generate the kinds of questions that a reporter would); insure that microphones and other equipment work; make a list of all these items and any others that occur to you to meet the needs of reporters. A list should include coffee, back-up technicians who can fix an electrical or apparatus breakdown, back-up experts to elaborate on the main points of the conference, invitations to editors and others from concerned and cooperating nonprofit and government agencies, suggested

The Detroit Institute of Arts

5200 Woodward Avenue
Detroit, Michigan 48202

Public Relations Department
(313) 833-7963

NEWS RELEASE

DETROIT, MI—Cranbrook Academy of Art and its influence on 20th century architecture and design will be explored for the first time in a major exhibition, organized by The Detroit Institute of Arts and The Metropolitan Museum of Art. Scheduled to open in Detroit December 12, 1983 to February 19, 1984, "Design in America: The Cranbrook Vision 1925–1950," will travel to the Metropolitan Museum of Art, New York City, and museums in Helsinki, Paris and London.

Approximately 200 masterworks produced by more than 30 Cranbrook faculty and students will trace the development and influence of the Academy from its beginnings in the 1920s until the 1950 death of Eliel Saarinen, who guided the unique institution through those years.

Works through the early 1960s will be included to show the continuing influence of Cranbrook on these individuals.

Located in Bloomfield Hills, Michigan, the campus and educational concept of Cranbrook Academy of Art, a part of the Cranbrook Educational Community, was a creative collaboration of Detroit philanthropist George Gough Booth and Finnish-born architect Eliel Saarinen.

Excellent faculty drawn to Cranbrook included sculptor Carl Milles, ceramist Maija Grotell, and textile designer/weaver Marianne Strengell, as well as the Saarinen family—Eliel's wife Loja, a textile designer and weaver; their daughter Pipsan, also a weaver and designer, and son Eero, who became one of the most important architects of the 1950s. He designed Dulles airport (Washington, D.C.), the St. Louis Arch, and collaborated with his father on the General Motors Technical Center (Warren, Michigan).

The working environment stressed an interdisciplinary, non-dogmatic approach that attracted designers Charles and Ray Eames, furniture designer Florence Knoll, sculptor Harry Bertoia, architects Ralph Rapson and Harry Weese, textile designer Jack Lenor Larsen and painter Zoltan Sepeshy. These faculty and students had a decisive influence on the 20th century arts in America and Europe.

"Design in America: The Cranbrook Vision 1925–1950" was initiated by Jay Belloli, former curator of Modern Art, The Detroit Institute of Arts, and by R. Craig Miller, assistant curator of American Decorative Arts, The Metropolitan Museum of Art, with the assistance of Roy Slade, president, Cranbrook Academy of Art.

The following scholars participated: Robert Judson Clark, associate professor, Department of Art and Archaeology, Princeton University; David G. De Long, associate professor, Graduate School of Architecture and Planning, Columbia University; Martin Eidelberg, professor of Art History, Rutgers University; John David Farmer, director, Museum of Art, University of California at Santa Barbara; John Gerard, curator of Collections, Cranbrook Academy of Art/Museum; Neil Harris, professor of History, University of Chicago; Joan Marter, associate professor of Art History, Rutgers University; Mary R. Riordan, director, the Muskegon (Mich.) Museum of Art; Davira Spiro Taragin, assistant curator of Modern Art, the Detroit Institute of Arts; Christa C. Mayer Thurman, curator, Department of Textiles, the Art Institute of Chicago.

A comprehensive catalogue, published by Harry N. Abrams, Inc., New York, and educational programs will complement the exhibition. "Design in America: The Cranbrook Vision 1925–1950" is assisted by grants from the IBM Corporation, the National Endowment for the Arts, and the National Endowment for the Humanities.

10/7/82

FIGURE 2–5.   Courtesy of the Detroit Institute of Arts, 5200 Woodward
Avenue, Detroit, Michigan 48202.

questions to be asked that reinforce the purpose of the conference, follow-ups with reporters who don't attend by sending news kits, prompt responses for information from the media.

Radio and Television News Appearances.

Be informed, do your homework, and know what it is that you want to say. Be prepared for questions that may be completely off base. If you cannot answer because you don't have the information, say so. Fumbling on the air doesn't help the nonprofit.

Speeches.

Again, do your homework; either write it out entirely or make notes of your key points. Keep it brief and watch your audience for reaction. (People frequently fall asleep even during interesting speeches, so don't be put off balance by that.) Use films and slide presentations only if they complement your speech and do not repeat the same message. Don't wander; you will be doing well if you can get across one idea in a speech. Speak simply, concisely, and sincerely. Know your subject.

COUNTLESS WAYS OF GOING PUBLIC

Contacts with the public through the media—news releases, news programs and news conferences—are just the tip of the iceberg of ideas that flow from a good management plan. Organizations can adapt the following techniques to reach the media as well as to reach specific target audiences:

Open Houses.

One of the simplest ways of making contact with the public is by arranging public days at the nonprofit's facility.

Ground-Breaking Ceremonies.

Here is an opportunity for friends of the nonprofit, political and community leaders and the media. Rather than sending photos of the ground-breaking to the papers, send architectural drawings of the new building. The public is interested in new buildings, so play up this fact.

Photographs.

Use black and white glossies (unless color is requested). Eliminate pictures of people shaking hands, holding drinks, exchanging awards. The accompanying explanation sent with the photo should clearly specify who is where in the photo and spell all names correctly. A photo is an important news release.

Fairs.

Arrange a job fair to bring job-seeking consumers together with employers and other community agencies. This is an opportunity for nonprofit cooperation. Even in a tight job market a job fair can offer resumé writing, job-seeking skills, information on job-training programs, and volunteer opportunities that enhance job experience and readiness.

Radio-TV Interviews.

Talk shows as opposed to news programs have been well-received. Consumers discuss their experiences, their lives and jobs. Again, it is crucial to be informed and do your homework. The person to be interviewed must be an effective communicator—articulate, witty and animated. Talk shows are interested in personalities and liveliness. Be relaxed, have a sense of humor, and be talkative.

Book/Author Parties.

Give parties for the promotion of books by and about consumers at department stores and bookshops; give author luncheons; arrange interviews and panel discussions, and reviews of the book in the media.

Radio/TV-a-Thons.

Promote available opportunities for consumers, and raise funds for the organization. (See Figure 2–6.)

RADIOTHONS CAN PAY OFF FOR NONPROFITS. WGMS, a commercial AM/FM radio station in Washington D.C., produced a 78-hour Radiothon fundraiser for the National Symphony Orchestra in March 1983. WGMS announced at the end of the 78-hour period that it raised $232,000 for the orchestra.

FIGURE 2–6.

Speakers' Bureaus.

Speakers, particularly consumers, should be scheduled to speak at civic, social, service and other meetings. Volunteers are excellent for speaking and raising community support for nonprofit organizations. All speakers, including volunteers, need training in effective public and media speaking. Training should include rehearsals of set speeches, videotape playbacks of the person delivering a speech, reviews and analyses of guests on television talk shows, practice in use of body language and gestures, the opportunity to analyze other public speakers. Formal training in public speaking will reap benefits to the nonprofit organization and can attract volunteers to the nonprofit's speakers' bureau.

Dedications.

Stage ceremonies at buildings that provide special facilities for consumers; at buildings that have provided outstanding leadership in your consumer movement; at parks, museums, and recreation centers with special consumer attractions. Dedications can attract selected audiences as well as the media.

Community Thank-You.

Arrange for lunch, banquet, reception, media announcements, direct mail, thanking the community for its support of your nonprofit's consumers.

Special Newspaper Section.

Such sections are sponsored by allies and agencies that work with your consumers, and include success stories, community stories, problem areas.

Display.

Use displays of photographs of consumers at work, at play, at home for use in that great display place, the local public library. Arrange for art exhibits of consumer artists in the library; help the library arrage a mini-festival of films and books about your consumers. Another great gathering place today is the shopping mall; use it for exhibits, displays, festivals, and fundraising events.

Proclamations.

Cooperate with other organizations within the town which share concern for your consumers to interest the mayor in designating a particular day or week as an "awareness" event. Draft a proclamation for the mayor that spells out the event and have the signing ceremony attended by consumers, the media, community leaders. (See Figure 2–7.)

SAMPLE PROCLAMATION FORMAT

TITLE: DESIGNATION OF DAY/WEEK/MONTH AS EVENT

FIRST PARAGRAPH: State the reasons for the event. The need. The supporting statistics. Accomplishments of the past year.
SECOND PARAGRAPH: Call for cooperation from others in support of the event and in solving the problem.
THIRD PARAGRAPH: "NOW, THEREFORE, the chief executive of the City/State/ Nation designates and proclaims the Awareness Event and its date(s)."
SIGNATURE: Of Mayor, Governor or President.

FIGURE 2–7.

Demonstrate.

If there are seemingly insoluble situations in your community that work against your consumers, organize a peaceful demonstration.

Follow Up.

Read your local papers, watch the television, and listen to the radio. The media gives you tips and clues on how to best present your nonprofit's story. If the newspaper runs a major article on unemployment in your community, for example, and fails to mention its impact on your consumers, call or write the editor with story ideas and suggestions of consumers to be interviewed for follow-up stories.

Local media particularly like tie-ins that relate a national or state story to the local community. The nonprofit can act on these and provide the local angle.

Initiate Ideas.

If you think that you have found a good story or that you have a concrete story idea, talk it over with a reporter or an editor who seems to have an interest in your nonprofit. How to find such a person? Follow your local media, clipping, noting, and storing names of reporters who have done pieces on your area of concern. Identify a reporter who has done several articles and you've identified a writing contact who may be interested in developing additional stories. The same holds true for radio and television stations, although you may have to contact the public service director at these to follow up.

A good tip is to write letters to reporters, thanking them for their stories or taking issue with them if you feel the need. Be sure to send a copy of your letter to the editor. Keep in touch with reporters, editors, and public service directors and let them know of your continued interest in their stories on your consumers.

President Ronald Reagan issued the Proclamation in Figure 2–8 through the White House Office of the Press Secretary on January 20, 1983. The Proclamation designates "RED CROSS MONTH, 1983."

American Red Cross volunteers are among the millions of citizens who quietly serve their fellow man. Since the first settlement on our shores, a volunteer spirit has characterized the American way. This spirit has been reflected in the actions of the neighbor who is always ready to lend a hand.

The services performed by the Red Cross provide us with benefits that would otherwise cost billions of dollars. Last year, it was the volunteer who—giving freely of his or her time, energy, and talent—made it possible for the Red Cross to collect and provide the ill and injured with nearly six million units of blood. Volunteers established shelters to feed and attend to disaster victims, conducted thousands of courses to improve the quality of life by teaching nutrition, first aid, water safety, home nursing, and preparation for parenthood. The volunteer reached out to our young people, to members of the military, to veterans, and to the elderly, and through personal contact eased their loneliness and fears.

FIGURE 2–8.

For 102 years, the American Red Cross has been an essential ingredient of American life, helping us to learn, to grow, and to prosper. In accordance with this year's theme, "The Red Cross. We'll Help. Will You?" I urge all Americans to donate their time and financial resources in support of Red Cross activities. By giving of ourselves, we give the greatest gift one human being can give another—the gift of love.

NOW, THEREFORE, I, RONALD REAGAN, President of the United States of America and Honorary Chairman of the American National Red Cross, do hereby designate March 1983 as Red Cross Month.

IN WITNESS WHEREOF, I have hereunto set my hand this twentieth____day of___January, in the year of our Lord nineteen hundred and eighty-three, and of the Independence of the United States of America the two hundred and seventh.

RONALD REAGAN

FIGURE 2–8 (continued).

President Ronald Reagan issued the Proclamation in Figure 2–9 through the White House Office of the Press Secretary on May 2, 1983. The Proclamation designates the "NATIONAL YEAR OF VOLUNTARISM."

Voluntarism is a cornerstone of the American way of life and a fundamental characteristic of our American heritage. The generosity and civic-mindedness of the American people has long been a noted aspect of our Nation. Since its inception, this has been a country in which neighbor has lent a hand to neighbor, and families have banded together to help one another in times of adversity.

Voluntary service remains as important today as it was in earlier decades. We cannot rely solely on institutions of government to provide remedies for our problems. Many of the solutions must be devised and supported by other individuals and private groups. Greater emphasis must be placed on developing increased community commitment to voluntary service and on developing more volunteer leaders.

NOW, THEREFORE, I, RONALD REAGAN, President of the United States of America, in recognition of the vital contributions volunteers make to our society, do hereby designate the period beginning on May 1, 1983 until April 30, 1984 as the National Year of Voluntarism, and I call upon the people of the United States and interested groups and organizations to observe this celebration with appropriate activities of voluntary service and efforts to attract additional persons to this valuable and rewarding tradition.

IN WITNESS WHEREOF, I have hereunto set my hand this twenty-ninth___day of April____, in the year of our Lord nineteen hundred and eighty-three, and of the Independence of the United States of America the two hundred and seventh.

RONALD REAGAN

FIGURE 2–9.

Letters to the Editor.

Write them; they are read. Many radio and television stations also accept "letters to the editor." Suggest ideas for editorial treatment—things such as special commemorative events, discrimination against consumers in the community; housing and public transportation problems. Use your facts.

Op-Ed Opinion Articles.

More newspapers are giving column space to individuals or organizations to present a specific point of view. These op-ed columns are widely read, valuable to the nonprofit, and should be used with intelligence and care. Again, know exactly the point the organization needs to make.

Columnists.

Like editors, columnists welcome ideas. A column is widely read and important to the nonprofit. (See Figure 2–10.) An organization can produce and market its own columns and/or columnists. Consumers and volunteers are good sources as columnists. (See Figure 2–11.)

The National Spokesman reports that responses to such letters printed by Ann Landers or Dear Abby are "dramatic." "A Dear Abby column last June (1982) which included the address of the EFA (Epilepsy Foundation of America) brought 2,000 to 3,000 letters. In addition, both columnists handle the subject very, very well. Their stance was very positive in regard to epilepsy."

THE IMPACT OF COLUMNISTS

From the National Spokesman,[2] a publication of the Epilepsy Foundation of America (EFA):

"Ann Landers and Dear Abby usually give advice to the lovelorn.

"But four times in the past year, epilepsy has been the topic of discussion in their syndicated newspaper columns.

"In the latest discussion, in January (1983), Ann Landers printed a letter from the father of a three-year-old boy who has convulsive (grand mal) seizures.

"The father was worried about his son's condition, not because of the seizures, but because of 'the attitude of ignorant people' he feared his son would encounter throughout life.

"In his letter to Ann Landers, the father defined epilepsy, told what to do when someone has a seizure, and gave reassurance to people who suffer from the condition. Then he made a plea for understanding and acceptance."

FIGURE 2–10.

---

[2]*National Spokesman*, March 1983. The Epilepsy Foundation of America.

Cancer answer line

FIGHT CANCER

American Cancer Society

The Cancer Answer Line, a question-and-answer column about cancer, will appear on the first Monday of each month in The Alexandria Gazette. Those with questions should write the American Cancer Society, Attn: Debra L. Burnley, 346 E. Maple Ave., Vienna, Va. 22180. Although every letter cannot be answered in print, the Cancer Society will respond in writing to all who ask questions. Those with questions may also call 938-5550 from 9 a.m. to 5 p.m. weekdays.

Q: I enjoy being in the sun, but I am concerned about how to protect myself against skin cancer. Can you offer any suggestions?

A: To help protect yourself from skin cancer, one should:

• avoid repeated over-exposure to the sun — especially between 10 a.m. and 3 p.m.;

• use a sunscreen preparation to absorb ultraviolet rays or use a sunblock preparation that will deflect ultraviolet rays;

• wear protective clothing, such as long sleeved shirts and wide-brimmed hats.

The key to saving lives from skin cancer is early detection along with prompt and adequate treatment of a skin abnormality.

Q: I just found out that my friend's child has cancer. Is cancer in children common? Are there many types of childhood cancers? What are the symptoms?

A: Cancer is actually rare in children, though it is the chief cause of death by disease in children ages 3 to 14. Childhood cancers are different from adult cancers. They tend to grow more quickly because body tissues are growing rapidly and the cancer grows right along with hem.

The main childhood cancers are:

Leukemia — a cancer of blood-forming tissues. In leukemia, abnormal immature white cells increase greatly and invade other tissues and organs. These white cells are not able to function at their normal task of fighting disease which makes the leukemic child vulnerable to infection or hemorrhage. The child may have a wan appearance and/or listless behavior. New drugs and combined drug treatments have extended lives in some cases for more than 15 years.

Osteogenic Sarcoma — a bone cancer which develops most often in the forearm or lower leg. There is usually no pain at first, but eventually swelling and difficulty in using the arm or leg is noticed. Any chronic disability or swelling should be brought to the physician's attention. Treatment is surgery which may be combined with radiation and chemotherapy. This form of cancer is responding to aggressive treatment.

Cancers of the nervous system — are known as neuroblastomas. Except for leukemia, they are the most frequent form of cancer in children. They occur in certain nerve fibers of the body and can appear anywhere — though usually in the abdomen. The first sign may be swelling of the abdomen. The treatment of choice is a combination of surgery and drugs, and chances for recovery are excellent.

Brain tumors — very early in their course are likely to cause blurred or double vision, dizziness, difficulty in walking or handling objects and unexplained nausea.

Eye tumors — occur in children usually under the age of 4. The first sign may be a squint. Later a pearly glint may be noted in the pupil. If this cancer is detected early, cure is possible. Treatment is usually surgery, though radiation is sometimes used in combination with drugs.

Cancer of the kidney (or Wilms tumor) — is usually detected by a swelling or lump in the child's abdomen. Treatment is surgery combined with radiation. In selected cases, chemotherapy has also been effective.

FIGURE 2–11.   Courtesy of the *Alexandria Gazette,* 717 N. St. Asaph Street, Alexandria, Virginia 22313.

Newsletter.

Write, produce and distribute to members of your organization a lively, informative newsletter on what your group is doing for and with consumers. A newsletter maintains visibility in the community, emphasizes continuity of goal and purpose, and offers the opportunity to reach highly selected audiences. Keep your newsletter focused on what your group is accomplishing and the persons involved, and do a professional job either in house or on contract.

Public Service Advertising.

Develop written, filmed or recorded public service announcements of 10, 20, 30, and 60-second lengths. These public service announcements are a way to talk about your nonprofit's services, successes, needs, your contributions to consumers. The announcements must be carefully timed and delivered to the public service director of radio and television stations. Public service directors should be high on your list of contacts as they are frequently willing to discuss their needs for public service materials and can help you produce the right materials. (See Figure 2–12, page 46.)

Another's Paid Advertising.

Encourage businesses to advertise their products of interest to your consumers, to feature your consumers in their ads, and to support the nonprofit through their own paid advertising.

Paid Advertising.

Use paid advertising as necessary. It's effective in reaching audiences.

Direct Mail.

This is a most successful means of raising money. Although printing and mailing costs are high, individual contributions are all important. One successful way to use direct mail without having to pay for it is to arrange with local public utilities to be included in their billings.

These are a few ways to reach selected audiences; to "go public" through the media and through community activities; to broaden the basis of community support and funding.

COST EFFECTIVE SOLUTIONS

Volunteers.

Attract a group of media, advertising, and public relations people from the community to advise on the nonprofit's plan and programs.

FIGURE 2–12. Courtesy of the Illinois Division of the American Cancer Society. Created by Bentley, Barnes & Lynn Advertising, Inc.

Universities.

In universities you have a rich resource. University art departments can produce posters, letterhead and publication designs, graphic services, advertisements for newspapers and magazines. University public relations and advertising departments can produce campaigns as class projects. The business departments can produce marketing and management recommendations to help the small nonprofit. The university gains by affording student experience and by building student portfolios and resumés.

Many universities have film departments, which can produce television public service announcements, and radio stations, which can produce radio materials for public service.

University students are a good source of energetic fundraisers.

For-Profit Services.

Legal, advertising, marketing, financial, public relations firms do "pro bono" (free) work for nonprofit organizations. Representatives of these firms should be on the nonprofit's board of trustees and contacts should be continually developed for assistance.

COOPERATION

The success of the nonprofit in the community depends on its cooperation with other groups within the community. Many nonprofit organizations cannot afford to go it alone. They need the understanding and active support of the community. This plan outlines a number of ways to find and create this community understanding and support.

CHAPTER 3

Identifying and Communicating with Different Constituencies

The community is the nonprofit's oyster. The community may be the city in which the nonprofit is located, the state, or the nation. Frequently, it is two or more of these—or it should be. The 1980 census graphically spells out the loss of population in major industrial cities and the growth in suburbs and smaller communities. A major population shift is also taking place with increases in population in western states and declines in northeastern and middle western states. Constituencies are on the move. The nonprofit will move with these changes or be left behind. The inner city museum that doesn't reach out for support to the suburbs or, as the Detroit Institute of Arts does, to the entire state, is going to be left with a shrinking community base. This same reaching out for a changing constituency is a requirement for nonprofits as diverse as labor unions, political parties, trade associations, universities, and hospitals. For most nonprofits, the base is not shrinking, it is changing. Identifying the constituency requires planning and development today.

CONSUMERS: THE KEY CONSTITUENCY

The consumer is the nonprofit's key constituency. Profit-making firms have long known that a satisfied customer is the best advertisement. The same holds true for the nonprofit. The satisfied member, student, client, patient, patron is the nonprofit's best advertisement in the community. Equally, the consumer is a source of funding, volunteers, political and community support. To be satisfied, the consumer must be involved in the operations of the nonprofit. A hands-off, authoritarian approach will alienate the consumer and cost the nonprofit its most effective constituency.

INVOLVING THE CONSUMER

The consumer needs a stake in the nonprofit, a return on his or her use of the nonprofit's services. This return takes many forms. It can be as simple as a sense of belonging, or as sophisticated as an active role as a member of the board planning the directions of the nonprofit. It can be an accrual of social position in the community or a belief that the consumer is contributing to a major social change. The stake and the return require planning based on the size and nature of the nonprofit. It requires an analysis of the nonprofit's consumers and a determination of their goals, their interests, and their abilities to contribute to the nonprofit.

UNIVERSITIES: LEADERS IN CONSUMER INVOLVEMENT

America's universities are blessed with articulate, attractive, energetic consumers. Students as allies of the nonprofit university are proving indispensable to the health and wealth of their institutions. There are, of course, some additional unique aspects to the universities' consumers: they are more or less a captive audience, they embody leadership characteristics, they are adventurous, and they have excellent contacts throughout the community. It is only fairly recently, however, that this consumer group became a viable force for the nonprofit university.

Students in the 1960s looked at the nonprofit university as the enemy. Reacting against authoritarian rules and regulations which treated the student less as a consumer and more as a child, students wrested real changes in their relationships with the nonprofit management and board of trustees. These changes are still very much alive on college campuses and have opened the way to a new partnership approach between the university and its consumer. Students are involved in policy committees, in determining directions of coursework and programs, participating in decisions on investments, rating faculty on their performance. Students are making real contributions to the day-to-day operation of nonprofit universities.

The university is also profiting from this student involvement in its operation. Students are operating campus organizations and facilities at savings to the nonprofit; students are actively involved in recruiting potential students, and students are in the forefront of fundraising drives.

Recently, students have been publicizing their universities through publications and guidebooks which are a source of profit as well as a strong advertisement for the university. This rating, particularly in the highly competitive market for new students, is going to become even more important to the future of the nonprofit. It demands more analysis of consumer needs and desires and involvement of the student/consumer in the operation of the university.

CONSUMERS IN OTHER NONPROFITS

Hospitals realize the importance of a happy patient and of the need to involve patients in the direction of the nonprofit hospital. Patient responses to the hospital are scrutinized. Questionnaires and personal interviews are being used to determine the patients' reactions and recommendations. These recommendations, when implemented, are a public source of positive consumer contribution to the work of the nonprofit hospital. An example of this is the phenomenon of "birthing rooms" in hospitals where a mother can give birth in a home-like atmosphere. These birthing rooms are a response to consumer demand and are proving to be a valuable attraction to the hospital's consumers.

Human service agencies frequently assert that their consumers are not a viable source of assistance. Steps can be taken to turn this around. The service delivery agency has not benefited from the universities' consumer revolt. The consumers of these agencies also may not be the articulate and attractive consumers that the university attracts. They may only share a commonality with students in the fact that they are a captive audience of the service delivery agency, dependent upon the services for wellbeing. They may not be goal oriented and they may not know how to channel their energies in a positive way. They may have low incomes and great needs. They are not the profile of the upward mobile, but perhaps just the opposite.

But, beyond their need for the service, they undoubtedly have other needs. The first is their need for self-worth and for belonging to something that gives them a sense of self-worth. These additional needs can be identified by the nonprofit through questionnaires and interviews. They can also be turned to the advantage of the nonprofit and used to benefit both the service consumer and the organization providing the service.

ANTICIPATING CONSUMER CONCERN

Fellowship House in South Florida is a nonprofit community center for mentally ill people. The House offers social skills, housing alternatives, work experience, preparation and job placement. Its multitude of services to mentally ill people does not include psychiatric or psychological treatment. For that, Fellowship House's consumers must use established facilities within the community.

Fellowship House works with approximately 500 people a year. It demonstrates cost effectiveness and public accountability through the diminished costs for hospitalization for people who are in its programs. The community can easily understand that instead of the $150 a day for institutional care, Fellowship House's costs average $8.23 a day.

Fellowship House takes an unusual approach to its consumers. The usual way of doing business in the human service delivery area is to refer to the users of the services as "clients." Research done at Fellowhip House found that the philosophy of "everyone having something to offer" was most attractive to consumers. Consequently, its consumers are "members" of the House, not "clients." This distinction is more than semantic. A member of an organization belongs to something and has more responsibility to see that the organization succeeds. Subtle, yet effective and worthy of wide duplication. A "member" has a stake in the nonprofit, unlike a "client" who is in a passive role. The importance of assigning roles to the consumer and the dignity that goes along with this cannot be over-stressed. Fellowship House enjoys broad community support. One of the reasons is its concern for the dignity and worth of its consumers. This principle can be applied to the consumers of all nonprofit organizations.

RESPONDING TO NEW CONSUMER INTERESTS

The American Automobile Association, a nonprofit organization formed to encourage safety and enjoyment of automobile travel, has responded in a variety of innovative ways to its members' changing needs. As auto travel in the United States declined, the Association responded by introducing full travel services for trips abroad, including planning airline and ship tickets, making hotel reservations, supplying maps, and arranging car rentals while abroad. The AAA introduced mobile diagnostic vans in selected cities as American citizens have begun to keep their cars for longer periods than in the past. The AAA identifies trends affecting its member/consumers and provides a service to answer the trend to keep consumers satisfied and to maintain its viability as an organization. The Association calls the attention of its members to new services through mailings and other direct contact. It also uses its services as the basis for news stories to generate media notice that reaches both the existing member and the potential member.

SATISFYING CONSUMER SOCIAL NEEDS

The Corcoran Gallery of Art in Washington, D.C., has tough competition from public nonprofit museums such as the National Gallery and the Smithsonian Institution. As a private, nonprofit museum, however, the Corcoran recognized its advantage in its respected art school. Art schools attract working artists and the Corcoran's shows of new artists are popular and unusual Washington events. The Corcoran recognized the importance of its young artists and shows of new art to Washington's affluent young professionals. It identified an opportunity to build support among this group by highlighting its own youthfulness. The Corcoran revived a "masked artist's ball" as one of its key attractions for new Gallery members. The ball has become a major social event for young professionals as well as a highly successful fundraising effort. The Corcoran identified and responded to the Washington "singles" scene and has become an important resource for this group.

STAFF: AN OVERLOOKED RESOURCE

The staff of any nonprofit can be an important resource if it is recognized as a major constituency. The staff is on the job, a captive audience. If the nonprofit is the traditional pyramidical hierarchy, the staff may be cut off from needed information and unable to make the contributions that could enhance the success of the nonprofit. Two-way communication is extremely important in all phases of the nonprofit but particularly between management and staff. Staff contributions to programming and decision making is needed. There is a well-documented rise in employee dissatisfaction in the United States. The nonprofit is not immune. In fact, because of low pay scales, heavy work loads, and unclear goals, the nonprofit may be more vulnerable to employee dissatisfaction. A well-managed nonprofit can overcome these deficiences and make full use of its staff as a constituent partner.

ALUMNI: AN IMPORTANT CONSTITUENCY

Universities were the first nonprofits to recognize the importance of this constituency and to make concerted efforts to involve alumni. Initially, alumni were identified as a source of funding. This role has now grown, and alumni today are crucial to many universities not only in raising money but also in recruiting students, in lobbying for government and private support of universities, in providing career information and jobs, in helping to decide on programs the university offers, and in planning the direction of the university. Alumni serve on boards of trustees, in other volunteer capacities, and as staff and faculty of universities. Alumni are crucial.

Many universities are not, however, making full use of this valuable resource. It has been lost, overlooked in rapid expansion plans and in the pressures of dealing with student demands. Today, no university can afford not to

A TELEFUNDING SCRIPT

Hello, is this (name of the person being contacted)?

This is Sally Smith. I'm a junior at _____ College. I know that you are a graduate of the College in _____ and that you've been an active supporter of its _____ campaign for the 80s. I hope that we can count on your help again this year. I'd like to tell you some of the uses that your donation went to last year. The college was

PERSONALIZE   able to restore three of the main campus buildings, thanks to you and other alumni, and I'm sure you have memories of (names of buildings). This year, with your contribution, the college is setting aside money for students who are in need of funds for the new computer-required course. Funds will be available for students to borrow to purchase their own computers for the new course.

You may have some questions that I'll be happy to answer.

DONOR TALK

That's an important point. I'm from California also and I chose _____ College for the same reasons that

IMPROVISE   you did. I've also had a number of part-time jobs since I've been here, and I think that the field you are in sounds like a good one and I'm going to find out more about it.

I really want to thank you for talking with me and for your continued support of the college. You'll be receiving a

SPECIFY   donation form and return envelope for your convenience within a week. May I check your address again with you? We have _____.

Again my thanks. Goodbye.

FIGURE 3–1.

have its alumni involved in all aspects of the university. Many public nonprofit (state-supported) schools have been slow to recognize the importance of their alumni. A telling example of this is a comparison between the 25th class reunions of the private, nonprofit Harvard College in Cambridge, Massachusetts, in 1979 and a similar 25th reunion at a public nonprofit, the University of Michigan in Ann Arbor, Michigan, in 1980. Harvard College's reunion for its graduates of 1954 was a weeklong on-campus celebration complete with lectures, dinners, dances, concerts, and other events. Alumni paid a fee for room and board. This weeklong celebration covered its costs and realized the largest single class contribution in the college's history. The University of Michigan, on the other hand, did not schedule a single event for the class of 1955 during its 1980 Homecoming Weekend. The contrast between the two approaches to alumni is telling.

Alumni clubs, organized and supported by colleges, should be found in major cities throughout the United States. Many nonprofits use a sophisticated mix of fundraising approaches including alumni clubs, special events, publications, direct mail, and one of the newest techniques, "telefunding."

Telefunding is a brilliant use of a university's student constituent to reach out to the alumni constituent. Quite simply, telefunding is a student telephoning alumni at home throughout the United States. Whenever possible, students whose home is in the same area as the alumni to be called make the contact. This further personalizes the call. The students call during the week, usually to coincide with the dinner hour. Telefunding is personal, a student chatting with an alum, forceful in getting the college's need across, flattering to the call's recipient ("Gee, the old school remembers me") and predictably, with postal costs on the rise and with the competition for dollars in the nonprofit area, one of the new means to raise money. (See Figure 3–1 for a sample telefunding script.)

George Washington University in Washington, D.C., recently began telefunding ("George Calling" or "Martha Calling," depending on the sex of the alum and student), and found in its first year of use that contributions exceeded those raised from alumni by other means.

TARGETS WITH CONSTITUENCIES

Telefunding is by no means limited to schools. Most nonprofits can adapt this method to reach their consumers, alumni, or volunteers for purposes of fundraising or political support.

Often colleges pay students for telefunding. This is an added inducement to the student and a small price for an eager, persuasive, effective fundraiser. Typically, WATS lines are used to keep telephone costs down.

As telefunding becomes more common, its uses will become more sophisticated than they are today. Graduates of particular disciplines within a university will be contacted by students in that discipline: engineers by engineering students; business graduates by business students, etc.—highly selective, highly targeted, and highly effective adaptations to telefunding.

This selectivity, or market segmentation, has already begun, as we've seen when students from the East phone graduates living in the East.

George Washington University's Drama Department launched a "friends of the Drama Department" group to raise funds and support directly from alumni and from others interested in drama. The department identified the need to go beyond the university's fundraising efforts and to directly seek support for its own programs. This selective effort may conflict with the university's overall fundraising audience and could impinge on the university's ability to raise general monies. It can, however, attract new funding from sources that otherwise might not be interested in giving to the university: theater patrons, high school theater departments, community theater groups, and professionals concerned with the theater. It's creating another target inside the larger alumni audience.

NATURAL ALLIES

The drama department example illustrates how one constituency can, and should, lead to others. All nonprofits that offer a needed service can find natural allies. These allies can provide support and further the goals of the nonprofit. The College of William and Mary in Williamsburg, Virginia, a public nonprofit, identified the parents of students and former students as a valuable natural ally. The college established a parents' organization which provides a newsletter and tailored programs and special events for parents. The parents become an informed support group for the college as well as a source of short-term and long-term funding. The College of William and Mary has turned an overlooked group into a contributing constituency.

Examples of natural allies are everywhere. The Friends of Fort Ward in Alexandria, Virginia was formed in 1982 to provide community support to the publicly owned and operated Civil War fort. The Friends experienced a growth rate in paying members of 500 percent within the first six months of existence by contacting other historical associations, history departments at local universities and community colleges, high school history clubs, organizations of reenactment groups, civic associations in neighborhoods near the fort, and political and community leaders. All were natural allies waiting to be tapped.

Museums have natural allies in artists, art schools, interior designers, antique dealers, and gallery owners. Hospitals have allies in the burgeoning self-health movement, in joggers and dieters, in groups of parents of disabled children, in alcoholic support groups, in herpes support groups, in the multitude of community health support and interest programs.

VOLUNTEERS

Where do you find them? Often they are right under the nonprofit's nose, among the consumers, the natural allies, the alumni. Don't overlook the families of the nonprofit staff or the employees of profit-making and nonprofits interested in career growth or change.

CORPORATIONS

Ask not what can the corporation do for me, but what can I (the nonprofit) do for the corporation? Corporations respond to cost effective, visible ways to assist a needed nonprofit service. Corporations can be the source of volunteers, of in-kind contributions, of meeting and office space, of equipment and supplies, of donated materials for distribution, of professional public relations, accounting, marketing and other needed advice, of transportation, of a multitude of useful items. In return, the corporation wants to benefit its own employees, support a needed community service that enhances the life of the community and that responds to the needs of an accountable nonprofit. The approach to the corporation must be planned, feasible, and a contribution to the corporation goals.

FOUNDATIONS

Do your homework and identify those foundations with an interest in the area of your nonprofit. Plan, identify the needs that you will fulfill through a foundation grant, and approach the foundation with skill and personal attention. Use your board of trustees and community supporters to design the right approach and select the right people to make it.

GOVERNMENT

There are untapped new opportunities at all levels of government. Local, state and national governments can support those nonprofits that have community acceptance and that provide a needed community service. The shift in population to western cities with underdeveloped social services and new population demands is an opportunity for the well-managed, nonprofit service agency. Find the right office to deal with (don't rely on your contacts; other agencies can help), find out whom you are dealing with, and plan your approach. These governments need you to provide needed services.

MEDIA

People working in the media are an important audience for the nonprofit. Close working relations can be developed with reporters and broadcasters in newspapers, magazines, television, radio, and the wire services. Media contributions to the nonprofit should be recognized and honored by the nonprofit. This is another form of contact. Media representatives should be invited to be on the board of trustees. Contacts should be made with the publishers and owners of media outlets in the community. The publishers and owners are frequently overlooked as nonprofits tend to pursue reporters and broadcast journalists. Media people change jobs frequently and constant contact is necessary to keep up with who is on the job.

OTHER NONPROFITS

These comprise an important constituency. Nonprofits can pool resources, exchange ideas, purchase supplies cooperatively at savings, produce public-awareness campaigns that benefit cooperating nonprofits, and work together for mutually beneficial legislation and public funding.

CRITICS

Critics of the nonprofit can become valuable resources in attracting public attention and support. The criticism must be answered fully and effectively. Secrecy in a nonprofit organization that depends on public funding is a thing of the past. Today's educated public demands accountability from all groups that receive its monies. Fundraising agencies must account to the public for the expenditure of funds as well as the effectiveness of their programs.

How can criticism be turned into support? A look at the growth rates of the Sierra Club and other environmental groups can be attributed to the Federal Government's expressed intention to sell or lease government-owned lands and its disdain of environmental groups. This generated public awareness of these groups and public knowledge of the response that the groups gave to the government. A host of new supporters agreed with the groups and became contributing members. The criticism of these groups, fully responded to by the groups, was the impetus for a dramatic increase in community support for environmental causes.

Nonprofit organizations are commonly criticized publically for their failure to account for the use of their donated money, for their failure to achieve stated goals, for their mishandling of consumers, and for arrogance in refusing to be fully frank with the public. These sins can damage a nonprofit unless it can publically respond with honesty and a willingness to change its ways if needed.

CHECKLIST: THE ABC's OF CONSTITUENCIES

A. ASSESS
- Identify the organization's assets.
- Ask the consumer/user by telephone, questionnaire, or interview.
- Ask the community by phoning editors, political and community leaders; setting up booths at conventions, meetings, shopping centers.
- Identify the competition to identify your unique contribution.
- Find out if you have any for-profit competition.
- Check the possibility of government support.
- Investigate other private nonprofits.

B. BUILD
- *Consumers.* Are they involved? Are they paying for services in cash or in volunteer time? Are they used in fundraising, in public appearances, in promotional materials? Are their wishes actively taken into account in the language and programs of the nonprofit?
- *Staff.* Provide clear objectives, obtainable goals, full knowledge. Establish opportunities to affect change.
- *Alumni/former users.* Are they being addressed on a continuing basis? Are they involved in the running of the organization?
- *Natural Allies.* Are families, other organizations, for-profit groups with similar interests contacted?
- *Corporations.* What does the nonprofit offer the corporation?

- *Volunteers.* Are they being used for full benefit to the organization? What are they getting in return?
- *Foundations.* Have you identified foundations interested in your work for continual contact?
- *Government.* Can the nonprofit produce cost-effective, accountable, and community-supported services with government funds? What community needs are not being addressed by government programs? Look for the gaps in services that the government could fund. Be competitive and offer more efficient services than the government itself can provide.
- *Media.* Does the organization have friends in the media to call upon for assistance and direction?
- *Other Nonprofits.* How can you cooperate to benefit all concerned through purchases of materials, equipment, and professional services?
- *Critics.* Are you making the best response to critics and turning criticism to the organization's advantage?

C. COMMUNICATE

- For maximum effectiveness and recognition establish a flow of information to and from your constituencies.
- Use cost-effective and personalized communications:
  Telefunding
  Newsletters that reach more than one constituency
  Direct mail
  Questionnaires
  Interviews
  The media
- Be open, frank and accountable.

CHAPTER 4

Public Relations Research and Assessment

Stop, look, listen, and ask. These four steps are the fundamentals of successful research, assessment, and evaluation. In turn, research, assessment, evaluation are the foundations on which an effective public relations program is built.

All nonprofits deal in information. Information is the nonprofit's distinctive value to the community and to its member/publics. While nonprofits produce a dizzying array of services, they share information production in common. Information for the nonprofit is a product, a major product. This product, information, must be used to the advantage of the nonprofit. Information can be gathered by research and it can be news for all of the nonprofit's publics.

INFORMATION AS NEWS

More Americans went to museums to see the traveling art exhibition "Tutankhamen" than to any other single exhibit. This simple counting of attendance, this elementary research, is still news to the media years after the Tutankhamen treasures were returned to Egypt. Every major art exhibit mounted today is compared in attendance and popularity to that show. The research on the exhibit's attendance was the basis for national news stories and increases in overall museum attendance. The museum gained public visibility as an exciting place. The museums that hosted the exhibit were not the only beneficiaries of the media excitement about it. Other museums benefited as well by media-promoted interest in all museums. The research on the attendance at the exhibit consequently had major impact on museums, on the general public, on the media, and on museum attendance. Museums became "the place to be seen," and "Tutankhamen" spawned a host of other major exhibitions at museums throughout the country.

INFORMATION AS FUNDRAISER

The proliferation of media stories sparked by the depression and the needs of people for shelter and food brought increased donations to those charities which are directly concerned with these needs. In 1982 donations to the New York Times Neediest Cases Fund, sponsored by the *New York Times* newspaper, exceeded by more than 20 percent all past records. Religious donations were also up in 1982. One reason for this increase is that more churches became involved in feeding and sheltering programs. This outpouring of public concern and money was a result of the extensive media coverage based on the information available through nonprofit organizations concerned with food and shelter needs.

INFORMATION AS CATALYST

In a matter of days, the following disparate group of nonprofit organizations organized to protest the government's proposed regulations to prohibit nonprofits from engaging in "advocacy" while using government funds. Armed with an outpouring of information about their own programs, members and concerns, these organizations appeared at Congressional hearings, which in turn generated media news. The information provided by the nonprofits was crucial. These organizations cooperated on this mutual effort despite their wide range of members, activities, and views.

LEGISLATION AND NATIONAL SECURITY SUBCOMMITTEE
Tuesday, March 1, 1983
SCHEDULE OF WITNESSES
National Conference of Catholic Charities
American Lung Association
League of Women Voters of the United States
National Urban League
Appalachian Mountain Club
American Association of Retired Persons
American Association of Museums
The National Network of Runaway and Youth Services, Inc.
National Association of Manufacturers
National Council of Technical Service Industries
Disability Rights Education and Defense Fund, Inc.
American Civil Liberties Union
Wisconsin Community Action Program Association, Inc.
Association for Retarded Citizens, Pennsylvania
Computer and Communications Industry Association
The Fairness Committee Against Tax-Funded Politics
Chamber of Commerce of the United States
Professional Services Council
Electronic Industries Association
National Committee for Responsive Philanthropy
American Heart Association
National Council of Senior Citizens

Information sometimes just happens. For most nonprofits, however, information must be sought, produced, developed, and distributed. Information is in constant flux. The nonprofit can use the following steps to insure that it is keeping up with the need for timely and useful information:

UNCOVERING YOUR ASSETS

Stop assuming that the nonprofit's management knows what it is offering to its member/public. The member/public may perceive the nonprofit's service very differently. It may be selecting one service over all the others as the most important reason for supporting the organization. The nonprofit offers its members something, and members respond to this offering. The information that is needed is the reason the member has selected this particular nonprofit.

A small professional organization of writers and editors offers its members newsletters, working lunches, training programs, seminars, and a forum for exchanging ideas, problems, job tips. The organization also offers an annual awards program to honor the members' best work. The organization's management has had longstanding problems in attracting members to its programs and special events. Management surveyed its members and found that the awards program was the major service for the members. The awards program, designed as an adjunct to the professional activities, became the organization's strongest program and a major source of income and information.

One way to uncover the most important program of the nonprofit is to query the users of the nonprofit's services. Users can be asked in a number of ways to reduce inaccuracies and to produce valid information for the nonprofit. Some users may dislike the nonprofit the day they are asked about it, so questions must be designed to identify this and any other errors that may otherwise creep in undetected. Indirect questions can give the nonprofit a clue to its most important user attractions.

Asking questions can be done in person, through written questionnaires, and by telephone. A good use of member/users is to involve them in the design and execution of the survey. The more involvement a nonprofit offers its users, the more valuable the user becomes and the more information the nonprofit can gather.

Similar tactics can be used for all the nonprofit's constituencies. Some suggestions:

Staff.

All levels of staff should be questioned as to their understanding of the nonprofit's mission and goals and their ability to contribute. Staff information can be developed in many ways: anonymously through written questionnaires and suggestion boxes, and openly at staff meetings. All staff should, however, be questioned at frequent intervals in order to keep the communication channels open. If the staff is unclear as to the mission, the purpose, and the information of the nonprofit, chances are that the member/users are going to reflect this lack of understanding. Staff bias is reflected in member/user attitudes. Staff is too important to overlook. Small staff gatherings, perhaps self-directed, in specific work areas of the nonprofit, are a means to involve staff at all levels in the success of the nonprofit.

Alumni and Former Members.

These provide a source of information about changes that are affecting the nonprofit. Seeking their opinions not only helps to keep this group involved, but also can lead to some interesting observations about the nonprofit, some of which, of course, may be quite negative. A few years ago, several well-known private schools and universities decided to sexually integrate their campuses. In some instances, alumni were asked for their opinions in advance of the change. In others, alumni were notified of the change when it became public knowledge. Many alumni in the first instance felt their important views were ignored. In the second instance, alumni bitterness was much deeper. As a result, some schools continue to feel the effect of alumni wrath concerning the change. This points up a warning: don't seek advice after the fact. Asking for opinions means just that. The opinion is to be weighed by management before a decision is taken. Alternatives may be offered which could be very attractive.

Natural Allies.

Don't overlook corporations, foundations, government. Seeking the views and opinions of these groups affords the nonprofit opportunities to identify resources (including potential sources of funding), to identify the unexpected needs, and to clarify the goals and programs with these key constituencies.

Volunteers.

Like staff, the volunteer's association with the nonprofit affords insights from a viewpoint that is different from that of management or even staff. Volunteers should be included in the planning of volunteer questionnaires and research projects, and used to collect information from each other as well as from other constituencies. The volunteer can do telephone surveys; operate booths at conventions, meetings, shopping malls; write follow-up letters; and generate needed information—even about his own feelings.

Media.

The media can be most useful in doing public opinion sampling for a nonprofit. As information is news, and as many media outlets currently do opinion sampling, the needs of the nonprofit could be included in ongoing or new media studies. The president or chief executive officers of the nonprofit should be in constant communication with media leaders in the community to determine their views on the nonprofit, its programs, and goals.

USING OTHER'S RESEARCH TO SUPPLEMENT YOUR OWN

The nonprofit does not have to do all its own research. There are opportunities for cooperation within the community. Many of these opportunities are within the nonprofit's constituencies. There are also opinion polls and surveys frequently presented by other sources, major corporations, the media, political opinion firms, that can be used by the nonprofit to its advantage in developing community support. These surveys provide useful clues to social changes that must be incorporated into the nonprofit's planning.

LISTEN FOR CLUES

Listen to the general public. What are its needs, its directions, its desires? The media offers many clues, and a study can be designed based on these clues to determine programs and planning in the nonprofit. The American Red Cross determined through a survey that its safety, nursing and health services component was the least frequently mentioned of its services in the media. Yet health and self-health interests were found to be important public concerns. Based on these findings, the American Red Cross determined to target health promotion and related skill training to meet public needs and to further its safety, nursing, and health services.

One result was that the American Red Cross offered 5,822 courses in "preparation for parenthood" during 1982. The American Nurses Association, a professional nonprofit, determined that instructor training in this "preparation for parenthood" course merited continuing education units for professional nurses. This increases both the appeal of the course as well as its credibility. Additional programs coming out of the American Red Cross's listening to the public are teenagers taking courses in babysitting and volunteer nurses earning continuing education units for instructor training in home nursing. Listening has stimulated new and attractive visibility for the American Red Cross' safety, nursing, and health services.

IDENTIFYING NEW IDEAS THROUGH QUESTIONING

The American University's Division of Student Life held a September 1982 informal meeting of a group of women who had returned to higher education after an absence of a number of years. This important target audience, known at the American University as "women in transition," is one that the University is actively seeking.

Among the important concerns identified by the participants were (1) the need for a center/commons area with telephones and typewriters for the exclusive use of the mature woman for study, peer support, and refuge from younger students; (2) evening office hours for all areas of the University (registration, deans' offices, etc.), not just the office dealing specifically with the mature woman; (3) tutoring in mathematics to overcome "math anxiety;" (4) more and better advice on course work and career development; (5) babysitting services; (6) carpool-matching services; (7) briefings on academic rights and responsibilities; (8) safe and plentiful parking.

These contributions can be valuable to the University in shaping programs of greater appeal to women returning to higher education.

A new idea that came from the questioning was the recommendation that a similar program be established to attract men back into higher education.

ASKING THE RIGHT QUESTIONS

Asking questions is the basis of research, assessment and evaluation. It is essential that the right questions be asked to get the answers that the nonprofit needs to be more efficient, more effective, more attractive.

Start at the beginning and find out where the nonprofit is in reaching its constituencies; in determining their opinions; in meeting publically expressed needs; in the use of tools to reach constituencies. How effective are these tools?

QUESTIONING THROUGH PRE-TESTING AGENCY MATERIALS

Pre-testing public service advertisements, new designs for letterheads and logos, new publications, on a group that includes members/consumers, volunteers, staff, representatives of other nonprofits, media professionals and the general public is a valuable way of establishing two-way communications with key audiences.

Pre-testing can be both questioning and evaluating. Responses can indicate the effectiveness of the materials being pre-tested (before release) and can evaluate the appropriateness of the materials for specific audiences. Pre-testing is valuable in helping to determine how clear the organization's goals are to specific audiences as well as assessing the contribution of the specific program being pre-tested to the organization's goals.

Pre-testing has long been used by commercial advertisers and product manufacturers. Film companies offer "sneak previews" to test audience response to a new film and use the information to determine how the film will be marketed—or even if the film should be marketed.

EVALUATION

Evaluation means determining how cost effective and productive your tools are. In the past, public relations offices would rely on counting the column inches of agency-originated stories the newspapers ran. This reliance is outmoded. Clipping services can provide the amount of coverage that an agency gets in the press, but evaluation determines the effectiveness of this coverage and its contribution to fundraising, membership, volunteers, legislative developments. Evaluation is more than counting. It is determining the cost effectiveness of various programs and the goals accomplished by these programs.

The models presented in Figures 4–1—4–5 are a systemized approach to evaluation. Apply these techniques to your organization's constituents and programs. The results will benefit your organization's planning for success.

RESEARCH, ASSESSMENT AND EVALUATION MODEL (BASED ON SPECIFIC PROGRAMS)

PROGRAM	RESEARCH	ASSESSMENT	EVALUATION	PROPOSALS
University alumni publication.	Published four times a year. Features news items about alumni activities. Low cost, no color newsprint paper. Regular columns from university president on happenings and plans. No advertising.	Questionnaire included in publication shows reader interest and value of publication. Younger alumni not interested. Readers mention "sameness" of articles.	While relatively low cost, postal increases are driving costs up, as are printing costs. Publication is self-supporting from alumni dues. Publication does not raise additional funds. Alumni office staff spend disproportionate amount of time on publication.	1) Broaden the list of recipients of the publication to include donors to the university and interested others—parents, foundations, corporations, government. 2) Change the format to a magazine style quarterly and investigate the use of color and better paper stock. 3) Interest younger alumni by running free job-wanted ads. 4) Seek advertising from corporations and organizations doing business with the university. 5) Feature corporate stories on alumni in a corporation, with accompanying institutional advertising. These corporations can be identified through campus recruiting and alumni surveys. 6) Strengthen the editorial content by contracting with faculty, students, and alumni for specific articles of interest to the university's community. 7) List specific university needs in each issue and the amounts of donor dollars needed for specific items; fundraising is a major target of alumni publications. 8) The president should be free of a regular column in an alumni publication. He should be used for major consumer magazines and daily newspaper op-ed pages and reprints shared with alumni and donors.

FIGURE 4–1.

RESEARCH, ASSESSMENT AND EVALUATION MODEL (BASED ON AN URBAN ART MUSEUM)

CONSTITUENCY	RESEARCH	ASSESSMENT	CURRENT EVALUATION	PROPOSALS
Museum visitors.	Admission fees.	Fees do not indicate names, addresses for follow-up.	Need more revenue from fees to meet operating costs.	1) Survey other art museums in urban areas for pricing information.
	Sales/shops and restaurants.	Sales off.	Need more sales from shops and restaurants.	2) Design 2/3-minutes simple questionnaire for each visitor in a one-month period. Seek specific info on pricing, hours, programs, services such as shops/restaurants, public transportation, parking, security. Seek names and addresses.
	Comments: letters, calls to staff and remarks to docents and guards.	Unreliable because of bias.	Need reliable indicators of visitor preferences.	3) Design 8-minute personal interview for random selectees (each 50th visitor) for staff use on proposed new features: day-care center for visitors; shopping mall programs; film festivals; classes in furniture restoration, antique buying, etc.
	Group tours.	Mainly schoolchildren.	Need more group tours.	4) The restaurant should produce menu tie-ins with exhibits. Restaurant to cater outside of museum as well as at museum and nonprofit events within the museum. Restaurant should advertise in newspapers, be reviewed by food critics, initiate a "special"—Sunday Brunch, Saturday tea-dance.
				5) Shop. Design a sales brochure for mailing. Buy mailing lists. Pick a specialty unique to urban area.
				6) Group tours. Schedule staff/volunteer appearances at senior citizen centers, convention centers. Offer highly selective programs to specific audiences. Tie in with local department store promotions and loan objects for specific promotional use.

FIGURE 4-2.

RESEARCH, ASSESSMENT AND EVALUATION MODEL (BASED ON URBAN ART MUSEUM) - 2.

CONSTITUENCY	RESEARCH	ASSESSMENT	CURRENT EVALUATION	PROPOSALS
Museum staff.	Guards are employed by city; are union members.	Must negotiate guard hours with city and union.	Need flexible hours to suit working professional visitors. More city and union participation.	1) Assign one senior staff to work with city and union. Invite city and union officials to be on board and in on committees' planning future.
	Curators are highly specialized.	Curators are compartmentalized.	Need curators to do more public speaking and outreach. Need income from their teaching, writing, professional services.	2) Assign senior staff (curator) to investigate cooperative credit courses with high schools/colleges. Offer credit and teacher/expert training at museum.
	Staff newsletter.	Newsletter is poorly and cheaply done.	A lousy newsletter is worse than none.	3) Develop and place curator articles in newspapers and special interest (travel, social) publications.
	Yearly staff parties.	Staff parties—little mixing.		
	Occasional all-staff meetings.	Staff meetings—top down sharing.	Need greater staff participation and contribution to planning.	4) Seek outside funds for newsletter.
	Weekly top staff meetings.			5) Form working groups (quality circles) involving each employee in specific work areas.

FIGURE 4-3.

RESEARCH, ASSESSMENT AND EVALUATION MODEL (BASED ON URBAN ART MUSEUM) - 3.

CONSTITUENCY	RESEARCH	ASSESSMENT	CURRENT EVALUATION	PROPOSALS
Museum volunteers.	Quantity.	Outnumber staff 5 to 1.	Goal is 10 to 1 volunteer/staff ratio.	1) Advertise in "help-wanted" sections for volunteers who want valuable job experience for their resumés.
	Quality.	Poorly trained.	Need training programs for volunteers in fundraising, political and public speaking.	2) Arrange with schools and colleges for credit to be given to volunteers for specific work.
	Commitment.	For social prestige.	Need greater commitment.	3) Write job descriptions for each volunteer.
	Reliability.	Varies.	Need higher reliability.	4) Establish progressive ladder wherein volunteer will move on to new duties as performance merits.
	Fundraising: actual; potential.	Insufficient.	Need more money from volunteers and friends.	5) Establish training for volunteers in public speaking, lobbying, fundraising techniques.
	Staff comments.	Staff find volunteers take too much time and contribute too little to daily operation.	Trained volunteers would be asset.	6) Cover volunteer personalities and activities in member/staff newsletter.
				7) Honor volunteers with awards and educational program opportunities.
				8) Design questionnaire for volunteers to gain their thoughts on plans and programs.
				9) If feasible, offer assistance with babysitting, transportation, meals, discounts on purchases, and loans of art.

FIGURE 4-4.

RESEARCH, ASSESSMENT AND EVALUATION MODEL (BASED ON SPECIFIC PROGRAM)

PROGRAM	RESEARCH	ASSESSMENT	CURRENT EVALUATION	PROPOSALS
Fundraising dinner dance.	Annual event.	Considerable staff time used.	Need to sustain volunteer commitment.	1) Produce and distribute a questionnaire to volunteers for recommendations.
	Established in community.	Little consumer/user participation.	Need to lessen staff time.	2) Investigate holding the event at another nonprofit organization and having catering done by a nonprofit's restaurant.
	Good volunteer leadership.	Competition for fundraising keener.	Need to involve consumer/users.	3) Contract for an event coordinator to ease burden on staff and to plan event. Contractor must have strong ties to existing volunteers and could be recruited from among them. All volunteers should be honored and rewarded for their work with event.
	Raises needed money.	Nonprofit cause not as visible as in the past.	Need to up the level of profit.	4) Consumer/users should be on planning committee for event and corporations and volunteers solicited for donations to provide tables for consumer/users.
	Produces community visibility.	Need more visibility in community from fundraising event.	Costs at hotel and for catering up substantially.	5) Consumer/users and volunteers should be scheduled for pre-event publicity to focus on the programs and services resulting from fundraiser.
			Media coverage of event and the reasons for it need improvement.	6) Produce a program with advertising from cooperating firms and organizations.

FIGURE 4-5.

STOP, LOOK, LISTEN, AND ASK

Every constituency, every program, must be researched, assessed and evaluated. No opportunity should be overlooked to foster closer relations with constituencies and to insure that programs are cost-effective and productive. The application of these methods can make better use of available resources.

As an organization becomes familiar with this process, and the process becomes an integral part of the organization, questions will flow and answers will follow.

The more you ask, the more information you will have to use in building support for the nonprofit. The sample forms shown in Figures 4-6—4-9 indicate ways to obtain valuable information at low cost from important audiences.

Evaluation takes either a spoken or a written form. The value of the written evaluation is that it can be anonymous and readily assessed by the organization.

SAMPLE #1:   EVALUATING BOARD MEETINGS (EVALUATION TO BE DONE BY
             BOARD MEMBERS)

Please use the scale of 1 to 10 (1 being poor and 10 being excellent) to evaluate the board meetings:

	POOR							EXCELLENT		
1. FREQUENCY OF MEETINGS	1	2	3	4	5	6	7	8	9	10
2. STAFF PREPARATION	1	2	3	4	5	6	7	8	9	10
3. INFORMATION RECEIVED	1	2	3	4	5	6	7	8	9	10
4. IMPORTANCE OF MEETINGS	1	2	3	4	5	6	7	8	9	10

Please answer TRUE or FALSE

1. I feel that my role as a board member is important to the organization's
   operations.   TRUE   FALSE
2. I find the materials sent to me in advance of the meetings prepare me
   sufficiently.   TRUE   FALSE
3. I believe that board recommendations are incorporated into ongoing operations
   of the organization.   TRUE   FALSE
4. I find staff presentations at meetings useful and frank.
                                 TRUE   FALSE
5. I believe the organization to be important to the community.
                                 TRUE   FALSE

Briefly note other comments:

A. Topics for future board meetings:
B. Suggestions for new board members:
C. Recommendations for involvement of board other than meetings:

FIGURE 4-6.

SAMPLE #2: EVALUATING A TRAINING PROGRAM

On a scale of 1 to 10 (1 being poor and 10 being excellent), evaluate the following general aspects of the training program. Circle the number that corresponds to your evaluation.

	POOR							EXCELLENT		
1. ORGANIZATION OF THE TRAINING	1	2	3	4	5	6	7	8	9	10
2. LENGTH OF SESSIONS	1	2	3	4	5	6	7	8	9	10
3. QUALITY OF PRESENTATIONS	1	2	3	4	5	6	7	8	9	10
4. DISCUSSION OPPORTUNITIES	1	2	3	4	5	6	7	8	9	10
5. LENGTH OF TRAINING PROGRAM	1	2	3	4	5	6	7	8	9	10
6. LENGTH OF INDIVIDUAL SESSIONS	1	2	3	4	5	6	7	8	9	10
7. RELEVANCE OF INFORMATION	1	2	3	4	5	6	7	8	9	10
8. CONFERENCE SETTING	1	2	3	4	5	6	7	8	9	10
9. LUNCH/REFRESHMENTS	1	2	3	4	5	6	7	8	9	10
10. SPEAKER PREPARATION	1	2	3	4	5	6	7	8	9	10

BRIEFLY DESCRIBE OR IDENTIFY:

1. THE MAIN IDEA(S) YOU GAINED FROM TRAINING.

2. TOPICS FOR FUTURE TRAINING.

3. OUTSTANDING SPEAKERS AND SESSIONS.

4. WEAKEST SPEAKERS AND SESSIONS.

5. SUGGESTIONS FOR FUTURE TRAINING PROGRAMS.

FIGURE 4–7.

SAMPLE #3:   EVALUATING A MUSEUM VISITOR'S EXPERIENCE

The museum is interested in providing the most valuable and pleasant experience possible for its visitors. Your taking three minutes to respond to our questions will help us in improving our program and meeting your needs.

1. Is this your first visit to the museum?   YES   NO
2. How frequently do you visit the museum?
     WEEKLY   MONTHLY   YEARLY
3. Were the guards courteous?   YES   NO   NO COMMENT
4. Were the staff members helpful?   YES   NO   NO COMMENT
5. Did you take a guided tour?   YES   NO
6. If you took a guided tour, was the guide informative and interesting?
   YES   NO
7. How much time did you spend in the museum?
     1 HOUR   2-4 HOURS   MORE
8. Did you eat in the restaurant(s)?   YES   NO
9. If you ate in the museum restaurant(s), please rate the food:
   GOOD   AVERAGE   POOR
   The service:
   GOOD   AVERAGE   POOR
10. Did you shop in the museum shop?   YES   NO
11. If you shopped, did you buy anything?   YES   NO
    How was the service?   GOOD   POOR
    How were the prices?   FAIR   HIGH
12. Which of the following programs would you attend if they were available?
    Children's tours and hands-on programs: _____
    Senior citizens' programs: _____
    Film series: _____
    Lectures: _____
    Musical programs: _____
    Auctions: _____
    Openings: _____
13. Are you a member of the museum?   YES   NO
14. If you are interested in being on the museum's mailing list, please print your name and address below:

15. Comments and suggestions:

Thank you for your time and help. We look forward to seeing you again.

Signed: The Director of the Museum

FIGURE 4–8.

SAMPLE #4:   EVALUATING A PROSPECTIVE MEMBER FOR A PROFESSIONAL
ASSOCIATION

Dear Prospective Member,

We are an association of professionals—of people like you—and we would like
to interest you in joining us. The enclosed brochure outlines our programs,
services, and fees.

First, though, we'd like to know your concerns and interests. If you will take a
few minutes to answer the following questions, it will help us provide the kinds of
services that respond to your needs as a professional.

Please circle the number from 1 to 10 which most accurately reflects your
professional interests and needs. (1 is NO INTEREST, 10 is HIGH INTEREST.)

	NO INTEREST							HIGH INTEREST		
Lobbying and legislative development.	1	2	3	4	5	6	7	8	9	10
Publications.	1	2	3	4	5	6	7	8	9	10
Awards programs.	1	2	3	4	5	6	7	8	9	10
Exchange of case studies.	1	2	3	4	5	6	7	8	9	10
Annual meetings.	1	2	3	4	5	6	7	8	9	10
Training workshops.	1	2	3	4	5	6	7	8	9	10
Professional standards:	1	2	3	4	5	6	7	8	9	10
Tests.	1	2	3	4	5	6	7	8	9	10
Evaluation of materials.	1	2	3	4	5	6	7	8	9	10
Directory of professionals.	1	2	3	4	5	6	7	8	9	10
Information on available jobs.	1	2	3	4	5	6	7	8	9	10
Site visits of professional interest.	1	2	3	4	5	6	7	8	9	10
Tours of professional interest.	1	2	3	4	5	6	7	8	9	10
Library of information resources.	1	2	3	4	5	6	7	8	9	10
Evaluation of your programs.	1	2	3	4	5	6	7	8	9	10

Do you belong to other professional organizations?   YES   NO
Are these organizations useful to you?   YES   NO
What are the most important services that you identify in other professional
organizations? Please note in order of importance to you.

Thank you for your time and help.

Sincerely, Chief Executive Officer

FIGURE 4–9.

CHAPTER 5

How to Generate Favorable Publicity for Your Nonprofit Organization

Competition for public attention is keen. The public is surrounded by the clamor of the communications media vying for its attention. Corporations with advertising budgets that exceed the Gross National Product of dozens of nations flood the public's view with compelling and imaginative messages. The proliferation of cable television channels, radio stations, newspapers, magazines, specialized newsletters, catalogues, coupon mailings, third class mail offerings of everything from resort homes to vacuum cleaners, has left the public reeling. The competition for the public's time and dollar is ferocious. The nonprofit organization is up against well-funded and sophisticated competition.

There is equal competition in news. News space for nonprofits can be hard to get. Competition includes war and crime, depression and inflation, fascination with the lives and times of politicians, royalty, movie and rock stars. Frequently, the news that the nonprofit wants to generate is not considered "news" by the media. What the media identifies as "news" about the nonprofit is often negative: employee strikes, financial mismanagement, legal action against the nonprofit by users, investigations of abuse and misuse of public funds.

The news that a nonprofit wants to generate—the honors awarded, the successes of programs, the achievements of users—is either overlooked or bumped from the "news" by a fast-breaking development of greater interest to the media's public.

Attracting positive attention to the nonprofit is tough. Public relations tools and resources assist in getting the nonprofit a share of positive public attention, time, and dollars.

GETTING READY TO GO PUBLIC

The nonprofit organization, because it is the recipient of public funds, is frequently in the public eye whether or not it wants to be there. No effort, regardless of expense or skillfulness, can mask mismanagement, misuse of funds, inefficiency, poor quality services, or unhappy users, volunteers or staff. The public demands a frankness and fullness from any organization receiving public funds. The media take these demands to heart and can be rigorous in pursuit of suspected wrongdoings. The nonprofit must meet the media and the public with an openness about its operations and a willingness to fully discuss legitimate issues concerning the public.

This public demand for accountability can work to the benefit of the nonprofit organization. The nonprofit is assisted by local, state, and federal government through property tax exemptions and income tax deductions as well as through subsidized use of the mails. The nonprofit also benefits from Federal Communication Commission (F.C.C.) regulations requiring radio and television stations to donate certain public service time to nonprofits. The regulations are currently being revised. Nonprofit organizations can keep up with the regulations by contacting the Federal Communication Commission, 1919 M St. N.W., Washington, D.C. 20554, or through Congressional representatives.

While privately owned magazines and newspapers are not subject to government regulation regarding public service space for nonprofit messages, many of the country's magazines and newspapers donate space for public service messages from nonprofit organizations. There are countless opportunities to go public for the nonprofit that carefully examines and prepares to do so.

A CLEAR IDENTITY

Few nonprofits are as fortunate as the Red Cross. The Red Cross's logo—a red cross—is instantly identifiable. This logo conveys an understanding of the organization's purposes: that the Red Cross appears when there are needs to be met, misfortunes to be dealt with, disasters to be overcome. The organization is fortunate in having a symbol that is neat, clean, and recognizable. It didn't just happen, however; years of constant attention to the logo have gone into making it a successful symbol. The Red Cross continually monitors public opinion about the organization and adapts its programs to identified public needs. This constant attention to the image of the organization (based on performance, quality, and relevance of services) maintains its prominence locally and nationally.

A clear identity is carefully planned, developed, and nurtured. Every program and activity of the organization is designed to complement and further the identification. Identity must move and change with the times, the demands of its users, and changes in other audiences. Needs change and so must the nonprofit. Attention to these changes and to the simplest of details in the organization's daily activities are ways to overcome muddied images and to foster a strong identity. Some of these simple details include the following factors:

LOGO: Does the organization use a logo? Does the logo convey to the public a clear understanding of the work of the organization? This can be determined by testing the logo's comprehension through random sampling of specific audiences. Is the logo used consistently by the organization on all public materials? Is the logo out of date and needing replacement? Is the organization better able to convey its purposes by using a line of copy on public materials? (See Figure 5–1 for examples of logos.)

A logo can be urgent . . . .

A logo can be traditional . . . .

A logo can be modern . . . .

A logo can provoke interest . . . .

A logo can be dignified . . . .

A logo can be in motion . . . .

FIGURE 5–1. Courtesy of American Red Cross Title, American Red Cross, Washington, D.C. 20006

Courtesy of Kappa Alpha Order, 3379 Peachtree Road, N.E., P.O. Box 18603, Atlanta, Georgia 30326. ® KAPPA ALPHA ORDER.

Courtesy of the Friends of the Kennedy Center, Washington, D.C. 20566.

Courtesy of PROJECT ORBIS, Inc., 330 West 42nd Street, New York, New York 10036.

Courtesy of the Colonial Williamsburg Foundation, Williamsburg, Virginia 23187.

Courtesy of WETA Television 26 Radio FM 91, Box 2626, Washington, D.C. 20013—the major public broadcasting service of the greater Washington area. Logo design by Herb Lubalin.

LETTERHEAD: Perhaps the only contact an organization will have with a specific audience is by letter. This is the case with organizations soliciting funds through mass mailings. Does the letterhead convey a clear identity for the organization? Is the letterhead design used on publications, posters, other public materials of the organization? Are important names affiliated with the organization needed on the letterhead? Is the letterhead overwhelming the body of the letter or is it an effective background? A letterhead can be too contrived and consequently prove to be a distraction rather than a clear, forceful symbol of the nonprofit. Good graphic artists abound in the United States. Universities and art schools are good sources of advice on the design of logos and letterheads. Don't overlook the envelopes in which the letterhead is sent. The envelopes should coordinate with the letterhead and encourage the opening of the envelope. A good graphic artist is invaluable in determining this, as are test mailings for public response to the envelope and letterhead.

Redesign: New Name, New Image, New Vitality.

The Board of Directors of the Society of American Florists, a nonprofit association, felt that "society" connoted a private club and not the professionalism of a national trade association. Additionally, the association's responsibilities had expanded greatly, the membership was international and members represented all aspects of the floral industry, not just retail florists. The Board also did not want to lose the recognition of the acronym—SAF—since the association was known within the floral industry by that acronym.

The result was a new title for the association which incorporates and safeguards the acronym while responding to the expansion of the association (Figure 5–2). The new logo and letterhead incorporate vivid color to add to the foreward movement of the design while reinforcing the dynamism of the organization and clarifying the society's role as an aggressive representation of its members. Note that the new design incorporates a new member service—a toll-free telephone number.

The old traditional design . . . . SOCIETY OF AMERICAN FLORISTS
901 North Washington Street, Alexandria, Virginia 22314   Telephone (703) 836-8700

The new bold design . . . .

901 North Washington Street • Alexandria, VA 22314
Telephone: Toll Free 800/336-4743 • In Virginia: 703/836-8700 • TWX 710-832-0607

Reprinted courtesy of "SAF—The Center for Commercial Floriculture."

FIGURE 5–2.   Courtesy of SAF—the Center for Commercial Floriculture, 901 North Washington Street, Alexandria, Virginia 22314.

COLOR: Color can convey warmth and indicate that a message has greater meaning for the recipient. Color can be used to create and maintain an identity while conveying the organization's mission. The use of green for environmental groups reinforces the idea of nature; the use of red in the "Red Cross" reinforces the goal of insuring supplies of blood from donors to hospitals and to people who need blood. Color can be subtle in conveying the goals and reinforcing the work of the nonprofit.

APPEARANCE: The nonprofit has the responsibility to its users and other publics of maintaining its offices and worksites in a professional and organized manner. Even the nonprofit that is overwhelmed by users and short of funds and staff has an obligation to present itself as effectively, humanely, and professionally as possible. As some nonprofits are located in low rent sites, cleanliness and order may be all that can be achieved. More affluent nonprofits can provide worksites that reflect the purpose of the nonprofit while not overwhelming or intimidating users and other publics. A clean, organized, and professional worksite reinforces the purpose of the organization while conveying a respect for users, donors, volunteers, and staff.

MANNERS: Have the staff been trained in telephone use and in public contact? This training should be done on a continuing basis and the importance of public/user manners must be reinforced and recognized vigorously. Some of the worst offenders in manners and attitude towards users and other publics are the public nonprofit organizations (government). Rudeness cannot be tolerated by a nonprofit. A large university recently criticized its employees for their rudeness to students. It organized training sessions to improve contacts between staff and students. Rudeness or an apparent lack of interest can, and does, result in negative publicity when a user complains to the media. It can also lead to the loss of donor dollars.

MORE MANNERS: Every contributing volunteer, donor, staff, user, alumnus, and media representative should be recognized for all accomplishments and assistance. When large numbers are involved, the thank-you must necessarily be less personal, but it can still be most effective in recognizing the contributions to the organization. Thank-yous may take the form of donor and volunteer lists in newsletters, letters to the editor, personal handwritten notes, awards, recognition in other forms. The important thing is to recognize the contribution. Thank-yous reflect the professionalism of the nonprofit, strengthen its identity, reinforce its concern for its publics, and accentuate its contributions to the community.

STYLE

Applying the above recommendations moves a nonprofit closer to a particular style, a style that distinguishes it from other organizations. Style is determined by appearances, programs, professionalism, attitudes, manners. A style can add luster to an organization and can generate a pride among staff and users. In turn, this luster and pride enhance the effectiveness of the nonprofit in the community. While style is elusive, nonprofits across the nation have successfully captured it. That's why we hear women's organizations described as "responsive," labor unions as "fighting for the little man," universities as "concerned about students," hospitals as "caring." These comments are made possible and plausible by style.

THE MEDIA NEEDS THE NONPROFIT

In addition to fulfilling government requirements, the nation's newspapers, magazines, radio and television, including the burgeoning cable systems, need the nonprofit to provide news, information, special programs, human interest stories, community-related stories, speakers for talk shows and interview programs, a myriad of opportunities to attract attention.

The successful nonprofit will use these opportunities to its advantage; it won't be caught off guard by media interest. To insure that this does not happen, nonprofit management must maintain a constant two-way communication with volunteers, staff, users, and interested publics. Shared information can prevent many a crisis that results when one hand does not know what the other is doing. The successful nonprofit will also be realistic in its public contacts; it will not claim "services" that it cannot provide, or unsubstantiated "successes."

Knowing in advance that the public and the media will scrutinize every aspect of a nonprofit helps the organization to keep itself in order. Wolf Trap Farm Park, a public nonprofit performing arts center in Virginia, announced in December 1982 that a gala fundraiser it was planning to hold would raise $400,000 to construct a new theater for the Park. The fundraiser was subsequently held in February 1983 and the *Washington Post* began to query the organizers of the fundraiser as to how much money was actually raised. The *Post* reported a few weeks after the event that Wolf Trap had not tallied the results of the fundraiser. Was that the end of the interest? No. In a story on April 13, 1983, the *Washington Post* reported that Wolf Trap netted $85,972 for the "gala fundraiser" and that expenses amounted to $188,613.[1]

The lesson is clear: be cautious in estimating the amount you may be able to raise from a fundraiser or from a fund drive and be prepared to tally up the results for the media immediately following the event. The media is not going to go away and will not be brushed off when it feels that a story is there.

"No comment" is an expression that is sure to bring the media back time and again until the "no comment" may be turned into highly critical publicity. Avoid a "no comment" by being realistic, factual, and honest. If you don't know the answer to a question, say so, and then find out the answer and get back to the media. Refer media questions to the person in the nonprofit who does know the answer. Unpleasant facts cannot be hidden once there is a hint to the media. While the media may initiate queries before the nonprofit is prepared to deal with them or before the answers are gathered or, in some cases, even thought of, the queries must be answered quickly and responsibly.

The successful nonprofit will get its side of the story out to the media, or be prepared to get it out, as soon after the incident is known as possible. A nonprofit that cooperates effectively with the media on a news story will find that the media will often reciprocate by giving the nonprofit's side equal treatment,

---

[1]"Wolf Trap Gala Nets $85,972," by Phil McCombs, the *Washington Post*, April 13, 1983.

by turning to the nonprofit for other news items in the future, and by a willing-ness to use materials produced by the nonprofit.

Nonprofits that do not produce "news" can have more difficulty meeting the media's needs. There are opportunities, though, for backgrounders on major news stories that affect the nonprofit, for interview and talk shows that are not consistently topical, for public affairs programming on radio and television, and today, the possibility of nearly unlimited access to burgeoning cable television outlets.

Controversy makes news, and the nonprofit with the controversial issue—abortion is an example—can develop many opportunities for access to the media. The noncontroversial nonprofit also has opportunities, although development may be more difficult. Regardless of controversy, however, the nonprofit must professionally plan and orchestrate its approaches to the media, highlighting its contributions to the community, and identifying its valuable program and human resources.

The nonprofit that has a reputation among media as honest, factual, and re-liable will improve its access to the public through the media.

REACHING BEYOND THE PUBLIC TO YOUR PUBLICS

The media, press, radio, and television reach the general public. The non-profit must reach the general public as well as its own publics. Many of the meth-ods used are overlapping, and the cost-effective nonprofit will produce materials that can be used interchangeably, that can reach both the general public and highly specialized publics.

There are three main methods of going public: the written word, the spoken word, the special event. All three can be developed to reach specific audiences as well as the general public. All three deserve the same quality of time, attention to detail, planning, and foresight.

Just as all materials must be given the same careful attention, all publics must be courted as carefully as the general public through the media. Each prod-uct must be evaluated and the following standards must be applied:

What is the purpose?
Who is the audience?
What does it contribute to the nonprofit's goal?
How many audiences can be reached?
Is the presentation factual and honest?
Is it understandable to its intended audience?
Is it needed?
Is it cost effective in generating the response desired?
Is it well done and carefully planned and produced?

If any product doesn't meet these minimal standards, it should be aban-doned, or rethought and redesigned. Asking questions and demanding answers from each activity or product will save the nonprofit resources and highlight the materials produced as valuable additions to the community or to the body of knowledge. Hastily produced materials that don't meet minimal standards can result in a nonprofit's losing its credibility with its publics, and can make going public difficult and damaging. Successfully competing for public attention requires planning and careful consideration of every activity, whether it is written, spoken, or special.

CHAPTER 6

The Written Word: a Potent Tool for the Nonprofit

Words have poured forth from the nonprofit sector since the printing press was first invented. The Roman Catholic Church used the invention to reproduce the Bible. To this day, the Bible remains the largest single published work in the world, with an immense impact on social development.

The written word continues to influence developments and to shape public opinion—if perhaps on a more modest level than before. It is a powerful tool for the nonprofit, essential to the development and continuation of community support.

The versatility of the written word allows the nonprofit to use it to reach several publics at the same time. Each production should be evaluated as to its effectiveness with specific target audiences as well as with the general public. This can provide far greater use of all materials while assisting the nonprofit in accomplishing a number of goals at the same time. Some words, however, will be aimed at a specific audience and may not be appropriate for general use. This, too, must be determined when the word is being produced.

Don't be misled by reports that newspapers are on the decline. The newspaper publishers association recently reported that major daily newspapers in the United States are on the rise. There has also been a proliferation in recent years of suburban daily and weekly newspapers that are hungry for the kind of hometown story that the nonprofit with community ties can and must provide. Specialized newsletters of other organizations also offer opportunities for nonprofits to get their word out. There are innumerable possibilities to be identified, developed, and used.

As publishing and postal costs increase, the nonprofit is obliged to produce effective, attractive written materials that meet a number of its needs at the lowest cost. The potential for multi-use of materials is unlimited. The nonprofit can also find many resources within the community to add to the effectiveness of its written word. Accompanying the increase in costs is the competition for readership. It is no secret that reading is falling off in the United States, despite the advances in the educational levels of the general public. While there are many reasons for this, it is a fact that must be taken into account by the nonprofit. A judicious and selective use of the written word can improve the organization's contacts with its community, enhance its competitiveness, and lower its costs. Each publication must be evaluated on its cost, its message, its audience, and its potential for cost effectiveness and accountability:

- Is there a less expensive way to reach a public?
- Is there a more effective way?
- Can one publication meet several needs?
- Is a cheap publication going to be read by the intended public?
- Is there a way to produce more attractive and professional publications on a limited budget?
- Is a publication needed?

VARIOUS VEHICLES FOR THE WRITTEN WORD

The questions listed above apply to every publication. Here are some approaches to cost- and impact-effective written words:

Annual Reports.

While these reports are legally required of private nonprofit organizations, they can be produced to meet the information needs of several publics: the volunteer, the staff, the user, the alumni, the donor (real and potential), the board of trustees, as well as the government. The annual report must be an honest appraisal and evaluation of the accomplishments of the nonprofit. As the report is frequently the major public accountability document, it will be scrutinized for cost-effective programs and for the nonprofit's use of donated monies. Trust can be established and conveyed by an annual report. An educated public will be looking at the report for honesty, accountability, and frankness. Public trust is at stake. A significant aspect of the report is clarity in defining the goals and accomplishments of the nonprofit. Unclear use of figures and murky writing will weaken the report and cost the nonprofit public support. The report is an opportunity to test its public's responses to ideas and directions.

As the report may be the single most important publication produced by a nonprofit, it should incorporate the organization's best efforts in research, planning, production, and marketing. The actual writing of the report is an ideal opportunity to involve talented volunteers and users. These first-hand experiences with the nonprofit will lend the report credibility and freshness. The report should feature the user, the alumnus, the volunteer. The staff's role is to provide the background, the framework for the words of these key publics.

Don't rely totally on your own resources to design an annual report. Hundreds of existing reports are effective guides to producing your own successful report. Begin a file of reports from other profit and nonprofit organizations and adapt from these examples the most effective techniques for your organization.

Tips on Building a File of Annual Reports.

1. Request a copy of the latest annual report from organizations in a related field. For example, hospitals can request annual reports from other hospitals in their geographic areas; from national specialized hospitals (children's, heart, women's); from for-profit hospitals.
2. Use the Foundation Center libraries (addresses listed in Resource chapter) to review foundations with an interest in your nonprofit's activities and request annual reports directly from these foundations.
3. Keep your eyes open for media mention of nonprofit annual reports and request copies directly from the organization.
4. Follow the awards programs of local art directors and graphic design organizations and request annual reports from nonprofits honored by designers.
5. Send a copy of your annual report to nonprofits in your field of interest and request a return copy of theirs.
6. Use these same techniques to build files on newsletters, promotional materials, college catalogues, etc. Don't hesitate to borrow good ideas from others.

Seek out talented users and volunteers as report writers, and remember that photographs of these same people can enhance the report's credibility. All photographs must have the written consent of the person photographed prior to publication. Photographs may be in black and white or color depending on the printer's requirements and budget for the production.

The report has many ancilliary markets: sections written by consumer/users and volunteers can be the basis for media features; the entire report can be the basis for a press conference; research done in the preparation of the report on the nonprofit's activities can be the basis for editorials, suggestions to columnists, radio and television talk shows. The report or specific sections of it can be effective in fundraising. (See Figures 6–1—6–3.)

The annual report is an opportunity for the nonprofit to turn a legal requirement into a valuable support tool. Planning, research, consumer involvement, frankness, probing the future, best possible use of available funds for design and production, and skilled marketing of the finished product can turn a report into an event for the nonprofit. A report can provoke comments and suggestions from key publics that will broaden the nonprofit's two-way communications with its audiences.

Research Reports.

Facts, facts, facts. Facts are what the nonprofit must dig for and use to further its aims. Facts are the basis for research reports which in turn are the basis for conferences and news coverages. Facts are news. Facts can be compressed into a release that gives the media ideas for coverage. Facts can be used effectively in fundraising and in reaching important audiences. Facts include samplings of opinions, cost-effectiveness of programs, numbers of user/patrons serviced, the size of the nonprofit's audience in terms of needs, the accomplishments of the nonprofit in saving dollars or in community service, and in critical analyses

MARKETING THE GOODWILL MISSION

1982 · STRATEGIES

TO ENSURE THE SUCCESS, productivity and management quality of the core vocational rehabilitation services, as well as the retail and contract programs just described, it is necessary to engage in other, equally important activities which focus on the effective mobilization of resources: people, community relations, legislation and fund raising. The following section will briefly describe these activities. Regrettably, it can only highlight the efforts and contributions of each local community's Goodwill Industries employees, clients and volunteers.

COMMUNICATIONS
New Slogan Sets National Identity

A critical part of Goodwill Industries of America's leadership responsibility in representing the 177-member Goodwill network is to build national public awareness and support for the Goodwill Industries movement. Only a high level of such awareness and support will make Goodwill's mission of helping disabled people possible.

In 1982, the Communications Department developed a national communications program to achieve that necessary level of public awareness. It did so in the face of increasing numbers of disabled persons and decreasing government participation and as part of a program to apply basic techniques of marketing to its operations.

As a first step, the Gallup Organization was commissioned in 1982 to measure what is known about Goodwill Industries and how it is perceived by the public. The study found that although 80 percent of the American public recognized the name, only 10 percent knew what Goodwill did. Those polled who were aware of the Goodwill Industries mission thought favorably of the organization and, in general, considered services to assist disabled and handicapped Americans very important.

Using this research as a basis, Goodwill Industries Communications Department began a public mass communications program to establish a national identity for the organization. It developed a new slogan, "Goodwill Industries. Our business works. So people can.", which identifies the organization and establishes it as a professional service with a meaningful purpose to society.

This campaign is directed toward building a national awareness and a single-purpose identity —addressing the needs of the present while building toward the future.

FIGURE 6–1. Reprinted with permission from the 1982 Annual Report of Goodwill Industries of America, Inc., Bethesda, Maryland.

of government programs. Grants are given for fact-finding if the proposed research need is documented and the approach to grant-giving organizations is effectively planned and executed. An example of how research attracts money is a 1982 report published by the nonprofit Urban Institute Press, "The Federal Budget and the Nonprofit Sector." The report was introduced at a well-publicized conference which announced the sale of the new report to the public and revealed newsworthy highlights. The report also attracted support from corporations and foundations for its preparation, as seen in Figure 6–4.

In addition to attracting the funding for research and production of the report, the news release announcing the publication was a compressed report of its own and attracted media coverage while emphasizing the importance of the report's findings which, in turn, motivated buyers of the report. (Figure 6–5 presents the news release.)

LEGISLATION
GIA Testifies at Key Congressional Hearings

Tracking Federal legislation affecting services and assistance to disabled and handicapped persons, as well as providing insight into legislative issues affecting Goodwill Industries, were essential parts of day-to-day operations in Goodwill's Government Liaison Department.

Among specific legislative and regulatory issues earmarked by the department for attention in 1982 were: financial support for programs serving the disabled; revisions in the review process of eligibility standards for Supplemental Security Income (SSI) and Social Security Disability Insurance (SSDI) beneficiaries; and reimbursement procedures for vocational and rehabilitation programs involving Social Security Act recipients. Provisions for disabled individuals in Federal employment and training programs, as well as the placement of the Rehabilitation Services Admin-

istration within the Federal Government, were also major issues involving not only the national office, but also local and "grass roots" participation.

Goodwill Industries of America, Inc. was requested to testify before

Congress on legislation affecting Federal funding for vocational rehabilitation and employment programs and efforts to seek increments in the appropriation levels. Goodwill Industries also worked closely with a number of

legislative and nonprofit groups seeking changes in the Fair Labor Standards Act to permit the integration of work activity center and sheltered workshop clients, testifying on this issue before the Labor Subcommittee of the Senate Labor-Human Resources Committee.

Looking ahead to 1983, several legislative and regulatory issues will require continued attention by the national office and local Goodwills. Priority items include maintaining funding for rehabilitation programs, reauthorization of the Rehabilitation Act and increasing the involvement of disabled individuals under the Job Training Partnership Act.

FIGURE 6–2. Reprinted with permission from the 1981 Annual Report of Goodwill Industries of America, Inc., Bethesda, Maryland.

The Urban Institute itself, which published the report, is a nonprofit organization founded to research social and economic problems and government programs and policies.

The Urban Institute's supporters indicate the interest of an important cross-section of American society in the facts that can be researched and produced by the nonprofit organization—facts that can, and do, influence the way our society works.

The introduction of "the Federal Budget and the Nonprofit Sector" illustrates the importance of research as a product of the nonprofit. The research plan attracted foundation and corporate support, which in turn made the report possible, which in turn attracted media coverage, buyers for the product, and undoubtedly influenced legislators and politicians, who in turn may become supporters of the nonprofit. Facts can produce a full circle of benefits for the nonprofit organization.

On Not Quitting When We're Behind

by John R. Coleman
President

FIGURE 6–3.   Annual Report, 1982. Courtesy of John R. Coleman, President, the Edna McConnell Clark Foundation, 250 Park Avenue, New York, New York 10017.

A federal judge in Colorado was hearing a case in which one of our biggest grantees was involved not so long ago. The state's Attorney General was presenting his defense of why Colorado was doing such a poor job on a particular social front. The blame for the mess clearly didn't belong on the Attorney General's shoulders, nor on his boss's. But he still gamely tried to make the best of the situation. After a while the judge took pity on him, leaned over the bench and said, "Look, why don't you just quit when you're behind?"

The story haunts me. There are times when I wonder if we shouldn't quit what we're doing and do something else. Look at the evidence:

— We're interested in controlling the tropical disease schistosomiasis (snail fever). Yet there are probably more people with this illness now than when we began our work on it.

— We're interested in reducing unnecessary use of incarceration for non-violent criminals. Yet our prisons and jails have never been so crowded, nor our states so committed to buying more steel bars.

— We're interested in decreasing unemployment among disadvantaged urban youth. Yet their disengagement from the world of work has gone up steadily since we launched our Jobs program in 1978.

Yes, it's probably true that fewer children are being shunted around endlessly from foster home to foster home since we began that particular work in 1973 — but that's the only arena where the surface evidence would suggest we're ahead.

But times of such self-doubt pass quickly. And we hope that something more than pigheadedness lies behind our conviction that we're involved in the right fields at the right time. To argue that way, we must of course be able to say that we have a strategy for change in each area — and we have to have some strong, informal sense that things might be worse if we and our allies weren't involved in those chosen fields.

Five years into a foundation presidency and hours away from the beginning of a four-month sabbatical, I'm led to wonder what strategy is all about in a foundation. What is it that we would like to see happen with the philanthropic dollars in this trust, and how do we see that coming about?

There's no way of convincing someone who doesn't work for a foundation why helping our Trustees figure out how to give away $14 million a year is hard work. And yet I'm convinced that it is, simply because there are so few excuses for failure. Once I was a college president and, if things didn't go well, I could charge that to a fractious faculty, a balky board, or a tenuous treasury. Now there's no one to blame if we fail to use our freedom and power to act both imaginatively and responsibly. I work with a staff of unusual skill and commitment. We have trustees who have supported both high-risk and unpopular endeavors. And we have enough money to make a difference in our chosen fields. That leaves the ability to select a strategy for change as the key variable — and that's where the hard work comes in.

In this past year we've talked often in the Foundation about the subject of strategy in grantmaking. That's an obvious enough topic in an organization such as this one that has deliberately chosen to do only a few things in hopes of having extra impact. But this year — and next year — in each of

FIGURE 6–3 (continued).

our four programs there's a special timeliness to pushing ourselves for clearer definitions of how we expect to see lasting change occur.

In the Tropical Disease Research field we have begun the process of looking for another focal point for our work; while there is still much to be done in seeking control of schistosomiasis, there is a time not too far away when we'll want to cut back on our grants there and apply what we've learned to still another among the most neglected diseases in the tropical world. In the Children's field a panel of experts is helping us define some of the most pressing problems facing families today; their deliberations should result in a listing and an analysis that will allow us to make an intelligent choice of a new direction to replace our longstanding concern with permanent adoption of hard-to-place children. In the Justice field the crises arising all over the nation from a fear of crime and a resultant over-reliance on incarceration dictate that we ask what we can possibly do to make our strategy for change still sharper and more persuasive. And in the Jobs field, our only wholly new endeavor in the past five years, the national despair about employment and the resolve of a few foundations to work together to show that youth and jobs can still meet give an urgency to agreeing on the elements of effective strategy.

Each Program Officer's essay for this year's report focuses on some detailed aspect of strategy as it involves a few of our grantees. The aim is to show strategy at work, with some continuing problems mixed in with what we immodestly see as some real success. This introductory essay grew out of our joint discussions on how one program here informs and, we hope, improves another. While we work in

separate fields, we share an interest in asking, "How can the Clark Foundation make the most difference?"

Ideally the framework within which each program evolves has these components:

1. An agreement on the major objective to which the program is to be addressed.

2. The establishment of some criteria by which to measure whether we are in fact moving towards that objective and whether we have either reached the objective or done as much as we should to attain it.

3. A determination of what in-between steps need to be taken along the way to ensure that progress is being made.

4. The establishment of criteria and a timetable to assess whether those in-between steps are in fact being taken.

5. A review process to see that the overriding objective still makes good sense and that we modify it in the light of new experiences and new events.

Selecting the Objective

People who hear for the first time that our primary concern is with the most disadvantaged come back with one of two responses, "Well, that's me", or, "That's a mighty broad mission". For the first response, I have no retort of note. But for the second I can offer both some disagreement and some agreement.

The disagreement comes with the realization that our statement of mission means we don't work in such fields as higher education, the arts and humanities, and

FIGURE 6–3 *(continued)*.

basic science. (The only exceptions are in our out-of-program grants which constitute about 10% of a year's funding.) The agreement comes from an awareness of how many people there are among the disadvantaged and how wide the choices still remain as to what selectivity we'll show among them.

The Trustees long ago decided that four fields was the best number for us. While we have no criteria which, when applied, leave only four natural choices for our work, we have found these questions valuable in the winnowing process:

— Is the problem one which affects large numbers of people?

— Is it one where there is good reason to believe progress can be made in dealing with it?

— Is it one where we think we at Clark might conceivably have some comparative advantage in seeking progress?

— Is it one where the amount of money we can bring to it is enough to make a difference, either alongside the money that others bring to it or, if need be, all alone?

— Is it one where our activity may in turn spur greater flows of either private or public moneys to this field?

— Is it one where our new experience can help us do a still better job on future grantmaking?

Using those questions, we could easily have come up with an array of programs quite different from the ones we now have. But I am satisfied that what we're doing meets each of those tests and that the current combination of fields makes for some deeply rewarding work. And when I watch how our program staffs work together and feel challenged by one another's work, I'm satisfied that each part of what we do is made better by the presence of the other parts.

Measuring the Progress

This is a tricky process, and the one that we in foundations seem to enjoy the least. Especially when one chooses social problems of unusual complexity, it is hard to tell whether one's efforts are in fact paying off. Hence that story about the judge in Colorado.

My biases here are known. The worth of intensive and expensive evaluations in much of what we all do collectively is vastly overrated. Someone once said that trying to measure most social programs is like trying to milk a he-goat into a sieve. While that puts the matter a touch too strongly, it is nevertheless true that evaluation has, along with computers, become one of our bigger growth industries. And we still don't know much about what works and don't often enough apply even what we do know. (Witness our dumping so many of the federal government's youth employment efforts even when some of them were stamped by the evaluators as clear economic successes.)

But none of this means we shouldn't try hard and ask ourselves as many questions as possible about our programs. Sometimes a good journalist can answer our queries as appropriately as a social science team can; that's particularly true when there are so many variables that the best one can do is make rough judgments. Common sense, a nose for logic and a tongue given to straight talk will go a long way in telling us most of

FIGURE 6–3 *(continued).*

what we really need to know. Even when it's very rough, the very act of doing one's best to see if there is movement ahead acts as a spur.

So what about those cases where the surface evidence suggests movement backward rather than forward? The choices are painful but clear. Present a convincing, hard-nosed case to our critics as to why things would have been worse in the absence of our efforts—or quit while we're behind.

And finally, what about those happy cases where most of the available evidence suggests that progress to the goal is so substantial and the momentum so strong that our foundation dollars are no longer as needed as they once were? That too is time to quit. Declare victory and go home, to think about a new arena where the chances for still more success seem strong.

Getting All the Pieces in Place

I suspect that the place where agents of change, such as those in foundation offices, fail most often is right here. It is in seeing that, before a certain ultimate and worthwhile result can be achieved, a lot of different pieces have to be put in place along the way.

Sometimes this means taking time to involve institutions which, if they're on our side, can be of inestimable value. Sometimes too this means, at a minimum, taking time to neutralize institutions which, if they're on the other side, can turn any good day into a bad one. Most change for the better is likely to involve the search for unlikely allies along the way. The aim is to identify those key actors and institutions which, once involved, can provide an impetus that is longer lasting and wider reaching than anything we can do on our own.

In the foundation world where we often try to make a few dollars go a long way, this means early attention to replication. We all say casually that we want it, but how often do we spell out how it is likely to happen? And what care do we put into seeing that the conditions are there for sustaining momentum long after our few dollars are in some past auditors' reports?

This problem of leverage and of a piece-by-piece plan for lasting change hangs over every one of our programs. It helps to explain why we are most anxious to find allies in other foundations who can show us how to do our work still better. And it helps to explain the presence of some of the grantees in our annual listing; what sometimes looks like a diversion from our central objective is, more often than not I hope, a search for a new path or a building of a neglected bridge along the old path.

Timing the Forward Movement

One part of strategy-building of use to us in our three domestic social programs could be adapted more fully from the Tropical Disease Research Program. That program has long had a Strategic Plan which spells out in concise but comprehensive terms what steps are necessary for progress in each part of that total effort—i.e., in epidemiology and control, biochemistry and drug development, and immunology and vaccine development. The director, his staff and advisors have put rough time estimates on each of the steps, and they regularly review the total plan to see if the steps are right and the timing is appropriate. It's a living document.

Those of us who are not hard scientists have much to learn from this model. (The first thing we have to learn, of course, is how to translate the scientists' language.) Properly adapted to the social action field,

FIGURE 6–3 (continued).

it can become a checklist and a map of considerable worth.

This example, incidentally, helps to explain why we are so comfortable here with a medical research effort that at first glance is so unlike the rest of what we do. The dividends—I suspect they flow both ways—from working side by side are real.

Reviewing the Goal

A foundation that is ambitious to bring about change needs, as we have suggested above, to define that goal with as much clarity as possible. But, like the steps to achieve that goal, the objective itself needs reexamination along the way. What may have made eminently good sense at one time becomes less than inspired or even

sensible at a later time. Events over which we have no control change not only the magnitude of the problem but also its shape. And what is learned along the way, the surprises that make all of this work so rewarding, may suggest that there's a still better way of looking at the whole issue.

This is where the freedom and the parallel responsibility in a foundation's work become somewhat awesome. The trustees and staff aren't usually stuck with what someone else has defined as the job to be done. There's room to choose and then to make a still better choice in the light of new knowledge.

Quit when we're behind? Give up that freedom and that responsibility to tackle tough issues in new ways? Go where it's safer and quieter? No, thank you.

FIGURE 6–3 *(continued).*

A survey of nonprofits show that they produce some of the most important research being conducted in the United States. Major medical facilities, universities, think-tanks, health- and issue-oriented organizations devote time and resources to research. But the fact that the research of major nonprofits such as Harvard University, Stanford University, and the American Cancer Society have national impact should not inhibit the small, local nonprofit from using research to strengthen its contributions to the community and to become more visibly important. Major research requires major funding, much of it from the government. Small research projects—for example, one designed to identify the needs and preferences of elderly people in a small town—can also be attractive to corporate and other funding sources. Planning and finding research funding may be the nonprofit's major program activity and major source of funding.

News Release.

This is the nonprofit's major means of contacting the media. As releases are such important, relatively inexpensive and visible signs of the nonprofit, they must be handled with skill, professionalism, and a devotion to fact. An effective news release clearly presents facts. The importance of these facts determines the news value of the release. Not all facts are equally important to all the media, and judgment must be used to determine where a release is to be sent and how it is to be distributed.

A release follows simple, professional guidelines in its appearance and makeup (Figure 6–6).

THE NONPROFIT SECTOR PROJECT

Lester M. Salamon, Director

The Urban Institute's Nonprofit Sector Project is a broad-gauged inquiry into the role and character of private, nonprofit organizations, the relationships between these organizations and other segments of American society, and the impact on them and those they serve of recent changes in public policy. The project involves several different types of analysis being conducted at the national level and in sixteen locales throughout the country. This report is one in a series that will be produced as part of this project over the next several years.

Support for this project has been made available by a wide cross-section of funding sources including corporations, national foundations, and local community foundations throughout the country. A list of these sponsors is provided below.

Sponsors

Amoco Foundation, Inc.
Atlantic Richfield Foundation
BankAmerica Foundation
The Buhl Foundation
Carnegie Corporation of New York
The Chevron Fund
The Chicago Community Trust
The Coca-Cola Company
Equitable Life Assurance Society
The Ford Foundation
The General Electric Foundation
General Mills Foundation
Howard Heinz Endowment
Independent Sector

Richard King Mellon Foundation
Metropolitan Atlantic Community
  Foundation, Inc.
The Minneapolis Foundation
John Stewart Mott Foundation
The New York Community Trust
The Pittsburgh Foundation
PPG Industries Foundation
The Rockefeller Brothers Fund
The Rockefeller Foundation
The Saint Paul Foundation
The San Francisco Foundation
The Shell Companies Foundation
United States Steel Foundation, Inc.

FIGURE 6–4.   Copyright © 1982. The Urban Institute, 2100 M Street N.W., Washington, D.C. 20037.

The Urban Institute
2100 M Street N.W., Washington, D.C.

Release: September 1, 1982   Contact: Anita MacIntosh
                                                    202/223-1950

PRESS RELEASE

NEW REPORT DETAILS IMPLICATIONS OF REAGAN BUDGET
PROPOSALS FOR NONPROFIT ORGANIZATIONS

Hospitals, universities, social service agencies, community-based organizations, arts groups, and other private, nonprofit organizations stand to lose $33 billion in revenues from federal sources over the period 1982–85 as a result of the latest Reagan administration budget proposals, according to new data released today. This represents a 20 percent reduction in the real value of the support these organizations receive through federal programs.

These losses are in turn but a part of a much larger reduction totaling $115 billion in federal spending in fields where nonprofit organizations are active, which will increase the need for nonprofit services as people formerly aided by federal programs turn to nonprofit agencies for help instead.

These conclusions are detailed in a major new report by Lester M. Salamon and Alan J. Abramson released today by The Urban Institute, a Washington-based public-policy research organization. Entitled The Federal Budget and the Nonprofit Sector, this report provides important new data on the scope and structure of the nonprofit sector, the relationships between this sector and government, and the projected impact on this set of organizations of the major budget changes proposed by the Reagan administration in 1981 and 1982, and partly enacted by Congress.

Among the other major findings of this report are the following:

■ Nonprofit organizations play a vital role in American life. These organizations supply a considerable portion of the health care, education, research, cultural life, social services, community organization, and public advocacy available in this nation. They therefore touch virtually all the nation's citizens, rich and poor, young and old.

■ Private, nonprofit organizations had revenues of approximately $116 billion in 1980. They therefore account for approximately 5 percent of the gross domestic product and almost one-third of the nation's service employment.

■ Nonprofit service providers received $40.4 billion in revenues from federal government programs in fiscal year (FY) 1980. By comparison, these

FIGURE 6–5.   The Press Release was reprinted with the permission of Lester M. Salamon, director of the Nonprofit Sector Project of the Urban Institute. The information in the release, the list of trustees, and the description of the Nonprofit Sector Project are from Lester M. Salamon and Alan J. Abramson, *The Federal Budget and the Nonprofit Sector* (Washington, D.C.: the Urban Institute Press, 1982).

organizations received $25.5 billion in private contributions from corporations, foundations, and individuals that same year. In other words, nonprofit organizations other than churches now receive a larger share of their total revenues from federal programs than from all of private giving combined.

■ This extensive nonprofit support from public programs reflects the fact that government has turned extensively to private, nonprofit organizations in this country to help it carry out its responsibilities. The result is an elaborate pattern of "nonprofit federalism" that links government at all levels to nonprofit organizations in a variety of close working partnerships.

■ The budget proposals advanced by the Reagan administration would sharply curtail these partnership arrangements. Under these proposals, the real value of federal support for nonprofit organizations would be 27 percent lower in FY 1985 than it was in FY 1980. Some types of nonprofit organizations would be affected even more than this. For example, federal support for nonprofit social service organizations would decline in real value by 64 percent, for community development organizations by 65 percent, and for arts organizations by 68 percent. For social service and community development organizations, these reductions in federal support would mean the effective loss of between one-fourth and one-third of their total revenues by FY 1985.

■ These are also the areas where the need for nonprofit services is likely to grow the most, however, as a result of the overall budget cuts that are proposed. Between FY 1980 and FY 1985, overall federal spending in fields where nonprofit organizations are active would decline by 26 percent in real value. In the social welfare field, however, it would decline by 57 percent, in education and research by 48 percent, in health services by 26 percent, in the arts by 42 percent, and in environmental activities by 94 percent.

■ To permit nonprofit organizations to offset the reductions in revenues they face and maintain their 1980 levels of activity, private giving to nonprofit organizations would have to increase by 24 percent in 1982, or twice as fast as it has ever grown. In 1983, 1984, and 1985, the rate of increase in private giving needed would be 40 percent or more.

■ For private giving to fill the entire gap left by the overall reductions in federal activity in fields where nonprofit organizations are active, private giving would have to grow in 1982 by 60 percent, five times faster than it has ever achieved. In 1983, 1984, and 1985, the rate of increase in private giving needed to fill this gap would be in excess of 100 percent.

■ Expressed in current dollars, instead of constant 1980 dollars, the proposed reductions in federal spending in fields where nonprofit organizations are active would total $158.2 billion during FY 1982–85, instead of $115 billion. In these same current dollar terms, the projected loss of nonprofit revenues from federal sources during this same period would total $46.2 billion, instead of $33 billion.

FIGURE 6–5 *(continued).*

Copies of The Federal Budget and the Nonprofit Sector are available from The Urban Institute Press, 2100 M Street, N.W., Washington, D.C., 20037.

The Federal Budget and the Nonprofit Sector is the first product of a major nationwide study headed by Dr. Salamon examining the fiscal health of the nonprofit sector and the impact on it of the major public policy changes now under way in the nation. It updates and expands on an earlier analysis the authors completed on this subject in 1981. Support for The Urban Institute's Nonprofit Sector Project has been provided by a broad cross-section of community foundations, corporations, and national foundations in all parts of the country.

The Urban Institute is a private, nonprofit research organization that examines the social and economic problems of the nation's communities. The Institute's President is William Gorham and its Board of Trustees is headed by William D. Ruckelshaus of Weyerhauser Corporation. Lester M. Salamon directs the Institute's Center for Public Management and Economic Development Research. Dr. Salamon earned his Ph.D. at Harvard University, and has served as deputy associate director of the U.S. Office of Management and Budget and as a professor of policy analysis at Duke University. Alan J. Abramson earned his M.A. and M.Phil. at Yale University and is currently at work on his doctoral dissertation. Both authors are also contributors to The Reagan Experiment, which will be released by The Urban Institute later this month.

FIGURE 6–5 *(continued).*

MODEL RELEASE

     FOR RELEASE: December 1, 19____

                          Contact: RHWriter/area code/telephone
                                       business/home (if needed)

HEADLINE: MUSEUM ANNOUNCES LUNCH SERIES FOR SENIOR CITIZENS

The City Museum of Art (WHO) announced today that a new noon lunch series for senior citizens (WHAT) will begin in the Museum Curatorial Staff Lounge (WHERE) on Tuesday, January 6, 19____. (WHEN)

The six-week series, entitled "Lunch with an Old Master," will feature weekly talks by different museum curators on popular paintings in the Museum's collections. (WHY) The popularity of these paintings was established by a survey of senior citizen visitors to the Museum last October.

The lunch series costs $45.00 for six lunches or $10.00 if purchased separately. Space is limited and advance reservations are required. Call _____ for reservations and information.

FIGURE 6–6.

This model in Figure 6–6 illustrates the professional standards of a release:

1. It must be typed, double-spaced or even triple-spaced (for weekly newspapers and small dailies).
2. It must contain the name and telephone number(s) of the person(s) to contact (originator) for more information at the top of the release.
3. It must include the date of the release either at the top of the page or at the end of the text (the date is at the top of the page following "FOR RELEASE" if that is the date that the release should first be used for publication or broadcast; if the release can be used upon receipt, place the date at the end of the release.)
4. It should have a headline that briefly explains the purpose of the release.
5. Its first paragraph must contain the WHO, WHAT, WHERE, WHEN, of the event or news; the WHY may be in the first or second paragraphs.

Most news releases need not exceed one typed page.

A useful and effective means of notifying assignment editors at newspapers and news directors at radio and television stations about a news conference or meeting which can attract news coverage is shown in the model in Figure 6–7. This model (and all models in the book) is for adaption to the organization's specific news release needs.

RELEASE: IMMEDIATE

                                          Contact: RHWriter (area code and
                                                             phone number)

HEADLINE: "SPECIAL TO ASSIGNMENT EDITORS."
TEXT:
WHAT: News Conference.
SUBJECT: "New Study Finds Citywide Increase in Donations to Nonprofit
            Organizations."
WHEN: Tuesday, December 6, 19____.
WHERE: Westside Recreation Center (THINK VISUALLY TO ATTRACT TELEVISION AND
            TO CREATE PHOTO OPPORTUNITIES).
WHO: The Mayor.

            The Director of the Office for the Elderly.

            The Author of the Study.

            The Director of the Corporate Giving Program.

            Four representatives from low-income, elderly, youth and minority
            nonprofit projects.

WHY: The City has vastly increased its donations in cash, kind, and
            volunteers to nonprofit organizations operating in the City. The
            News Conference will highlight some of the developments made
            possible by the increase in donations. Public and corporate
            cooperation has made a dramatic impact on the lives of low-income
            City residents.

DATE OF RELEASE

FIGURE 6–7.

That's it. Clean, simple, comprehensive, and proven effective in attracting media coverage of conferences and meetings.

All new publications that are free can be brought to the public's attention by the release shown in Figure 6–8, accompanied by a copy of the publication for editor or broadcaster review. Releases should be directed to the editor responsible for the content/interest of the publication. For example, a publication on job training programs would be directed to ATTENTION: BUSINESS EDITOR. A publication on coping with bugs in the vegetable garden would be directed to ATTENTION: GARDEN or FOOD EDITOR. And so on. Sending a release to the attention of a specific editor helps to insure its use.

RELEASE: IMMEDIATE

Contact: RHWriter (area code and phone number)

DIRECTION: "SPECIAL TO HEALTH EDITORS"
HEADLINE : "NEW PUBLICATION FOR NEW PARENTS"
TEXT   : "Tips for New Parents on Early Learning Problems" is the title of a new publication of interest to parents and teachers of children under six years of age.

Based on a study by the nonprofit community mental health center, "Tips" identifies ten common early learning problems with accompanying suggestions on dealing with these problems and information on where to go in the community for assistance.

"Tips for New Parents" is available without cost from Our Town Community Mental Health Center, 4 Main Street, Our Town. A copy may be requested by telephoning 666-6666 weekdays from 9:00 am to 5:00 pm.

ATTACHMENT: "Tips for New Parents"
Date   : November 5, 19___

FIGURE 6–8.

News releases have a multitude of uses. The Urban Institute's example illustrated the introduction of a new study and the fact that a publication of the study is available for purchase. The models address news conferences/meetings and free publications of free services of interest to the community. All of these releases illustrate that rules are made to be broken by professionals who have planned and researched their market. The Urban Institute press release does not follow strictly the "who, what, where, when, why" guidelines. Rather, it features highlights from the report to introduce the facts that the report is (1) important, (2) newsworthy, and (3) available for purchase. This release interests potential purchasers.

Releases are far too important to be limited to narrow uses. They can be the basis of a news story or they can provoke interest in broader news coverage. They can be designed to reach just one important person, or one specific audience. They are a fundamental tool of the nonprofit organization in marketing its information.

DISTRICT OF COLUMBIA DIVISION, INC.

NEWS RELEASE   CONTACT:
                                      Lois N. Callahan
                                      (202) 483-2600

DAFFODIL DAY SIGNALS THE START OF THE 1983 CANCER CRUSADE

On March 18, businesses all over town will blossom out in beautiful daffodils flown directly to Washington from the West Coast.

Daffodils are the symbol of spring and the symbol of hope for cancer patients. That's why on March 18, the business community through their purchases and donations will be spreading the joy of Daffodil Day among employees, customers, and hospital patients.

F. Davis Camalier, President of Camalier and Buckley and Chairman of Daffodil Day for the American Cancer Society, is urging businessmen and employers to support the ACS by purchasing some of the beautiful daffodils as gifts to employees, hospitals, nursing homes, or homes for the aged.

American Cancer Society volunteers will be accepting donations for freshly cut daffodils at downtown Washington locations on Daffodil Day. Advance orders may be placed for large quantities of the flower by contacting the American Cancer Society at (202) 483-2600. Gift cards will be provided so that sponsorship will be recognized.

Your American Cancer Society urges you to join in the fight against cancer by supporting Daffodil Day and at the same time adding some beauty and cheer to someone's day.

March 1, 19____

> **FIGURE 6–9.** Courtesy of the District of Columbia Division of the American Cancer Society, 1825 Connecticut Avenue N.W., Washington, D.C. 20009.

The example in Figure 6–9, a release from the American Cancer Society's District of Columbia Division, is of particular interest to volunteers, businesses, and friends in the community. The "Daffodil Day" release recognizes the contributions of the volunteer in charge of "Daffodil Day." It also serves to notify business people that a prominent community and business leader is promoting the day. The release suggests ideas to businesses on their participation with specific instructions on advance orders.

The second American Cancer Society release concerns an award to a prominent volunteer (Figure 6–10). This release not only recognizes the volunteer's contributions to the Society but also serves to promote attendance at the luncheon where the award will be presented. This release, then, goes beyond the

AMERICAN CANCER SOCIETY® DISTRICT OF COLUMBIA DIVISION, INC.

NEWS RELEASE

CONTACT:
Lois N. Callahan
(202) 483-2600

AMERICAN CANCER SOCIETY SALUTES BARBARA BOGGS SIGMUND

The American Cancer Society, Washington, D.C. Division, will honor Barbara Boggs Sigmund at the 1983 Annual Volunteers Luncheon on March 18 at the Washington Hilton Hotel International Ballroom.

Mrs. Sigmund, daughter of United States Representative Lindy Boggs (D. La.) and the late House Majority Leader Hale Boggs, will receive the Society's Hubert H. Humphrey Inspirational Award from Frances Humphrey Howard before an expected audience of one thousand volunteers and friends of the Society.

In 1977 the American Cancer Society paid tribute to Hubert Humphrey, whose valiant fight against cancer remains a lasting source of inspiration for cancer patients and all Americans. Upon his death an award was established in memory of Senator Humphrey with the criteria that it be presented to a person who best exemplifies the spirit of the great Senate leader. Mrs. Howard, sister of Senator Humphrey, has presented the annual citation for the past five years. Past recipients include Former First Lady Betty Ford, Edward M. Kennedy, Jr., The Honorable John S. Monagan, Marvella Bayh and Jack Pardee.

Barbara Boggs Sigmund, a political figure in her own right, was stricken by cancer during a race for a U.S. Senate seat in New Jersey last spring. She lost an eye to the disease but that did not hamper either her political campaign or the enthusiasm of Mrs. Sigmund.

A native of New Orleans, Barbara Sigmund divided her time between the Crescent City and Washington, D.C., after her father was elected to the U.S. House of Representatives. She attended the Stone Ridge Country Day School in Bethesda, Maryland and Manhattanville College of the Sacred Heart in Purchase, New York.

Prior to becoming a candidate for the U.S. Senate from New Jersey, Mrs. Sigmund served on the Princeton Borough Council. Then in 1976 she was elected to the Mercer County Board of Freeholders (county commissioners), serving as president in 1979 and 1980. Mrs. Sigmund was elected president of the New Jersey Association of Counties in 1981. She has also been a delegate to the last two Democratic national conventions.

Barbara Boggs Sigmund is the wife of Paul Sigmund, a Princeton University Professor. The mother of three children, Mrs. Sigmund is an active volunteer for the Society's New Jersey Division.

Noted syndicated columnist and Pulitzer Prize winner Jack Anderson will serve as Master of Ceremonies for the 12 noon luncheon program.

Dr. LaSalle D. Leffall, Jr., professor and chairman, Department of Surgery of the Howard University College of Medicine and National Medical Director of the American Cancer Society, will speak to the audience on the state of the art in cancer control.

Tickets for the luncheon are available by calling the American Cancer Society at (202) 483-2600.

March 1, 19___

> **FIGURE 6–10.** Courtesy of the District of Columbia Division of the American Cancer Society, 1825 Connecticut Avenue N.W., Washington, D.C. 20009.

audience of community supporters and reaches out to friends and associates of the person being honored, a new audience of potential friends. Note also that the honor is judiciously awarded to people prominent in the community, people who can bring attention and supporters to the organization. The involvement of community leaders serves to motivate others to volunteer and support the organization. Community leaders can help to confer a sense of importance to a nonprofit.

A news release is a fundamental tool for the nonprofit organization. It must, however, be used only for the sharing and promotion of factual information. Organizations that issue releases based on unclear or uncertain facts are only airing their own management weaknesses while opening themselves up to critical public scrutiny. There are ethics involved in all public contacts, and the press release is not exempt from ethical standards. Releases must be rigorously audited for honesty and purpose. The credibility of the organization depends upon this. One recommended way of auditing the validity of the organization's releases is to periodically query the recipients of releases for their views.

Newsletters.

Newsletters are the nonprofit's current chief means of reaching members, alumni, volunteers, consumer/users, boards of trustees, staff, and allied organizations. The nonprofit world is awash in newsletters fulfilling one or another need of specific audiences.

Newsletters are a means of signaling specific audiences that the organization is concerned. National organizations produce legislative newsletters to alert their members to the organization's advocacy on their behalf and to changes in the law that affect the membership. These newsletters, produced frequently, can be short and simple statements that serve the purpose of demonstrating that the national is actively at work on its members' behalf. Staff newsletters recognize staff accomplishments and serve as a two-way communicator between the board, management, and staff. Volunteer newsletters can serve to recognize achievements, offer training and other programs to volunteers, recruit new volunteers. Special interest newsletters aimed at specific audiences include those directed to the board of trustees from the executive director, university alumni newsletters, newsletters directed to consumer/users from management, and a more recent development, hospital newsletters directed to former patients.

Newsletters have one common feature that can be overlooked. They are excellent vehicles for advertising items of interest to the audience, of attracting paid advertising from organizations interested in marketing to the newsletters' audience, and for fundraising, particularly for specific items tailored to the concerns of the intended audience. Legislative newsletters can develop extra funds for special campaigns and advocacy programming. Alumni newsletters can identify pressing specific needs such as scholarships for currently enrolled students affected by the economic downturn. Staff newsletters can recruit resources, both volunteer hours and dollars, for unusual and urgent purposes. Newsletters can feature items to purchase from, or for, the nonprofit. No newsletter editor can overlook the advantage of raising funds from its specific audience if the appeal for these funds is specifically tailored to the audience's interests and abilities.

An effective newsletter, one that is read and responded to, adheres to rules, regardless of the budget available.

RULE ONE: Plan. Determine the specific goal of the newsletter.

RULE TWO: Know the audience. Use surveys and questionnaires (these can be done through the pages of the newsletter) to determine the content, direction and reader needs.

RULE THREE: Need. Could the newsletter be combined with other newsletters for greater cost effectiveness while retaining the specific audience? Or is a magazine format more effective?

RULE FOUR: Professionalism. Is the newsletter professionally written, edited, produced and marketed? Is it clearly understandable; is the type sufficiently larger for an aging population; is the use of color and photography merited; is it neat, clean, attractive; is it reaching its target audience?

Magazines.

Magazines are a more costly means of reaching audiences, but with the advantage that one magazine can serve the needs of a broad range of audiences. Effective magazines follow the same rules as newsletters and require constant monitoring for cost effectiveness and accomplishments. Huge mailing lists which magazines frequently accumulate are a major cost and frequently a major headache, as maintaining large lists is difficult. The size of a magazine's audience is, however, an attractive incentive to paid advertising, and to businesses and corporations with products of interest to the magazine's readership. Magazines are urgent concerns for organizations like the National Geographic Society. A good magazine is an expensive product, however, and is to be carefully planned, funded, and approached with caution. Competition for magazine readership is fierce. The majority of magazines published by nonprofits are essentially intended for single-target audiences such as university alumni magazines and donor magazines, similar to the one published by the National Trust for Historic Preservation.

Letters, Memos, Notes.

These are an integral part of the nonprofit's communication with its publics. Again, the standards are those of professionalism, legibility, clear writing, clear purpose, and a knowledge of the intended recipient. Brief, handwritten notes can be extraordinarily effective in this day of the word processor. People appreciate a personal touch and the handwritten thank-you to cooperating editors, suppliers, volunteers, and consumers gives a patina of humanity to the organization. Letters and memos are an effective way of communicating with audiences and can be significant tools.

Calendars.

Printed calendars of events of note are useful in retaining the interest of consumers and members, in building new allies in the community, and for the media, as many use calendars of events. Calendars can be colorful reminders of the nonprofit's use to its community and offer many organizations, such as hospitals and churches, the opportunity to develop new community support by offering a wide variety of programs of interest.

Bookmarks.

The public library is a community distribution center for nonprofit information. Bookmarks highlighting the organization's services are a contribution to the reading public as well as useful in reaching new audiences.

Flyers.

Flyers are simple, inexpensive, colorful hand-out publications for wide distribution through allied organizations, including libraries, universities, community centers, city halls. The flyer should highlight the services offered and recent accomplishments. Flyers should also "call for action" and seek volunteers, donations, program contributions.

Training Materials.

Training programs can incorporate written materials that provide several uses: as specific training materials, as sale items, as the basis for a news story or an interview. All training programs, including those for staff and volunteers, should be examined for multiple use of materials developed.

Programs.

Lectures, fundraising events, open houses, seminars, meetings, all are opportunities for programs that highlight the accomplishments of the organization and that further the goals and objectives of the event itself. Programs deserve the same careful production and evaluation as any written word. Meeting programs sent out in advance can be used to attract people to the meeting as well as to highlight the contributions of volunteers, donors, consumers. Programs are also useful for attendees to take back to their offices and homes for referral purposes.

Convention Materials.

A daily newspaper at an organization's annual convention is a good way to keep attendees informed about the program as well as to highlight the news value of the convention. The American Association for the Advancement of Science attracts media attention to its national meetings by sending conference materials highlighting speakers and potential news stories in advance to reporters (Figure 6–11). The national media coverage that the nonprofit AAAS attracts is not accidental; it is carefully planned and developed. Along with advance materials and press credentials, AAAS operates a press room at its conference and makes texts of speeches available in addition to daily releases. Convention materials can reach several objectives if carefully planned and produced and marketed: media interest; recognition of speakers, exhibitors, attendees, members; public recognition of the organization and its contributions to society; increased revenues for the organization through sales of publications and exhibit space and increased registration of attendees.

AAAS

American Association for the Advancement of Science, 1515 Massachusetts Ave. N.W., Washington, D.C. 20005

FOR IMMEDIATE RELEASE   CONTACT: Joan Wrather
(Mailed 3 March 19___)   (202) 467-5441

WORLD OF SCIENCE AND TECHNOLOGY TO BE EXPLORED AT 149th AAAS NATIONAL MEETING, 26–31 MAY 19___, DETROIT

Washington, D.C. . . . The many ways in which science and technology touch our lives—from medical advances to assembly line robots—will be described at the 149th national meeting of the American Association for the Advancement of Science (AAAS).

The meeting will be held 26–31 May 19___ in Detroit, Michigan. Headquarters for the meeting will be the Westin Hotel in Detroit's Renaissance Center.

Some 150 symposia will cover such diverse topics as genetic engineering, acid rain, automation and the economy, cancer in China, teenage suicide, high-energy physics, new food sources, and science and national security. The meeting's theme will be "Science and Engineering: Toward a National Renaissance."

David Adamany, president, Wayne State University, will open the meeting with the keynote address Thursday evening (26 May). The meeting will continue with several concurrent sessions through Tuesday afternoon (31 May).

In addition to the keynote address, other public lectures, free and open to the public, will be given by E. Margaret Burbidge, AAAS president and director, Center for Astrophysics and Space Sciences, University of California, San Diego; Sara C. Bisel, archaeologist and anthropologist working with the Smithsonian Institution; Nobel Laureate Gerald M. Edelman, Vincent Astor, Distinguished Professor, Rockefeller University; Dorothy T. Krieger, director, Division of Endocrinology, Mount Sinai Medical Center; Leon M. Lederman, director, Fermi National Accelerator Laboratory; Cyril Ponnamperuma, director, Laboratory of Chemical Evolution, University of Maryland; Derek deSolla Price, Avalon Professor of the History of Science, Yale University; and Theodore T. Puck, director, Institute for Cancer Research, University of Colorado.

Co-chairmen for the Detroit Advisory Committee are Robert A. Frosch, vice president, Research Laboratories, General Motors Corporation, and Harold T. Shapiro, president, University of Michigan.

The AAAS Science Film Festival, which is free and open to the public, will feature 50 of the best short science films recently produced. The Science Film Festival will open Friday (27 May) and run through Monday (30 May) in the Cabot Room at the Westin Hotel.

The annual exhibition of new scientific instruments and publications will be on display in the Ontario Exhibit Hall of the Westin Hotel, 27 May through 30 May. Also, adjacent to the Ontario Exhibit Hall will be the "poster sessions," with individual authors using visual aids to present their papers in an informal setting.

The AAAS meeting, as in the past, will be accessible to handicapped persons. Among the services will be a resource center for disabled attendees at the Westin Hotel, transportation for those in wheelchairs, interpreters for the hearing

FIGURE 6–11. Courtesy of the Office of Communications, American Association for the Advancement of Science, 1776 Massachusetts Avenue N.W., Washington, D.C. 20036.

impaired, special tours and sightseeing information, audiotaped highlights of the meeting program for persons with visual impairments, and a round-the-clock answering service to deal with emergencies.

The American Association for the Advancement of Science, formed in 1848, is the largest general scientific organization in the country. It currently has some 138,000 individual members who are scientists, engineers, and others interested in science, and some 285 affiliated scientific and engineering societies and academies of science.

Several thousand scientists, engineers, and those interested in science and technology attend the Association's national meeting, which is held in a different city each year. The last meeting was held in Washington, D.C., in 19___; the 19___ meeting will be held in New York City (24–29 May). The Association last met in Detroit in 1897.

NOTE TO MEDIA: Enclosed are advance press and hotel reservation forms. If you are planning to attend the meeting, we urge you to send the press registration form to us and the hotel reservation form to the AAAS Housing Bureau as soon as possible. Over the next few weeks, we will be sending you additional information about the meeting, including symposium highlights, a description of annual meeting newsroom facilities available in Detroit, and an advance press conference schedule. A preliminary program for the 19___ AAAS Annual Meeting, containing symposium titles, is reprinted in the 25 February issue of SCIENCE.

AAAS Annual Meeting
Detroit
26-31 May 1983

Advance Press Registration

First Name   Last

Street Address or P.O. Box Number

City   State   Zip-(USA)

Country   Area Code   Phone Number

Name of Institution or Company

FIGURE 6–11 *(continued).*

PRESS

Send confirmation to:

Name _____ Street _____

City _____ State _____ Zip _____ Phone No. _____

Other occupants of room:

Name _____ Name _____

Choice of hotel: 1. _____   2. _____   3. _____

Room: ☐ Single ☐ Double ☐ Twin   **Suite:** ☐ 1 Bedroom ☐ 2 Bedrooms   **Preferred Rate:**$_____

Please indicate special housing needs due to a handicap: ☐ Wheelchair accessible room.

Other: _____

Arrival Date: _____ **Time:** _____ ☐ a.m. ☐ p.m.

Departure Date: _____ **Time:** _____ ☐ a.m. ☐ p.m.

Be sure to list definite arrival and departure date and time. Reservations will be held only until 6 p.m. unless accompanied by 1 night's deposit.

For Convention Bureau use only			
RESERVATION FOLLOW-THRU	DATE & INITIAL	RESERVATION FOLLOW-THRU	DATE & INITIAL
Received at Housing Bureau		Received at Hotel/Motel	
Processed to Hotel/Motel		Confirmed to Guest	

MAIL TO: AAAS Housing Bureau, 100 Renaissance Center, Suite 1950, Detroit, Mich. 48243

- All hotel reservations must be submitted to the AAAS Housing Bureau in writing **(use form above; type or print).**
- Reservations must be received by the Housing Bureau **not later than 2 May 19____;** reservations received after that date are conditional upon space availability at the hotels.
- Rooms are assigned on a first come, first served basis. If the first choice hotel cannot accommodate you, the Housing Brueau will try to assign the second choice you requested.
- The Housing Bureau will send you acknowledgement of reservation received; confirmation of reservation will come to you from the hotel. All changes or cancellations must be made directly with the hotel.

HOTEL RATES*

Hotel	Single	Double & Twin	Parlor + 1 Bedrm.	Parlor + 2 Bedrms.	Parking (rates subject to change)
The Westin Hotel Headquarters Hotel Renaissance Center (No. of rooms blocked: 1,200)	$65	$77	$170 and up	$260 and up	$4.00 per 24 hrs.—Parking Lot B (see "Meeting Information" for details; see map for location). Valet Parking also available.
Hotel Pontchartrain 2 Washington Boulevard (No. of rooms blocked: 200)	$58	$73	$170 and up	$240 and up	$6.00 per 24 hrs.: Valet parking with in & out privileges for registered guests only.
Book Cadillac Hotel 1114 Washington Boulevard (No. of rooms blocked: 300)	$42	$52	$135 and up	$189 and up	$6.00 per 24 hrs.: Valet parking with in & out privileges for registered guests only.

The Book Cadillac Hotel also offers these special rates: **Triple occupancy, $62; Quadruple occupancy, $72.**

*Add 5%: 4% Michigan State Sales Tax plus 1% Transient Facility Assessment.

Charges for extra person in room: Westin and Pontchartrain, $15/night; Book Cadillac, $10/night. Inquire about roll-away beds.

Children are accommodated free of charge in same room with parents if no extra beds are required. Age limits are as follows: Westin, 17 and under; Pontchartrain, 18 and under; Book Cadillac, 16 and under.

25 FEBRUARY 19____

FIGURE 6–11 *(continued).*

THE WRITTEN WORD IS A VALUABLE ASSET

The written word remains one of the most valuable assets available to the nonprofit. It is the basis for media and public contact. As information is the major product of the nonprofit, the annual report, the research report, the free and for-sale publications, the news release, the newsletter, the magazine, the memo, the letter, the handwritten note, the program, convention materials, the bookmark, the calendar, the flyer, and the training materials reflect the purpose of the organization. The identity of an organization, its appearance, clarity, unique style, and contributions to the community are effectively conveyed by the written word.

Outstanding examples of the powerful written word abound in the nonprofit world. There are resources, both free and for purchase, that can help a nonprofit achieve the image and style that will distinguish it in a hotly competitive market. Resources are as close as the local public library.

Others are aware of the value of the written word, so keep abreast of the competition and build a file of effective written words.

CHAPTER 7

Broadening Contacts with the Powerful Spoken Word

The spoken word is a powerful means of broadening an organization's contacts and influence in the community. Television and radio reach huge audiences which are otherwise unavailable to the nonprofit. Speakers' bureaus and speaking engagements (featuring volunteers, service users, patrons, and staff) are a means of tailoring the spoken word to specific target audiences.

The spoken word is versatile. In television and public appearances it is visual. In radio and telephone communications, it can be urgent, informative, exciting. It appears in the form of films, interviews, talk shows, speeches, news broadcasts, public service messages, telephone calls to prospective donors, volunteers, legislators, and members. The spoken word can be used to identify and sustain sources of funding and support. It generates credibility and community support.

TELEVISION: TODAY'S LOUDEST VOICE

Television is the source of most news for 65 percent of those responding to a 1982 Roper Organization, Inc., study, "Trends in Attitudes Toward Television and Other Media,"[1] and enjoys a two-to-one advantage over newspapers as the "most believable news medium." The Roper study also finds that respondents rate television higher on performance than churches, police, newspapers, schools, or local government. And, the study finds, television is growing, with two-thirds of the respondents reporting that cable TV was available to them. Well over half of those respondents reporting the availability of cable also report subscribing to it. When presented with a list of descriptive words and phrases, the Roper study respondents selected "entertaining" as the most descriptive of television, with "informative" in second place. "Public-spirited" was near the bottom of the list.

---

[1]"Trends in Attitudes Toward Television and Other Media: A Twenty-Four Year Review." A report by the Roper Organization, published by Television Information Office, 745 Fifth Avenue, New York, NY 10151, 1983.

The Roper study substantiates the importance of television to the nonprofit organization . . . audience, credibility, growth. Making full use of the opportunities that television offers requires planned and thoughtful action.

Nonprofits should note that "entertainment" is the primary purpose of television viewing, with information in second place. This dictates that appearances on television, as well as materials developed for television, must take into account the entertainment factor. Heavy messages, dull formats, and complicated problems are to be avoided. Simple, visual, attractive—these are the words that describe television materials and appearances. People scheduled by the nonprofit to appear on interview and talk shows must be prepared to get the message across in a manner that is lively, entertaining, and easily comprehended. Items for television news must be scrutinized for the same characteristics—entertaining, visual, easily understood. People scheduled for appearances can rehearse, can use videotape equipment to train for TV appearances, can be prepared to be lively, talkative, and informative. "Yes" and "no" responses to an interviewer's questions on television are deadly and can be avoided by carefully selecting the nonprofit's representative and by rehearsing and preparing. Don't expect an interviewer to know anything about the nonprofit or the reason for the appearance on the program. The nonprofit representative must carry the ball and help the interviewer develop the questions that will bring out the nonprofit's message.

PUBLIC SERVICE: A BOON TO THE NONPROFITS

Television and radio stations in the United States offer opportunities for public affairs, including public service messages. These opportunities vary from station to station but are a major source of donations available to the nonprofit. Public affairs requirements for radio and television stations originated with regulations governing the use of airwaves. The Federal Communications Commission is the federal government agency responsible for granting and renewal of operating licenses for radio and television stations. The Federal Communications Commission has deregulated public affairs requirements for radio stations, but, at this time, television stations must meet certain requirements. Radio and television stations, however, offer public affairs and public service time because stations are anxious to demonstrate their involvement with their communities and because public service/public affairs time generates listener support. Radio and television stations need the nonprofit organization.

Because of a station's interest in reaching its community, public service time on radio and television can be successfully attracted by the smallest nonprofit organization. National nonprofits are in competition with these local groups. Those national organizations with local affiliates can readily adapt public service materials to reflect local ties. This local tie-in will give the national organization the opportunity to compete effectively for public service time.

Public service time is competitive and insistent. Competition requires local tie-in as well as high professional standards. Insistence requires that the nonprofit serve the station's community. Public service materials must incorporate competitiveness and community service.

Professional quality can be costly. Filmed 30- and 60-second public service announcements can cost thousands of dollars in production. Fortunately, there are relatively inexpensive alternatives to filmed announcements.

Regardless of their cost, all materials prepared must be professional, high quality, attractive, and indicative of the nonprofit's contributions to the community. These characteristics, combined with personal contacts with the public service directors of radio and television stations, will insure the nonprofit's success in competing for public service time.

PUBLIC SERVICE ANNOUNCEMENTS (PSAs)

Television.

Television uses public service announcements in 10-, 20-, 30-, and 60-second lengths. These PSAs can be produced in 16-mm film or in videotape. Color and sound quality must be of professional standards. Sixteen-mm filmed PSAs are the most expensive to produce. Videotape production is less costly and highly flexible, and there is a growing acceptance of videotape PSAs by television stations.

Whether the PSA is produced in 16-mm film or in videotape, national distribution to the nearly 1,000 television stations in the United States is costly. One way to cut these distribution costs is to request a television station to make its own copy of a videotape PSA and to return the original videotape to the nonprofit. Paralyzed Veterans of America have had great success in placing PSAs with stations that produce copies from the master.

Another way of cutting distribution costs is to send a "storyboard" to public service directors. A storyboard is a printed version of the filmed PSA complete with the script and photographs taken from the filmed version. The station's public service director can then contact the nonprofit to obtain a filmed or videotaped version of the storyboard. The advantage here, in addition to costs, is that a public service director requesting a specific PSA is more likely to use it than not. A stamped, addressed return card should be included with the storyboard to encourage orders.

The examples in Figure 7–1 of storyboards and a return card were produced by Planned Communication Services, Inc., of New York City and included in that for-profit firm's publication, *Public Service Communicator*. A growing number of nonprofits now use storyboards for cost-effective PSA distribution.

One storyboard is a PSA of the nonprofit Federation of American Hospitals. It is an example of a generic public service message that offers opportunities for tie-ins to local hospitals and organizations concerned with pre-natal care. The message is simple and direct, and the PSA is attractive and appealing.

The production and distribution costs of 35-mm slide/script packages are even less than videotape PSAs. Many television stations will take a package of slides with accompanying written scripts and produce a PSA for the nonprofit. A package of three slides accompanied by written 10-, 20-, and 30-second scripts offers the stations flexibility in using the nonprofit message in varying time spots. Ten-second messages are frequently used for station breaks (Figure 7–2).

Requirements of television stations must be adhered to strictly for successful placement of materials, filmed, videotaped or slide/scripts. Many television stations provide nonprofit organizations specific instructions on preparing public service materials.

KOCE Television in Huntington Beach, California, offers its local nonprofits the guidelines seen in Figure 7–3.

PCS Film Productions
A division of Planned Communication Services Inc./ 12 East 46th Street, New York, N.Y. 10017 (212) 697-2765

SPECIAL CARE FOR A SPECIAL SOMEONE -- :30 Public Service Announcement -- Color, S.O.F.

Motherhood is a big responsibility, so

keep in good physical and mental condition.

Take extra care with your appearance.

Exercise regularly. Your doctor can recommend the right amount for you.

Get enough rest and eat a well balanced diet.

Avoid alcohol, nicotine, and all unnecessary drugs.

Your baby's good health depends on you.

"We had twins!"

A Public Service of the FEDERATION OF AMERICAN HOSPITALS

FIGURE 7–1. Courtesy of Planned Communication Services, Inc., 12 East 46th Street, New York, New York 10017.

TEENAGER -- :30 Public Service Announcement -- Color, SOF

Alcoholism. It can affect
your whole life: keep you
awake at night,

cut you off from friends and
neighbors, distract you at
school and humilate you at
home.

If you're a teenager affected
by someone else's drinking,
do you know what it's doing
to you?

In Alateen, teenagers will
level with you about the
drinking in their homes.

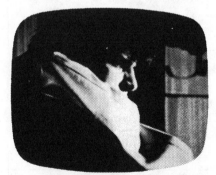

Contact Alateen through
Al-Anon, listed in your phone
book, or Al-Anon Family
Group Headquarters.

TITLE: AL-ANON
BOX 182
NY, NY 10010

FIGURE 7–1 *(continued)*. From Public Service Announcement "Teenager,"
copyright 1978 by Al-Anon Family Groups Headquarters.
Reprinted by permission of Al-Anon Family Groups
Headquarters, Inc., P.O. Box 182, Madison Square Station,
New York, New York 10159.

Dear Public Service Director:

Please use the attached request card to order

television public service announcements from

the PUBLIC SERVICE COMMUNICATOR.   The 16mm,

color, S.O.F. films will be sent to you free

of charge.

Thank you.

Please send me the following selection of
public service announcements:

G-1   (:30)_____   G-5 (:30)_____

G-2   (:30)_____   G-6 (:60)_____

G-3   (:60)_____   G-7 (:30)_____

G-4   (:30)_____

Comments _____

Please make any
call letter or
address changes.

FIGURE 7–1 *(continued)*.   Courtesy of the Federation of American Hospitals,
1111 19th Street N.W., Suite 402, Washington, D.C. 20036.

10-Second PSA

The Boys Clubs of America are open every day with a variety of educational, vocational, and recreational programs. Help turn a kid around. Support the Boys Club of _____.

15-Second PSA   Boys Clubs of America

How do you get a kid who's shut off to open up? By giving him a place to go, and someone to talk to. A Boys Club. Help turn a kid around. Support the Boys Club of _____. For information, call _____.

20-Second PSA   Boys Clubs of America

For over 75 years, the Boys Clubs of America have developed a tradition of turning kids around. Boys Clubs offer youngsters a place to go—off the streets—to develop skills, participate in group activities, and benefit from the guidance of professional youth workers who really care. Help continue the tradition. Support the Boys Club of _____, a member of the Boys Clubs of America.

FIGURE 7–2. Courtesy of BOYS CLUBS OF AMERICA, 771 First Avenue, New York, New York 10017.

PUBLIC SERVICE ANNOUNCEMENT
SUBMITTAL POLICY
KOCE-TV

1. Organization must be a qualified nonprofit group.

2. Request must be received a minimum of two weeks prior to the requested initial air date.

3. Format must be one of the following:

    a. Film: 16mm of 60-second length or less.

    b. Narrative: Written copy, 30 seconds or less in length, with optional color slide supplement. Copy may be in the format used on the attached samples or in a format of your own choosing provided it contains all required information.

    Your announcement would be enhanced by the use of your own slide, but if used, it must conform to the strict standards stated in the "Slide Guidelines" attached.

    c. KOCE cannot accept your public service announcements for airing unless they are written in broadcast form (see attached samples).

FIGURE 7–3. Courtesy of KOCE-TV Channel 50, Coast Community College District, P.O. Box 2476, Huntington Beach, California 92647.

PUBLIC SERVICE ANNOUNCEMENT

ORGANIZATION ORANGE COUNTY HUMAN SERVICES AGENCY/SOCIAL SERVICES

ADDRESS   1801 NORTH COLLEGE AVENUE

               SANTA ANA, CA 92702

CONTACT   LES RIDGE, (714) 834-2168

READING TIME   :10   SCBA FILE NO. #31581-267 GIL

SUBJECT   FOSTER PARENTS

VIDEO	AUDIO
SLIDE (If provided):	FOSTER PARENTS ARE EXCEPTIONAL PEOPLE
"BECOME A FOSTER PARENT - 834-2168"	WHO CAN GIVE OF THEMSELVES TO A CHILD WHO DOES NOT BELONG TO THEM. IF YOU CAN HELP FILL THE EMPTINESS IN A YOUNG LIFE, CALL ORANGE COUNTY SOCIAL SERVICES.
START DATE: 7/1/___ STOP DATE: 10/1/___	

FIGURE 7–3 *(continued)*.

<u>PUBLIC SERVICE ANNOUNCEMENT</u>

ORGANIZATION   CALIFORNIA STATE UNIVERSITY, FULLERTON

ADDRESS   FULLERTON, CA 92634

CONTACT   WALLY FARRELLY

READING TIME   10, 20, OR 30 SECONDS   SCBA FILE NO. #30681-268 EI

SUBJECT   ELMER ISELER SINGERS

VIDEO	AUDIO
SLIDE (If provided): Not provided	CAL STATE FULLERTON PRESENTS THE WEST COAST DEBUT OF CANADA'S ELMER ISELER (ICE lehr) SINGERS THIS SATURDAY, OCTOBER 3RD, AT 8:00 P.M. IN THE SCHOOL AUDITORIUM.
10 Second Cut-off	
	THE TWENTY-VOICE PROFESSIONAL CHOIR WILL PERFORM A VARIED PROGRAM OF MUSIC SPANNING FIVE CENTURIES, INCLUDING PIECES
20 Second Cut-off	BY SEVERAL CANADIAN COMPOSERS.
	RESERVED SEAT TICKETS FOR THE ELMER ISELER SINGERS ARE NOW AVAILABLE FROM CAL STATE FULLERTON. FOR INFORMATION OR
30 Second Cut-off	TICKETS, CALL 714-773-3347.
START DATE: 9/14/___ STOP DATE: 10/2/___	

FIGURE 7–3 *(continued).*

SLIDE GUIDELINES

Size and Format

All slides submitted for use on KOCE must be 35mm color transparencies with a horizontally composed image (mounted in glass preferred). Slides taken with a 35mm camera are approximately 24 × 36mm, however, only a 21 × 29mm area is transmitted on the air. All the copy in the slide (name, logo, telephone number or other pertinent information) must be limited to the central 19 × 24mm area. Television sets will cut off matter near the edges of the picture, therefore, all important material and lettering must be in the center of the slide (see example).

Copy

Keep the copy on the slide to an absolute minimum. The size of the lettering is of considerable importance. A simple test to determine if the lettering is acceptable for television would be to hold the slide before a window or other light source. If the copy can be read comfortably without magnification, the size should be adequate for television.

Example:

Color and Contrast

Slides for KOCE use should be bright in color. When selecting color, it is advisable to utilize a color wheel choosing opposite colors. After selecting contrasting colors for slides, both color and black/white reception must be considered, therefore, it is important to use a light/dark or dark/light contrast.

Packaging and Submittal

Slides should be packaged for mailing in corrugated material to insure against breakage. The slides submitted for KOCE broadcast will not be returned.

These guidelines are based on the formats of the equipment used in the television industry and are drawn up to assist you in preparing suitable slides for that purpose. If you have further questions, you are invited to contact Gail Bartosik, Program Services Manager.

FIGURE 7–3 *(continued).*

YOU MAY WANT TO OBTAIN AN SCBA NUMBER

While an SCBA number is not mandatory in order to obtain free Public Service air time from the broadcast media, it is highly expedient. When a radio or TV station Public Service or Public Affairs Director spots the SCBA identification number in the lower right-hand corner of your submitted copy, he or she knows that all the preliminary clearance work has already been done. The SCBA number signifies that your organization has been cleared as to non-profit status, that Internal Revenue Tax Exempt status has been proven in writing, a social service license has been submitted in case of fund raising, and the legitimacy of purpose and intent of your spots has been noted. The SCBA number speeds up the director's work and saves time in getting your spots scheduled for airing. SCBA clears your organization for every member radio and TV station in the L.A. & Orange County area. (However, clearance does NOT imply endorsement.)

HOW TO TELL IF YOUR ORGANIZATION IS ELIGIBLE FOR FREE AIR TIME AND AN SCBA NUMBER

If your organization is non-profit and has tax exempt status in writing from the Internal Revenue Service it quite possibly is eligible for air time. The same criteria apply for an SCBA number with the following exceptions:

1. Any event sponsored by a political, religious, philosophical or ideological organization.
2. Commercial trade associations or professional associations.
3. Commercial events for which the PREMIERE PERFORMANCE ONLY goes to charity.
4. Fund raising efforts sponsored by a non-incorporated group.
5. Controversial issues (materials may lend themselves better to editorials or Public Affairs programs.)

The groups just mentioned may apply directly to the stations for processing.

HOW TO APPLY FOR AN SCBA NUMBER

To request an original or renewal of an SCBA number, please send a self-addressed, stamped #10 envelope with 28¢ postage on it (please increase postage as postal rates rise per ounce), at least three weeks PRIOR to your needing it to:

> SCBA
> 1800 North Highland Avenue
> Suite 609
> Los Angeles, California 90028

You will receive an application, a fact sheet explaining all facets of the application, plus a Public Service List which will give each radio & TV station's requirements for length of spots, how to write them and whom to send them to. General information numbers are good for one full year, renewable on an annual basis. Fund raising numbers expire on the last day of the special event and coincide with the date on the Social Service license issued by the City or County Social Services Departments. You should apply for this Social Service license well in advance of requesting an SCBA number in order to expedite the process. There is a processing fee of $10 yearly payable to SCBA which covers all requests for information or funding numbers within that twelve month period.

1800 NORTH HIGHLAND AVENUE HOLLYWOOD, CALIFORNIA 90028
PHONE (213) 466-4481

FIGURE 7-3 (continued).

Cable.

Cable television offers both visual placement and a highly specialized audience. Cable systems are important new outlets for videotaped PSAs. The March of Dimes Birth Defects Foundation has been distributing PSAs to cable systems since 1971. It is probably the first organization to supply PSAs to cable systems on a broad scale.[2]

Planned Communication Services, Inc. in New York offers nonprofit PSAs to cable systems, and cable placement is growing in importance. Cable PSAs are prepared only in videotape (not 16-mm film), but otherwise follow the same rules that apply to other television PSAs—quality production, sound, color, and 10-, 20-, 30- and 60-second length.

Public Access to Cable Programming.

Government legislation authorizing national cable television systems requires "public access programming." The Federal Communications Commission is responsible for the regulations governing this requirement. This public access affords opportunities to develop and produce cable programs about the nonprofit's services to its community. Such programs become "national" in scope when marketed through other cable systems.

Cable promises endless opportunities in programming as well as in public service time. It also dangles the realization of all-text cable programming, all-health channels, responsive two-way communication through cable, hook-ups to home computers for information sharing, a plethora of Buck Rogers opportunities for the nonprofit.

Radio.

Radio stations are more specialized in audiences than television. Radio stations can identify their audience profile by age, income, interests. Radio's specialized audiences offer the nonprofit opportunities to get their message to specific interest groups. Minority people, for example, can be reached through targeted PSAs placed with radio stations aimed at minority groups. Young audiences can be targeted through radio stations aimed at the youth market. Arts nonprofits can use classical music stations to advantage in reaching important patron audiences. Radio is the opportunity to offer highly selective and specific PSAs.

Radio scripts differ from news releases. The words in a radio script are for hearing, not seeing. Difficult last names, for example, should be spelled phonetically in parentheses after the name. Every word must be timed and counted so that exactly 10 seconds (15, 20, 30 or 60 depending on the length of the PSA) of time is used, no more and no less. Radio runs on time and your PSAs must run on time also.

---

[2]Unpublished article by Andrew McGowan, Vice President, Planned Communication Services, Inc., 12 East 46th Street, New York, NY 10017.

Radio scripts can use language colorfully and do not necessarily follow the "who, what, where, when, why" rules of the news release. The example in Figure 7–4 of a radio script was produced by North American Precis Syndicate, a private, for-profit firm that produces and distributes written newspaper and radio script materials nationally. The script features a message from the nonprofit American Youth Hostels organization.

RADIO ROUNDUP
a collection of features, oddities, and helpful tips

NORTH AMERICAN PRECIS SYNDICATE, inc.
201 east 42nd street
new york, n.y. 10017

(173 WORDS, 69 SECONDS)

ECONOMICAL TRAVEL IDEA

For many health-conscious Americans, getting back to nature is more than just eating health foods. It's a whole way of life or at least vacationing—experiencing the world for themselves. Even on a tight budget, they travel by staying in hostels along the way—often backpacking, bicycling, or skiing between destinations. Membership in American Youth Hostels allows them to stay at any of more than 5,000 inns in 50 countries, including the U.S.

Lodging is sometimes less than two to five dollars a night—and half-price for children—for up to three nights. Sometimes it's in mountain lodges, college dormitories, national parks—even medieval castles, Swiss chalets and other interesting places. Most hostels offer fully equipped kitchens where you can prepare your own meals and a common room where hostelers meet. As a member, you can take advantage of other money-saving services like rail passes and charter flights. For a free leaflet write Department P, American Youth Hostels, Inc., Delaplane, Virginia 22025. Or call this toll free number: 800-336-6019.

FIGURE 7–4. Courtesy of Ronald N. Levy, President, North American Precis Syndicate, Inc., 201 East 42nd Street, New York, NY 10017.

The Nonprofit's Friend at the Station: The Public Service Director.

Most radio and television stations have a public service director or someone who fills the role. The public service director is responsible for the station's community relations. He or she is the nonprofit's best friend at the station and a relationship can be mutually rewarding. As the community relations person, the public service director is frequently responsible for selecting PSAs for use, for recommending on news coverage of community events, for producing public affairs programs of interest to the station's audience. Some public service directors, mainly in television, organize "ascertainment" functions to bring station executives together with community representatives to discuss the kinds of community issues that the station should cover.

You need to know the public service directors of radio and television stations in your area. These directors can help the nonprofit in producing PSAs—for both radio and television—as well as giving guidance on standards, content, and approaches. They are frequently willing to speak to nonprofit staff and volunteers and other nonprofit audiences about their particular medium and offer advice on getting better coverage. Knowing public service directors and keeping them advised on the nonprofit's activities is only a telephone call away.

The public service director of WRC-TV 4 in Washington, D.C., offers nonprofits a comprehensive booklet filled with information and specifics about the station's public service. The booklet additionally offers other sources of help and information. WRC-TV 4 also publicizes such events as "community leaders' luncheons" (Figure 7–5).

**COMMUNITY LEADERS
LUNCHEONS. . . .**

For several years, WRC-TV has held monthly luncheons at which representatives of community organizations discuss with station management the diversity of problems, needs and interests of the greater Washington community.

We have met with thousands of leaders representing local and federal government, social and civic agencies, the educational and religious communities and other groups.

Through these "Community Leaders Luncheons," WRC-TV is constantly learning more about the current interests and concerns of metropolitan area residents. These luncheons are your forum. They establish a continuing dialogue between you, the community and the WRC-TV management (see other side). They are of benefit to all of us.

We encourage your candid comments on how WRC-TV can better meet the needs and interests of our audience. Your opinions, criticisms and ideas are often the impetus to subsequent news coverage, community affairs programs and public service campaigns.

We welcome your recommendations and comments.

FIGURE 7–5.   Material provided courtesy of WRC-TV 4 and NBC, © 1983. The National Broadcasting Company, Inc. All Rights Reserved.

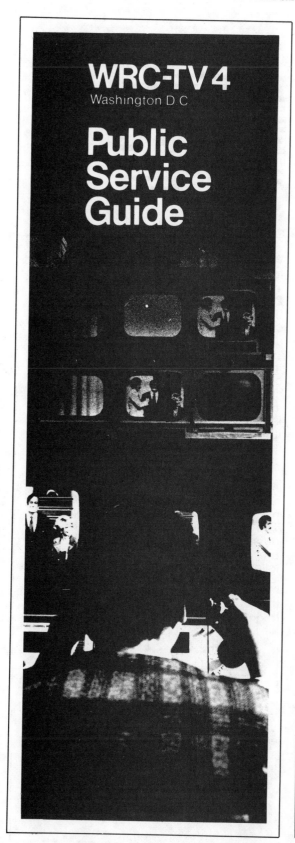

Public Service. It's all on us.

Each year, WRC-TV donates millions of dollars in air time, talent and facilities for public service announcements and programs on behalf of worthy causes. The result? A steady channel of information linking community groups, WRC-TV and the public.

This book tells you:
1. How to qualify for free public service announcements.
2. How to prepare public service announcements, if you do qualify.
3. How to submit material about your group for locally-produced program consideration.
4. How to submit information about your group for possible coverage by WRC-TV News.
5. How to get more information on WRC-TV community service.

If your group is involved in work that you feel is of importance to the community, read through the following pages. It's the first step to getting your message on.

FIGURE 7–5 *(continued).*

On PSA's

A Public Service Announcement (PSA) is one offered without charge to qualified non-profit, tax-exempt organizations for the promotion of programs, activities or services which serve community interests.

To qualify, your organization must be legally constituted as non-profit, IRS tax-exempt, and involved in the improvement of the community through an area such as health, welfare, religion, charity, safety, or other service.

WRC-TV's Public Service Department requires a listing of your group's officers, and a fact sheet outlining its background and aims, printed on official letterhead stationery. If you plan to solicit funds on the air, your organization must also, by law, provide us with its charitable solicitation number (issued by the D.C. Government Department of Licenses as proof of registration to raise funds).

Once you qualify for public service air time, WRC-TV will consider specific material for broadcast. You may submit an announcement to be aired for a short and limited duration, or for general use throughout the year. Announcements are seen throughout the broadcast day on a rotating basis.

In addition, WRC-TV schedules an early morning bulletin board, "Events 4 Washington," which highlights fairs, church bazaars and other one-day community events.

On PSA Preparation.

WRC-TV uses three types of material for spot announcements:
1) 2" broadcast-quality videotape,
2) 16 mm color, sound-on film, and
3) live announcements with 35mm color slides and written copy for on-air delivery by an announcer.

In each, the quality of visual and audio content must meet WRC-TV broadcast standards, and must conform to the 10-, 20-, 30-, and 60-second standard lengths of WRC-TV announcements. It should be pointed out the preference is for 30-second spots due to the greater availability of inventory.

Film and Videotape Spots can be more effective than slide announcements, but must be prepared by professionals. The audio portion of each film spot *must* contain one second of silence preceding and one second of silence following the sound-on film message.

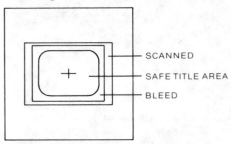

Live Announcements are the most economical PSA's to prepare. Slides should be standard 2x2" 35 mm color transparencies mounted in glass, containing pictures, logo, or lettered

FIGURE 7–5 *(continued).*

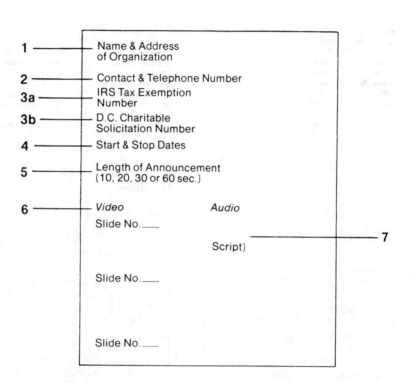

1 — Name & Address of Organization

2 — Contact & Telephone Number

3a — IRS Tax Exemption Number

3b — D.C. Charitable Solicitation Number

4 — Start & Stop Dates

5 — Length of Announcement (10, 20, 30 or 60 sec.)

6 — *Video*   *Audio*

Slide No.___

Script) — 7

Slide No.___

Slide No.___

copy to visually cover the announcer copy. The image must be composed horizontally, as indicated. Professional preparation is recommended.

Remember: Keep slides uncluttered; keep material centered on the slide, as television sets cut off matter near the picture (note example); mail slides in corrugated materials to prevent glass breakage.

Time your finished announcement's length with a stopwatch to make sure it can read *comfortably* within the required time. Make it conversational. Remember, you are asking people to do something.

Here's how to prepare your announcement for WRC-TV:

Each Piece of Written Copy *Must* Include:
1. Full legal name, address, zip code and telephone number of organization.
2. Name, title and telephone number of person to be contacted for additional information.

3. The IRS tax exemption number and the D.C. Charitable Solicitation number if fund appeals within the District of Columbia are involved.
4. Air dates that cover use of this announcement.
5. Length of announcement.
6. Material to be seen on viewing screen. Color slide number will be filled in by WRC-TV.
7. The message the announcer will read, concise and complete. The message should be typed in capital letters and double-spaced. Announcer's copy should be well-separated from the other material.

All material for use on WRC-TV should be submitted to:

WRC-TV Public Service Department
4001 Nebraska Avenue, N.W.
Washington, D.C. 20016

Inquiries can be made by calling 686-4087

Allow a minimum of two weeks for WRC-TV evaluation, processing and scheduling procedures.

FIGURE 7–5 *(continued).*

On Shows

Please consult your local TV listings or WRC-TV for current public affairs and religious programs.

These popular, locally-produced programs often explore significant community problems. WRC-TV also produces half-hour, hour and mini-series specials on subjects suggested by the activities and ideas of local groups.

If your group has a program suggestion of major interest to the entire Washington metropolitan area on a topic such as housing, education, safety, alcoholism, drugs, welfare, health, the arts, and youth:

Outline the idea in letter form, giving a brief sketch of the proposed program, indicating its visual possibilities, and its benefit to the community.

Include any brochures, fact sheets or other materials that would provide additional information on the topic you suggest.

All material for WRC-TV program suggestions should be submitted to:
WRC-TV—Director, Programs
4001 Nebraska Avenue, N.W.
Washington, D.C. 20016

On News

WRC-TV's News Center-4 often covers newsworthy organizational activities. To bring your group's activities to the News Department's attention, submit in writing all essential facts about your group or a special event, as far in advance of the event as possible. Your news story will be judged by whether it is of current and relative importance. Be sure, also, to include in your submission the name, address and telephone numbers of persons who can provide additional information.

Send your information sheet to:
Manager News Assignments
WRC-TV Local News
4001 Nebraska Ave., N.W.
Washington, D.C. 20016
or call 686-4117

FIGURE 7–5 *(continued).*

On Further Sources.

WRC-TV's Office of Community Services is another link between community groups, the station, and the public. It channels information about community needs and concerns to programming and news departments. In addition, the office handles arrangements for special group screenings of WRC-TV's programs, and operates a speakers' bureau that provides station personnel for appearances before community groups.

Write or call:
WRC-TV Community Services
4001 Nebraska Ave., N.W.
Washington, D.C. 20016
686-4087

Speaker's Bureau/Press
686-4034

"If You Want Air Time," a free handbook available from the National Association of Broadcasters, contains more information on radio, television, and public relations efforts, and the preparation of news releases. Write them at 1771 N St., N.W., Washington, D.C. 20036.

On WRC-TV

The date—June 27, 1947.

The occasion—Channel 4's (then WNBW) first evening of television programming. The schedule—a newsreel, boxing, a symphony performed by the Toscanini Orchestra, a variety show and a travelogue.

Since then, a list of WRC-TV4 "firsts" reads not only like a history of television, but a history of our time: The first televised Presidential Inauguration. The first TV pick-up from the White House. Congressional hearings in the '50s. The Kennedy-Nixon debates, and more.

WRC-TV now broadcasts from its own extensive home base in Northwest Washington, dedicated on May 22, 1958, by President Dwight D. Eisenhower. Ten hours of color programming a week in the '50s have since multiplied to over 125 hours of color a week.

Because of our prime facilities and location, WRC-TV provides not only fine community coverage to the Washington metropolitan area, but also important network programs to the nation, such as: "Meet the Press," "Today Show" interviews with topical Washington guests, and segments of the "NBC Nightly News."

We are proud of our close relationship with the greater Washington communities we serve, and of the increasing number of prestigious awards—evidence of WRC-TV's dedication to the highest quality programming.

FIGURE 7–5 *(continued).*

TIPS ON GAINING AND USING PUBLIC SERVICE TIME

- Deliver PSAs well in advance of the date that you'd like them broadcast. Stations require two to four weeks to process them.
- Include the nonprofit's name and address and the contact person's name and telephone number on all materials.
- Ask for the community's active support through PSAs.
- Offer the community information through PSAs.
- Recruit volunteers through PSAs.
- Know your station's broadcast range and specific audience so that your PSAs are appropriate.
- Use "calendars of events" regularly to spotlight nonprofit activities.
- Submit scripts to public service directors for their suggestions prior to filming, taping, or recording. This is particularly important if there are doubts or questions about the PSA.
- Feature consumer/users and volunteers from the community in PSAs.
- Involve public service directors in nonprofit programs.
- Be professional in your approaches to the media as well as in your products.
- Seek support for your PSAs from nonprofit allies in the community.
- Cooperate with other nonprofits on producing generic PSAs that will help all the agencies involved.
- Use public service time. If you can't produce professional PSAs within the nonprofit, contract out. Public service time is too important an asset to overlook or abuse.
- When producing a 60-second PSA, it may be cost effective to also produce 10- and 30-second PSAs from the same material.
- Generally, offer or send only one PSA at a time. Hold back the other lengths for later release—one at a time for maximum use and effectiveness.
- If you decide to use all lengths at the same time, offer the public service director a choice of lengths by using a story board with a stamped return card.

LOSING CONTROL: A CRISIS COMES SWIFTLY

A distinct advantage of public service is the control that it gives the nonprofit over the spoken word. There are other spoken words, however, and some may be angry and hostile to the nonprofit. Be prepared, as these emergency situations arise swiftly: a student demonstration against a university ruling; a patient's family suing for malpractice; service recipients protesting treatment; a donor accusing a museum of misappropriation of funds. Spoken words are turned against the nonprofit and the media follows, seeking a news story.

A critical news story develops as fast as a tornado. The successful nonprofit is prepared, its knowledgeable representatives identified at all times, and information about the critical issue is sought, verified, and shared. It is not a time for panic, for panic is a luxury to be indulged in after the crisis is professionally handled. It is also not a time for "no comment," for television and radio reporters are under deadlines that require immediate comment. The nonprofit is under two barrels in a crisis situation: the media's demand for information and the consideration of public trust. If the nonprofit wishes to have a "balanced" news story resulting from a crisis, it must produce the balance. That balance may be the announcement of an emergency meeting to review the consumer/user demands or the assignment of an immediate investigation into the alleged wrongdoings. A crisis requires immediate response and action, not passivity. The nonprofit must be alert to staff, consumers, and volunteers who can help balance the crisis situation on short notice. Credibility and accountability are at stake.

The Near Assassination of the President.

Most nonprofits will never have to confront the situation that George Washington University Hospital faced when President Reagan was rushed to that hospital after the assassination attempt in 1981. Besieged by hundreds of reporters, cameras, and microphones, the hospital could have lost its reputation as a leading medical facility in that first hectic half-hour. Instead, it produced Dr. Dennis S. O'Leary to speak to the reporters. It might have been throwing the lamb to the lions, but Dr. O'Leary calmed reporters—and a nation—by his knowledge and sureness.

It was a brilliant choice and a highly visible demonstration of being prepared for a crisis. Dr. O'Leary represented the nonprofit with authority and spoke with ease and assurance. He was able to make complicated medical procedures and hospital jargon completely understandable. Dr. O'Leary's expert and fearless performance in facing hysterical reporters, unanswerable questions, and allegations, is a standard to which all nonprofits can aspire in a crisis.

GENERATING YOUR OWN NEWS

The nonprofit needn't wait for a crisis to develop news about the organization. It can develop its own news stories, stories that are more likely to bring credit to the organization than those generated by crisis.

Nonprofit news includes developments in programs, resources, services; approaches that are unique and newsworthy; and human interest pieces about service staff, volunteers, and service recipients.

Essentially, alerting radio and television to news items is similar to those steps taken with the print media. News releases, news conferences, interviews, all can be arranged with some subtle tailoring to meet the needs of radio and television.

News Programs.

Radio and television news programs should be included in distribution of releases. They can also be sent videotaped or recorded news stories produced by the nonprofit. Some stations will use news items produced by nonprofits while others do all of their own reporting. The public service director can advise on this. In sending releases (not press releases when they are addressed to radio and television, but *news releases*), the designee should be the news director rather than the editor. If you want the release used exactly as you send it, then time it, count the words, and follow the radio/television news release format. If the release is to alert for coverage, use the brief announcement format.

Talk Shows.

All talk shows, from national ones like "Today" on television or "Larry King" on radio, to local programs on television or radio, require the same careful approach.

- Get the name of the show's producer.
- Write the producer well in advance (4 to 6 weeks) of the date you want scheduled.
- Choose your written materials with care. A persuasive letter should highlight the potential audience impact of the program, the significance for the audience, the unique qualities of the speaker(s) you are trying to schedule, and the most visual aspects of the program format you are recommending.
- Your package should be comprehensive but brief enough to read in no more than ten minutes.
- Select accompanying photographs or videotapes or tape recordings of the speaker(s). Again, these should highlight the unique qualities of the speaker(s) and the audience impact of the information/entertainment being offered.
- Select speaker(s) with attention to their visual and vocal abilities as well as their "entertainment" value in such things as quick thinking, sense of humor, ease before cameras and microphones.
- Telephone within a week following the sending of written materials to the producer. Offer any further information or persuasive tips. Follow up but don't bug and don't play games with producers of talk shows. If you've prepared materials carefully and persuasively, the producer will let you know.

Interviews.

Work with public service directors on arranging interviews for nonprofit representatives.

Radio stations will do telephone interviews. These can be set up by contacting radio news directors by telephone or by a news release. Radio station news directors frequently like to find reactions to news developments, and the stations in your area should be alerted to the experts that your nonprofit has in selected areas for telephone interview purposes. An example is a university professor with a specialty in Middle East affairs who can be queried on news developments in that area of the world.

Hearings.

Public hearings[3] on issues of community concern are an important way of attracting public support and attention. Political leaders should participate in

---

[3]See *Public Hearing Manual*, by Jean Mater, for full treatment of procedures and strategies. Englewood Cliffs, N.J.: Prentice-Hall, Inc.

public hearings on current issues and frequently can help to arrange such hearings. Hearings can be held in the morning to accommodate television crews filming for the evening news, can feature consumers, can highlight the nonprofit's response to the issues, and can further public support and funding. A hearing is an exchange of views between people testifying on an issue and being questioned by the panel of "hearers." Hearings are visual events, and all participants must be screened and prepared. The purpose of a hearing must be carefully thought out. Generally, a hearing is an opportunity to bring a problem/issue to the public's and to the government's attention. Know in advance the action(s) the nonprofit wants to take following the hearing.

Speakers' Bureau.

A nonprofit can offer a group of carefully prepared and trained speakers drawn from consumers and volunteers to represent the nonprofit at meetings throughout the community. All potential speakers should be trained in public speaking techniques and fully armed with information about the nonprofit, its services, programs, and problems. Speakers can be effective in attracting public attention, in attracting new members and allies, in attracting funds. There are opportunities in every community for effective public speakers at service organizations, community groups, lunch and dinner gatherings.

Exchanging Representatives.

Speakers representing the nonprofit should be scheduled to appear at allied nonprofit organization meetings, conferences, and seminars. Conversely, invitations should be sent to allied nonprofits requesting speakers for events. An exchange of information between nonprofits can increase understanding, cooperative programming, and share valuable information on mutual goals.

Training.

All speakers must receive training in public speaking to overcome aversion to appearing before groups, to learn the techniques of projection, audience relationship, body language, verbal clarity, and the all-important concept that only one idea can usually be successfully conveyed in one speech. Training in public speaking techniques is useful for all staff and volunteers in dealing with the public in person or on the telephone. Training is preparing to make the most of the powerful spoken word.

HIGH TECH: THE FUTURE IS NOW

"High tech" refers to teleconferences, cable talk-back capabilities, videotaped lobbying, telephone conference calls, telefunding, telethons . . . all the futuristic ways of "telling" the nonprofit's publics about the organization, its programs, its needs, its accomplishments. The nonprofit United States Chamber of Commerce has built one of the nation's most sophisticated teleconferencing centers, "Biznet." Biznet provides teleconferences to Chamber members throughout the United States. Teleconferencing has the capability of presenting the President of the United States "live" to audiences across the country, who can respond to the President's remarks by asking their own questions, and having them answered. Teleconferencing permits an outreach to audiences that may otherwise never attend a national conference or have the chance to question a national leader.

Teleconferencing offers the organization an opportunity to have ten or 50 conferences at the same time, with the same speakers, but in locations across the nation.

The impact of teleconferences on national meetings is yet to be evaluated. Similarily, the impact of talk-back cable is not yet evaluated. Some of these "tele" techniques offer a potential for reaching members, affiliates, allies, and other publics more effectively and less expensively than face-to-face contact. While the impact of high tech on the nonprofit is not clear, it promises to be profound.

Videotape lobbying offers an exciting dimension to organizations willing to invest in videotape equipment and to use it to dramatically illustrate the problems or progress of the nonprofit. Videotaping the need for a home for street people, for example, can graphically depict to government officials and other funding sources the plight of homeless men and women. Videotape produces a color, sound "film" that is easily transportable and can be played to any audience on a television set adapted for videotape use.

A well-produced videotape can have a profound impact on legislators and show precisely the points the nonprofit wishes to make.

CHAPTER 8

Creating Publicity
with "Special Events"

Every activity of the nonprofit is "special." Each activity, regardless of its size, requires the same careful attention to detail. All events, major or minor, require purpose, planning, and thoughtful execution. A meeting of the board of trustees is as crucial to the well-being of the nonprofit as a fundraising gala. A training program for volunteers, employees, or service recipients is a special event. Public service advertising, the nonprofit newsletter, an open house for the community, an awards banquet with a Hollywood star, are "special" to the nonprofit and to its future.

PUT PURPOSE INTO THE SPECIAL EVENT

The "special" in the event is generated by its purpose. Each event must be evaluated to determine its specific objective, its contribution to the nonprofit's goals, its potential for fundraising, its cost effectiveness, its acceptability to the nonprofit's publics, its potential for evaluation and duplication. Which specific audiences does the event reach and what are its contributions to community support and fundraising objectives?

Each special event must have the purpose of strengthening the nonprofit's community support or the support of a specific audience. Each special event must meet the criteria of furthering support for the nonprofit economically, politically, professionally.

CONTINUITY LENDS "SPECIALNESS"

Continuity's importance is easily seen by looking at the enormous number of days, weeks, and months that are designated as "National Red Cross Month," "National Clean Air Week," "Mother's Day." National observances are frequently declared by the President of the United States who is directed by Congress to declare the event to the nation. Governors and mayors do the same within their jurisdictions. A community learns to depend on a special event that is produced year after year, and continuity lends credence to the sponsoring organization as well as engendering support for the event. Many cities maintain calendars of charity balls, tennis matches, waterfront and neighborhood festivals, art shows, and other regularly scheduled nonprofit "special events." When a nonprofit wishes to introduce a new event, it should find a clear spot on the calendar of scheduled events so that conflict can be avoided. Mayors' and governors' offices, tourist bureaus, and other nonprofit organizations are the places to check before scheduling a first-time event. Once the event is established, be sure to keep these offices informed of its scheduled date, time, and place.

PUBLIC SERVICE CAMPAIGNS CREATE CONTINUITY

Nonprofits can gain needed continuity by regularly scheduled public service advertising campaigns. Depending on the nonprofit's budget, these campaigns can be released monthly, quarterly, yearly. A public service campaign thrives on planning and professional production, not on episodic news. Public service advertising campaigns can help the nonprofit to establish identity, image, recognition of its contributions to the community, and to generate urgency about its goals. Public service advertising usually cannot be controversial or involve funding appeals. Its function is supportive.

Public service advertising has outlets in cooperating media including newspapers, magazines, radio, television, cable. Its most important ingredients for success are continuity, quality of production and presentation, and cooperation from the media. The public service message must be simple, fresh, and attractive, and the nonprofit sustains its effectiveness by allocation of resources.

The headquarters of the National Easter Seal Society offers a quarterly public service advertising campaign to its affiliates throughout the country. This quarterly service is a comprehensive package of public service materials from which the affiliates may select and then place with local media. The materials in Figure 8–1 were among those offered to local Easter Seal affiliates in spring 1983 by the national office.

Easter Seal's package includes a wide variety of materials for use in public service campaigns. These materials include written radio and television public service announcements, 35-mm slides to accompany written television public service announcements, videotaped public service announcements for television use, posters for shopping malls, photographs for newspapers, and suggestions on using these materials. Additionally, local chapters can develop their own materials. All materials stress local names, addresses, and phone numbers.

Please note that the low prices charged for Easter Seal materials are a result of quantity production. Nonprofits not affiliated with national organizations can pool resources with other nonprofits and produce public service campaigns on broad themes which can then assist the work of all the cooperating organizations. Minority organizations, for example, may stress education or job training, while women's groups might target rape victim advocacy or pre-natal care.

Sharing with others is a way to offset the expense of continuity through public service campaigns.

Communications Department

NATIONAL EASTER SEAL SOCIETY

TO: Executive Directors of Intermediary DATE: April 4, 19____
and Local Easter Seal Societies

#828

FROM: Hope J. Boonshaft, Director of Communications

SUBJECT: 19____ SPRING QUARTERLY THEME PUBLIC EDUCATION PACKAGE—
A JOINT PROJECT BETWEEN NATIONAL EASTER SEAL SOCIETY AND
THE AMERICAN OCCUPATIONAL THERAPY ASSOCIATION

What is Occupational Therapy and who may avail themselves of Occupational Therapy Services, is the emphasis of the Spring Quarterly Theme for 1983. The National Easter Seal Society and the American Occupational Therapy Association have teamed up in a joint public education project, aimed at clarifying to the public what OT is and how it helps persons with disabilities become more independent.

The package offers a 30-second TV and Radio PSA featuring <u>General Hospital's</u> Leslie Charleson. It also offers a 30-second slide PSA for television with announcer scripts enclosed.

Our theme . . . "Occupational Therapy is a Special Way of Caring," is found on both the poster and brochure, again featuring Miss Charleson and OT clients in therapy.

A general release is enclosed, along with a photograph of Miss Charleson as she speaks for Occupational Therapy, together with a brief background on the actress who portrays a surgeon on the #1 rated daytime drama.

Also included are booklets on Occupational Therapy. One booklet, "About Occupational Therapy," answers common questions about OT in line drawings and may be ordered on the attached order form. The other, prepared by the AFL-CIO for the AOTA, offers a more sophisticated approach to OT: "Set Your Sights on a Great Life Through Comprehensive Rehabilitation." This particular booklet is available directly from the American Occupational Therapy Association, 1383 Piccard Drive, Rockville, Maryland 20850 at 40¢ each.

We have added an up-to-date listing of Independent Living Centers, compiled to assist the Clearinghouse on the Disabled with inquiries from persons with disabilities as to where they might live independently. The listing is arranged state by state.

There is a newspaper clipping from the North Peoria Observer on "Occupational Therapy, Helping Others Help Themselves" that should prove most informative.

FIGURE 8–1. Courtesy of the National Easter Seal Society, 2023 West Ogden Avenue, Chicago, Illinois 60612.

For further information, we have included a brand new bibliography that lists resources to encourage independent living by persons with disabilities. This publication (L-6) is available through the publications department of the National Easter Seal Society.

Finally, for your convenience, a check list of how to make full use of the Spring Quarterly Theme Packet, outlining accepted media placement procedures emphasizing local tie-ins.

Please use the order form below when ordering materials from this quarterly theme package.

ORDER FORM

19___ SPRING QUARTERLY THEME MATERIALS

Communications Department
National Easter Seal Society
2023 W. Ogden Avenue
Chicago, Illinois 60612

QUANTITY	ITEM	PRICE
_____	POSTER—"Occupational Therapy Is A Special Way of Caring" (Sold in lots of 25 only at $6.00 per lot)	_____
_____	BROCHURE—"Occupational Therapy Is A Special Way of Caring" (PR-39) $35.00 per M $20.00 per 500	_____
_____	BOOKLET—"About Occupational Therapy" 30¢ ea.	_____
_____	TV PSA featuring Leslie Charleson—one 30-second spot on 2" videotape (ES/FR/47). $20.00 ea.	_____
_____	Radio PSA featuring Leslie Charleson—$2.50 ea.	_____
_____	Set of three slides (not sold individually) at $6.00 a set.	_____
_____	Photo of Leslie Charleson with O.T. and clients (similar to photo featured on brochure and poster). 50¢ ea.	_____

SOCIETY _____

ADDRESS _____

CITY _____ STATE _____ ZIP _____

_____   _____
     (Signed)   (Date)

FIGURE 8–1 *(continued)*.

"INDEPENDENCE IS A SPECIAL WAY OF CARING"

LESLIE CHARLESON TO SPEAK FOR AMERICAN OCCUPATIONAL THERAPY ASSOCIATION—EASTER SEALS

Television star Leslie Charleson, who portrays surgeon Monica Quartermaine on the #1 rated daytime drama General Hospital, has agreed to serve as spokesperson for the American Occupational Therapy Association and the National Easter Seal Society in a joint public education project this spring.

Miss Charleson, whose character on television will bring added dimension to the quest for independent lives for all persons who are disabled, whether the disability be emotional or physical, is a recipient of a 1981–82 Emmy Award nomination for her character on General Hospital.

The popular young actress began her television career as a regular on another ABC daytime series, A Flame in the Wind (later changed to A Time for Us.) Miss Charleson has appeared on many television series including Adam 12, Barnaby Jones, Happy Days, Marcus Welby, The Rockford Files and Emergency to name just a few.

Established as a television actress, Miss Charleson co-starred with George C. Scott in the critically acclaimed movie, Day of the Dolphin, under the direction of Mike Nichols. She joined the cast of General Hospital in August of 1977, and remains one of the show's most popular characters.

Together, the Easter Seal Society and Occupational Therapists serve many persons each year through treatment centers in every state of the union. "It is truly an honor," Miss Charleson noted recently, "to be associated with two such fine organizations as the American Occupational Therapy Association and Easter Seals." Both organizations, Easter Seals now in its 64th year and AOTA in its 66th year, have helped hundreds of thousands of persons with disabilities lead purposeful, meaningful lives again, by helping them to help themselves.

Occupational Therapy is a health care service, based upon the use of purposeful activity as a means of preventing, alleviating, or overcoming a wide variety of physical, social, and emotional disabilities in people of all ages. Occupational Therapy is one of the many services provided by the Easter Seal Society through its 825 affiliates throughout the country.

"Health care today is based on the team concept," Miss Charleson continued. "The physician is assisted by a nurse, a physical therapist, and an occupational therapist. That same teamwork carries over to major health care non-profit organizations, such as Easter Seals and the American Occupational Therapy Association who have teamed up for this joint effort to make the public aware of the many advantages of Occupational Therapy, and of the many places where Occupational Therapy may be received.

"Independence is one of our most precious rights. Living independently with a disability is the goal of occupational therapists. In traditional and non-traditional settings, occupational therapists provide a vital link to the person with a disability in getting back to the mainstream of life."

Concludes Miss Charleson, "Independence is a very special way of caring. And two health care agencies who truly care are Easter Seals and the American Occupational Therapy Association. I'm pleased to be able to help them."

FIGURE 8–1 *(continued)*.

RADIO PUBLIC SERVICE ANNOUNCEMENT

FEATURING

LESLIE CHARLESON

THIRTY SECONDS

THIS IS LESLIE CHARLESON .... WHAT DO PERSONS WHO HAVE SUFFERED STROKES OR ACCIDENTS, OR CHILDREN WITH LEARNING DISABILITIES HAVE IN COMMON? .... ALL WILL BENEFIT FROM OCCUPATIONAL THERAPY. OCCUPATIONAL THERAPY IS A HEALTH AND REHABILITATION SERVICE BASED ON ACTIVITIES RELATING TO DAILY LIVING. OCCUPATIONAL THERAPISTS PROVIDE SERVICES TO INDIVIDUALS OF ALL AGES, HELPING THEM TO OVERCOME THEIR DISABILITIES .... FOR MORE INFORMATION, CONTACT THE AMERICAN OCCUPATIONAL THERAPY ASSOCIATION OR YOUR LOCAL EASTER SEAL SOCIETY.

PUBLIC SERVICE ANNOUNCEMENT

FEATURING

LESLIE CHARLESON

THIRTY SECONDS

VIDEO		AUDIO
Wide shot: Miss Charleson, OT, and client standing at kitchen stove; client in therapy.	V.O. LESLIE CHARLESON	THIS IS LESLIE CHARLESON ... IN ORDER TO PORTRAY A DOCTOR, I SPENT TIME IN HOSPITALS OBSERVING REAL DOCTORS WORKING WITH PERSONS WITH DISABILITIES ... AND THAT MADE ME AWARE OF THE COPING SKILLS THESE PEOPLE NEED TO LIVE INDEPENDENTLY.
Med shot: waist up of the three women.		
Cut to OT treatment ... pan into individual being treated as she cooks over the stove, being assisted by therapists.		HELPING DEVELOP THIS INDEPENDENCE ... LIKE OUR HOMEMAKER IN THE KITCHEN, IS THE WORK OF OCCUPATIONAL THERAPISTS AND THE EASTER SEAL SOCIETY.
CU of therapist and client, then to client alone as she cooks.		
Zoom to Leslie Charleson to upper left-hand corner of frame, drop in double logo AOTA/Easter Seal slide. Super: Contact the American Occupational Therapy Association of your local Easter Seal Society.		OCCUPATIONAL THERA- PISTS PROVIDE STEPS FOR MAINSTREAMING THE MILLIONS OF PERSONS WITH DISABILITIES .... INTO VITAL, PRODUCTIVE INDIVIDUALS, CAPABLE OF LIVING HEALTHY LIVES IN THEIR COMMUNITIES.

FIGURE 8–1 *(continued).*

TWENTY-FIVE SECONDS
(with 5 seconds for local tag)

VIDEO		AUDIO
SLIDE 1: General Hospital's Leslie Charleson in kitchen with OT and clients. SLIDE 2: Child in harness. SLIDE 3: Double logo: The Easter Seal Society and the American Occupational Therapy Association.	V.O. ANNCR:	RELEARNING HOUSEKEEPING SKILLS SUCH AS MEAL PREPARATION CAN BE THE KEY TO INDEPENDENT LIVING FOR PERSONS WITH A DISABILITY .... THANKS TO OCCUPATIONAL THERAPISTS, HUNDREDS OF THOUSANDS OF PEOPLE ARE HELPED BACK TO THE MAINSTREAM OF LIFE EVERY YEAR .... OCCUPATIONAL THERAPY IS A SPECIAL WAY OF CARING .... FOR MORE INFORMATION CONTACT (NAME OF LOCAL EASTER SEAL SOCIETY OR AMERICAN OCCUPATIONAL THERAPY ASSOCIATION).

FIGURE 8–1 *(continued).*

Leslie Charleson, far right, who plays Dr. Monica Quartermaine on "General Hospital", the number one rated daytime drama, observes occupational therapy coordinated by Carolyn Young, far left. Clients are James Gaddy and Penny Nichols. Miss Charleson is spokesperson for the Easter Seal Society and the American Occupational Therapy Association who have teamed up for a joint effort to make the public aware of the importance of occupational therapy in helping persons with disabilities lead independent lives.

NATIONAL EASTER SEAL SOCIETY • **2023 W. Ogden Avenue** • **Chicago, Illinois 60612**

SUGGESTED USES FOR THE SPRING QUARTERLY THEME PACKET

The Spring 19___ joint project between the National Easter Seal Society and the American Occupational Therapy Association is designed for maximum utilization at the local level. Each of the components—the three-slide presentation, the 30-second video PSA featuring Leslie Charleson, the 30-second radio spot also featuring Miss Charleson, together with the suggested general release and photos—should be taken to your local radio, television and newspaper markets for placement during the spring.

The packet should also be used as a guide when placing stories on your own local Easter Seal programs, volunteers, and fundraising activities.

The poster and brochure, prepared as companion pieces, are most useful in a variety of ways. Posters and brochures may be distributed to schools, hospitals, and civic organizations to heighten public awareness of what Occupational Therapy is and how it helps persons with disabilities to help themselves.

The poster and brochure make an attractive incentive for distribution to potential sponsors and volunteers, for fundraising purposes, as well as general information on AOTA and Easter Seal program services. They should be included in requests to the media for event coverage, as a general reference.

Investigate your various treatment centers for OTs who have distinguished themselves in one way or another and go to your local print and electronic media with a press release on the accomplishments of the OTs, and how they relate to your local society.

Keep an active photo file of noteworthy OTs or clients who have recuperated via treatment and would make good human interest subject matter for your television and newspaper features department.

When sending the quarterly theme packet to your local radio, television or newspaper, write a cover letter that will include details of OTs and clients that may be of local interest to that particular market.

For fundraising activities, send all or part of the packet to prospective participants as a public educational tool, together with a localized press release and perhaps case studies of local OTs and clients.

Send packets to newspaper assignment desks, health editors, feature editors; as well as radio assignment editors, feature editors, television assignment editors, health editors, and feature editors.

FIGURE 8–1 *(continued).*

PLANNING THE SPECIAL EVENT

Ask questions before, during, and after the event. After the purpose of the event has been found to be sound, build your questions about the event on these points:

- How much funding must be allocated? Determine a budget.
- How many resources must be allocated? Determine the staff involvement in both time and ancilliary resources such as printing, advertising, volunteers.
- Who will be responsible for the event? If a volunteer committee is established to handle the event, are staff and service users and trustees involved also? If not, there could very likely be problems during or after the event.
- Where will the event be held? Are there alternative sites? Can the event be handled more inexpensively at an alternative site?
- If the site selected is a hotel, is it a union hotel? If it isn't a union hotel, will this cause a problem for people whom you are inviting, including any stars? Lena Horne refused to attend a fundraising luncheon because it was being held in a nonunion hotel. At the last moment, the organizers had to change hotels. The resulting confusion could have been avoided by careful preparation.
- If your event includes food, is the kitchen kosher? Are there alternative selections available for vegetarians? Have you kept the menu simple and light to take into account today's concern with weight and overeating. Chicken, that versatile bird, is the ideal choice for large meals as most people will not object to it.
- Will handicapped people, women, minorities feel comfortable at the event? Is the site equipped to handle people in wheelchairs or people who have difficulty walking? Is there available parking easily accessible for elderly people and others who must use personal cars? Is there a parking fee or is this fee included in the price of the site? Is public transportation readily available to the site?
- If the site is costly to rent, what about using another nonprofit's facilities? There are dozens of private and public nonprofit sites available in major cities. Small towns frequently offer at least one or two. Don't restrict your search to museums, universities, and historic houses. Inquire about using city halls, public libraries, public transportation facilities such as bus garages. A site is only restricted by the demands of availability and funding, audience considerations and the nature of the event, i.e., a bus garage would probably not be an appropriate site for a seminar unless perhaps the subject were transportation. Relating the site to the topic is a means of stressing the importance of the topic: education at a community college or university; health at a hospital or mental health center.
- What events in the community will compete with your event? By all means you should avoid whenever possible competing with a similar organization on the same date. You should usually avoid holidays and three-day weekends. Maintain a calendar at least a year in advance, marking down those events scheduled by other community nonprofits and fitting your event into a logical time, with ample lead time for preparation and promotion.

- Determine how much to charge for the event. You've determined your budget and you need to clear your costs and preferably more. If it is a fundraising event, realistically project exactly what you plan to make from the event based on the price of the tickets and the number of attendees the event will attract. Always plan, at a minimum, to cover actual costs through ticket sales.

- Where are the logical sources of donations? How does the donation help the donor? If an event is planned that includes clothing, a fashion show, a raffle, invite local merchants to participate in the event. One sure way is to involve the local merchants in the planning of the event to insure that their own needs are met. If donors are being asked to sponsor an event, what advantages does the nonprofit offer in return? Donations are a two-way street, and both parties must gain if the relationship is to be successful and sustained.

- Who can attract the most attention and attendance? Careful selection of the headliner at an event is crucial to its success. Is a political leader, an actor, a singer, a well-known personality, an author, a leader in the community the best choice to headline an event? Determining the featured personality depends on factors including the nature of the event, the personality's relationship with the nonprofit or the nonprofit's interest, whether the event's purpose is information or entertainment, and how the personality relates to the nonprofit's audiences. Nonprofit theaters benefit from using theatrical personalities, while some nonprofits may be publically embarrassed by inviting inappropriate theater personalities. The keys in this area are appropriateness, the nature of the event, the sensitivities of the nonprofit's users, volunteers and patrons.

- Can the nonprofit handle controversy? Politically controversial figures can be a cause of conflict within the organization. If prepared for conflict, the nonprofit may benefit from controversial speakers. Universities traditionally have invited this conflict by seeking controversial political figures as speakers and as recipients of honorary degrees. The university maintains that this is the tradition of upholding free speech, and the results of such an invitation frequently provide wide public attention to the university. Cause-oriented nonprofits can also benefit from controversy as it is a means of attracting broader public attention. For some nonprofits, however, controversy is rigorously avoided and the nonprofit consistently maintains a low profile. This attitude, too, can pose difficulty in that the public may assume that the nonprofit is accomplishing little of value. Both high and low profiles can be of use to nonprofits, but both must be prepared for and planned carefully to work to the advantage of the nonprofit.

- Who will handle the myriad of details associated with a special event? Is one staff person assigned to work with volunteers to insure that all details are covered in advance? Nothing is more damaging, or less professional, than a nonprofit flubbing details; one or two may be forgiven by the nonprofit's audiences, but beyond that, beware. Prepare your lists—lists of things to do; lists of emergencies; lists of everything associated with the event.

CHECKLIST FOR AN EVENT

Budget.   Are costs being met by ticket sales alone?

Resources.   Are staff, volunteers, service users available and capable of handling the event?

Selection of site.   Affordability, appropriateness, accessibility to elderly and disabled attendees; alternatives.

Selection of program.   Attractiveness. Appropriateness. Controversial. Factual. Contribution to information or an entertainment.

Selection of time.   Conflicts with other community events. Competition with other nonprofits, holidays, vacation time, long weekends.

Selection of headliner/ speaker.   Appropriateness. Attractiveness to nonprofit's community, including users, volunteers, trustees, staff.

Donors.   What's in it for the donor? What does the nonprofit offer in return for a donation? Is the donation appropriate?

Criticism.   Is the nonprofit prepared for controversy and criticism?

Details.   Logistics:
- Room size.
- Availability of transportation.
- Advance adequate notice to media and to invitees.
- Set-up of room. Head table. Name cards for table and name tags for attendees.
- Appropriate handouts to invitees of literature or souvenirs, depending on the occasion.
- Equipment. Is it all functioning properly—lighting, sound systems, film projectors, videotape equipment, air conditioning, heat, microphones?
- Ambience. Is the setting appropriate, functional, clean, attractive? Are there flowers, candles, carafes of water for speakers, coffee for morning participants; tea and soft drinks for afternoon conferences? Is the food well prepared? Is the service pleasant?
- Style. Is the special event lending credence to the style of the nonprofit? Do invitees feel welcome, special, needed? Are service recipients, volunteers and staff playing an active role as both participants and hosts? Have staff been briefed and encouraged to mingle and meet, to greet and gratify? Are donors being recognized and hard workers being honored? Are awards being given to the right people?

CHOOSING AN APPROPRIATE EVENT

Match the event to the goal of the nonprofit. Arts' nonprofits attract affluent supporters and patrons. Arts' nonprofits have access to personalities and celebrities of interest to affluent audiences. These same personalities may be offensive to the supporters of human service delivery agencies. Social events may also be offensive to certain nonprofit audiences, and events such as seminars, workshops, and conferences would be far more attractive and effective.

Film and television personalities may be a draw for some groups and a disaster for others. Remember that when a "star" donates time to a special fundraising event, the sponsoring organization is usually responsible for the star's travel and expenses. These can be monumental as some stars travel with a retinue, and the expenses of the entire group must be covered by the sponsoring nonprofit. The star must be a major drawing card whose presence will sell (in advance) sufficient tickets to cover all expenses. To avoid surprise, have everything that you expect from the star, and everything that the star expects from you, in writing and signed by all concerned parties. Everything, including all union and broadcasting clearances, must be in writing. Without specific written agreements, signed by all concerned parties, the star's presence may prove to be a financial and possibly a legal embarrassment to the organization.

Personalities as fundraisers accomplish the objective of attracting attention to the nonprofit's cause. Support is another matter. While the general public may be avidly interested in your star, the specific audiences of the nonprofit may be insulted. Careful planning and questioning must be done before an invitation is issued. A personality that works well for one group may not work at all for another.

An educated public is donating its time and money to those nonprofits which it believes to be valuable community resources. Special events have the best chance to succeed if the nonprofit is fully aware of its particular audiences and is sensitive to their objectives when planning an event. The days of ignoring the service recipient, the nonprofit's consumer, are rapidly coming to an end. Today's consumers, whether a student deciding on a school or a doctor determining a hospital for a patient or a parent choosing a youth group for a handicapped child, are the determining factors in the success of a special event.

NOW . . . CHOOSE FROM A TO Z

- A. Auctions, antique shows, advertising, awards, alumni.
- B. Breakfasts, boat trips, brunches, buffets, bus excursions, building site ceremonies, basketball tournaments, bowling parties, block parties, bike races, ballet matinees, bake sales, bird watching.
- C. Cooking demonstrations, circuses, counseling, conferences, camping trips, candy sales, craft fairs, cookie sales, cat shows, caroling parties, Christmas parties, corporate ceremonies.
- D. Dances, designer shows, dog shows, decorator show houses, demonstrations, dinners.
- E. Exercise classes, energy fairs, estate sales, educational aids, exhibits.

F. Fund drives, fun fairs, follies, fashion shows, feature film premieres, folklore festivals, flower shows, founder's day, foreign tours.

G. Games, gambling for fun and funds, garden tours, garden shows, garden parties, golf tournaments, galas, graduations.

H. House tours, honors, holiday parties, horse races, health fairs, Hannukah parties, hikes, hay rides, holiday fairs.

I. Investment seminars, investitures, Independence Day parties, international seminars.

J. Job fairs, jousting exhibits, jumping events, jazz festivals, jazzercise parties.

K. Kitchen sales, kindergarten days, kite flying, kilt parties, klieg light events.

L. Lawn parties, legislative events, legislators' receptions, legal seminars, legal assistance and counseling, luncheons.

M. Marathons, marches, mixers, mime exhibitions, meetings.

N. Neighborhood involvement, nautical events, national celebrations, neon art exhibits, new ideas.

O. Outings, open houses.

P. Parades, processions, plays, polo exhibitions, pet competitions.

Q. Quilt shows, quiche parties, quadrilles, quality events.

R. Raffles, rugby tournaments, receptions, radio-thons.

S. Symphonies, street fairs, sales of anything and everything, skating parties, special Olympics events.

T. Telethons, tea parties, tea dances, tennis matches.

U. United States celebrations, United Nations parties, ukulele parties.

V. Vaccination counseling, vanilla ice cream socials, Valentine's Day parties, vegetable sales, violin concerts.

W. Walks, walk-a-thons, ward parties, weaving sales, save-the-whale events, wild animal protection parties, work-outs, world events forums.

X. X-ray clinics, xylophone recitals.

Y. Youth fairs, yard sales, your own ideas for events.

Z. Zoo parties.

CHAPTER 9

How to "Position" Your Nonprofit Organization

Finding your place in the sun depends on the needs, interests, and attention span of the nonprofit's community. These can change quickly, and the astute nonprofit must make rapid decisions to stay abreast.

Shifts in position are frequently not as dramatic as that which occurred when the polio vaccine first appeared in the 1950s. The cure for polio, long sought, threatened the existence of the nonprofit which had mobilized the effort to seek this cure. The March of Dimes had a national organization, a professional staff, a network of committed volunteers, and deep community interest. With the vaccine, it appeared that the March of Dimes had met its goal and would slip silently away. The March of Dimes, however, did not disappear. It evaluated the needs of its community and determined to continue with a new, unmet goal: that of either preventing or dealing effectively with birth defects. The organization positioned itself, and 20 years later it remains one of the nation's leading non-profit organizations. In determining its position, it selected a goal that was related to its original goal, thereby maintaining staff and volunteer expertise and commitment. It also selected a broad, long-range problem that would help to insure the organization's future viability.

The March of Dimes is an outstanding example of positioning. It demonstrated its ability to meet change. In positioning itself, the organization retained its commitment to the future and to the health of its community. It reached for a new goal that was consistent with its capabilities and expertise. It identified a need that was unfilled and to which it as an organization could offer national leadership. It retained its strengths and avoided identifying a goal that would result in weakening the organization. It read its positioning indicators and responded with intelligence and direction.

KNOWING YOUR CONSTITUENCY

An organization's constituency may be the members of trade or professional or labor union associations; the doctors who select hospitals for the patients; the students and parents who choose schools and universities; the volunteers who provide the strength of community service organizations; the recipients of human service delivery agencies and their families; the donors to museums and arts groups; the subscription holders of theater and dance companies. Each nonprofit has a specific constituency to which it is answerable and for which it is responsible.

Most nonprofits have several constituencies of varying degrees of importance. All of these constituencies have particular needs and desires. These fluctuate, and the successful nonprofit stays current by questioning, by involving, and by satisfying at least some of the identified needs and desires.

Questioning.

It is preferable that the nonprofit do its own questioning of key constituencies first, since otherwise it is likely to find itself in a position that many universities were in after a 1983 study commissioned by the National Academy of Sciences which rated graduate programs in biochemistry, economics, geosciences, history, microbiology, political science, psychology, and statistics. This study was based on reputation ratings by more than 5,000 professors from 228 schools.

George Washington University's faculty was displeased with the results of the survey, which found several of the school's graduate programs at or below average. One faculty member felt that the study was "misleading" as most of the school's graduates went into private business or the government and so would not have had the opportunity to rate various graduate programs. "Part of the population was missing."[1]

While this is a cogent argument, who is responsible for seeking the opinions of the university's graduates who are in business and government? It is an example of the importance of questioning your own constituency before someone else beats you to it in a way that may not be a complete and accurate assessment. George Washington University could have, and should have, surveyed its own doctoral graduates for their assessment of their education. This should be done on a continual basis, not only for the value of the answers, but also to maintain constituent involvement in the nonprofit.

Questioning can be handled in many ways. The approach depends partially on the constituency being addressed and partially on the nonprofit's capabilities.

Face-to-face questioning. Useful with staff, trustee, volunteer and user/recipient. Inexpensive and ongoing through meetings, telephone conversations, informal avenues. There are weaknesses in face-to-face questioning such as group and peer pressure, biases, personal ambitions, vendettas, but the offsetting strong point is that management should not be caught completely unaware.

---

[1]"Faculty Disagree with Survey Ratings," Christopher Murray, the *GW Hatchet*, George Washington University, March 24, 1983.

Telephone questioning. A growing and sophisticated source of information from key constituents. With WATTS lines and the latest in low-cost long distance telephone networks, telephoning can be inexpensive and reliable in keeping abreast with constituencies.

Being informed on social and economic trends. Social and economic trends can be followed and analyzed more easily today than ever before. Good sources of these key indicators are the national newspapers, the *Wall Street Journal* and *USA Today*.

Significant examples of some trends as they relate to the nonprofit include:

Working women. How does this affect the nonprofit's volunteer programs as women have always been the traditional strength?

Baby boom. What does this mean for nonprofits involved in the health, education, and other aspects of a child's life?

Single parents. Are their needs being met by nonprofits in the community? What opportunities does this group represent?

Long-term unemployment. Are training and educational needs being adequately and imaginatively met for this new market?

Student demands. These demands are usually job-related and job-oriented. Are there opportunities for new initiatives and programs drawing from existing, underutilized resources?

An aging population. Does the nonprofit effectively reach this constituency, and what program potential does this group offer?

Tracking major social and economic trends and applying the lessons of these trends to the nonprofit can result in a sensible and cost-effective way of keeping the nonprofit current to its present and potential constituencies.

Written questioning. Perhaps the most quantifiable and least subjective of all questioning techniques. Written questioning can be designed to give the organization a tight and precise view of what constituents think about the services, programs, and directions.

Written questioning is also a low-cost means of broadening and identifying new constituencies. Mass mailings of questionnaires can produce new sources of strength for an organization. An example of a brilliant use of a questionnaire in a mass mailing is a 1983 letter and questionnaire sent out by the League of Women Voters. Entitled "National Elections Project: Issues Not Images," the letter accompanying the questionnaire flattered the recipient by leading off with the following salutation:

> You have been chosen, as part of a select sampling of the American voting-age population, to take part in a national study of American elections. Your participation is strictly voluntary. But your help is needed.
>
> Your response will help form the basis for a project of major national significance designed to improve the working of our electoral process. Details below.[2]

---

[2]"League of Women Voters National Elections Project: Issues Not Images," sampling, spring 1983. The League of Women Voters, 1730 M Street NW, Washington, DC 20036.

The letter is stamped in bold red, PLEASE RETURN ENCLOSED SURVEY FORM WITHIN 12 DAYS.

This approach merits particular attention. It appeals to the intelligence of the recipient as well as to the recipient's concern for the country's future. The letter accompanying the questionnaire asks that the recipient become a "Friend of the League" and make an appropriate donation.

The approach also merits attention to the skillful way it introduces two-way communication. Questioning can be a means of involving constituencies, even new potential constituencies, in assisting the nonprofit. It can strengthen an organization's ties with its community while identifying new directions. (See Figure 9–1.)

League of Women Voters
National Elections Project: *Issues Not Images*

You have been chosen, as part of a select sampling of the American voting-age population, to take part in a national study of American elections. Your participation is strictly voluntary. But your help is needed.

Your response will help form the basis for a project of major national significance designed to improve the workings of our electoral process. Details below:

Dear Friend,

"Why bother?"

That's what millions of Americans said during the 1980 presidential elections. Barely more than half of the voting-age population cast ballots. That means only 27.4% of those eligible to vote elected our current president. And in 1982, 60% of those eligible failed to vote.

Campaigns are dominated by slick 60-second TV ads, canned speeches, and staged media events offering little serious discussion of issues and even less opportunity for genuine communication between voter and candidate.

After the election, a new administration may confront the familiar problem of trying to build consensus for new programs and policies with an electorate that considers itself unrepresented and ignored. The result, of course: resentment and alienation among many voters, and a demand for a change of leadership.

So the vicious cycle continues. And who are the real victims? You and I. Those of us who try hard to stay informed, learn about issues, and choose wisely come election day.

We at the League of Women Voters are troubled by what may happen to our nation should this dangerous trend continue, and we need your help with an exciting new venture to treat this critical problem at its source.

FIGURE 9–1.   Courtesy of the League of Women Voters of the United States, 1730 M Street N.W., Washington, D.C. 20036.

We have formulated a full three-year plan that will institutionalize debates among candidates and greatly improve the quality and depth of communications between candidates and voters. Our goal is to offer alternatives to the media packaging that now dominates campaigns.

We call this plan the National Elections Project.

You may recall that in 1976, and again in 1980, the League of Women Voters sponsored an historic series of debates between major candidates for the presidency—the first such debates since 1960. Perhaps these national forums helped you make your decision about how to vote.

I hope so. Because we at the League take you—the voter—very seriously.

In fact, to guarantee the success of our National Elections Project, we've decided to ask you which problems and issues that arise during national elections are most important to you.

Because I believe you share our special interest in improving the process by which you and I select our national leadership, I hope you'll take a few moments to answer the questions on the enclosed National Elections Project Survey.

We at the League of Women Voters truly care about your opinion. I sincerely hope you'll help us out.

Let me explain why your participation in this survey is so important to the future of our democratic system.

The League has many long years—more than 60 years—of experience studying, participating in, and monitoring the American electoral process.

So we know that two or three debates in a nine-month presidential campaign just aren't enough to help you and me effectively evaluate candidates and their stands on issues.

We also know that presidential contests are not the only important political contests that take place. Congressional and state elections are just as critical in affecting national policy. Moreover, every election, despite the many issues involved, is a contest between the major parties to determine which philosophy of leadership can best govern our nation during the coming years.

The issues are complicated, and the need for better communication between candidates and voters is urgent.

The League's National Elections Project is offering a series of quality political events starting now and leading up to the presidential contest of 1984. These events will be a variety of open, public forums—many on national television and radio—providing opportunity for serious discussion among candidates, party leaders, and the American voter. The result?

—No longer will candidates be seen only in slick 60-second TV ads designed to disguise, not reveal, their positions on important issues.

—No longer will the process by which political parties choose candidates be so ill-understood by the average American voter.

—No longer will you and I have to choose between candidates while wishing we knew more about the candidates' real positions.

—No longer will more than half of the voting-age population ignore national elections because they feel candidates don't represent their views.

FIGURE 9–1 *(continued).*

Already, during the 1982 elections, we succeeded in sponsoring a series of nationally televised Congressional Leadership Debates. For the first time, millions of voters heard key congressional leaders from both the Democratic and Republican parties articulate their party's views on major national issues—national security/defense spending and the economy.

These debates were unique in American history. Never before have national debates been held in a mid-term election year. Never before have opposition leaders in Congress faced off in such a public forum.

And this is but one example of the League's critical role as national arbiter of public debate. Before the crucial 1984 elections, we plan to sponsor a series of television programs on major campaign issues such as the effects of negative advertising, the politics of nominations, and how primaries and state caucuses function.

These important national media events will be held in addition to hundreds of state and local league-sponsored candidate events and a series of nationally televised presidential primary forums and presidential debates.

But we simply cannot afford to set our latest ideas into motion until we know whether or not you're as excited about this project as we are. I hope I can count on your support.

The first thing you can do to support the National Elections Project is to give us your answers to the important questions on the enclosed survey form.

Second, I'm asking you to please consider making a contribution to the League to help make this exciting project succeed. Unless thousands of individual, concerned Americans like you give your support, we simply cannot move forward. Let me tell you why.

Our success with the 1976 and 1980 presidential debates proved that the League has the respect of both political parties, the credibility, the political know-how, and the experience to meet the important goals of the National Elections Project.

But you probably thought the presidential debates were paid for by the TV networks or by the politicians. Not so.

Those exciting national events were financed in large part through the generosity of thousands of individual Americans. People like you.

There is simply no other way to do it. The cost of planning, producing, and publicizing such events is enormous—hundreds of thousands of dollars.

I hope you'll consider giving your support to the National Elections Project and help sponsor some of the most important political events ever held in our nation's history.

Please take a moment to answer the questions on the enclosed survey and return it to us here at the League today.

Along with your survey, I hope you'll become a Friend of the League by enclosing a check (all contributions are tax deductible) to help get the National Elections Project underway.

FIGURE 9–1 *(continued).*

There's much to be done if we are to succeed in improving the electoral process for all Americans. Please act now.

Sincerely,

Dorothy S. Ridings

Dorothy S. Ridings
President

P.S. If you receive a duplicate of this mailing, please forgive us. It's more expensive for us to remove duplicate names from our mailing lists than it is to send out extras.

National Elections Project Survey

Issued by:
League of Women Voters
1730 M Street, N.W.   Washington, D.C. 20036

Instructions:

You may record your answers by putting a check mark in the appropriate box. Please be assured they will be held strictly confidential by the LWVEF National Elections Project. Please complete the entire survey form and return within 12 days to LWVEF/National Elections Project, 1730 M Street, N.W., Washington, D.C. 20036.

Part I:

The National Elections Project should educate voters about the following topics:

Please choose three.

☐ Campaign advertising
☐ Political news coverage
☐ Presidential nominating process
☐ How political parties operate
☐ Campaign financing
☐ Voter registration laws
☐ Significance of congressional elections
☐ Key issues in congressional and presidential elections

FIGURE 9–1 *(continued).*

Part II:

Before the League of Women Voters proceeds with our plans for the National Elections Project, we'd like your opinion on the following important issues:

1. Should television news devote more attention to reporting on political campaigns, or are you satified with the extent of election coverage now?

   ☐ More attention   ☐ Satisfied   ☐ Undecided

2. Many candidates argue that paid television advertising is the only way they can directly present themselves and their issues to the electorate, without the "interpretation" that can accompany news coverage.

   a. Do you believe that television news coverage of candidates is generally objective, or slanted to reflect reporters' or stations' views?

      ☐ Objective   ☐ Slanted   ☐ Undecided

   b. Do you think that television advertising is an effective way for candidates to present themselves and their issues?

      ☐ Yes   ☐ No   ☐ Not what I've seen so far

   c. Do you believe that negative advertising placed by an independent group (not by a candidate's opponent or the opponent's party) should be regulated in some way?

      ☐ Yes   ☐ No   ☐ Undecided

3. Did you watch either the debate between Jimmy Carter and Ronald Reagan or the one between Ronald Reagan and John Anderson sponsored by the League in 1980?

   ☐ Yes   ☐ No

   If yes, how important were the debates to your understanding of the candidates' views?

   ☐ Very Important   ☐ Somewhat Important   ☐ Not Important

   In 1980, the League invited not only major party candidates, but other "significant candidates"—as determined by their standing in public opinion polls—to participate in the debates. Do you agree with this approach?

   ☐ Yes   ☐ No   ☐ Undecided

4. Thinking of campaigns you've followed in the past, would you like to see more of the following kinds of information about a political candidate seeking your support?:

   Issue Positions   ☐ More   ☐ Satisfied

   Personal
      background (values,
      aspirations, accom-
      plishments)   ☐ More   ☐ Satisfied

   Likely advisors   ☐ More   ☐ Satisfied

   Source of
      campaigns
      contributions   ☐ More   ☐ Satisfied

FIGURE 9–1 *(continued).*

Part III:

Important: Please complete entire survey form and return within 12 days.

☐ I've completed my survey and am returning it for tabulation.

☐ I want to do more. Enclosed is my tax-deductible contribution to help launch the National Elections Project. My check is for:

    ☐ $100 ☐ $75 ☐ $50 ☐ $35 ☐ $25 ☐ $20 ☐ Other $_____

Please make your check payable to the League of Women Voters Education Fund and return along with your completed survey form to: LWVEF/National Elections Project, 1730 M Street, N.W., Washington, D.C. 20036.

A copy of the last financial report filed with the New York Department of State may be obtained by writing to: New York State Department of State, Office of Charities Registration, Albany, New York 12231, or to LWVUS.

Contributions to national programs of the League of Women Voters are separate from membership dues.

FIGURE 9–1 *(continued).*

KEEPING THE TOP IN TOUCH

The pressures of leading a large nonprofit organization are many. Time is scarce. Nothing, however, beats knowledge at the top . . . the knowledge that top management can acquire through continual contact with constituents. Successful nonprofit managers make the time to eat in the school cafeteria, visit patients in wards, teach classes, attend social functions hosted by constituents, meet alumni, be accessible to service recipients and users. Management analysts attribute the practice of providing the same cafeteria for all employees (including top management) as a factor in the cohesiveness and purposefulness of the Japanese corporation. In our hierarchical system of management, top management frequently eats with each other in sequestered dining rooms. This holds true for the nonprofit also, and the nonprofit manager who eats with staff, who attends the hospital's community classes, who leads tours of the facility for parents or tour groups will have a better grasp of what these key constituent groups think and feel about the organization. It is this kind of highly personal questioning that keeps the top in touch.

LEARNING FROM THE COMPETITION

The nonprofit can learn from competing for-profit providers in the same area of interest. Study and analyze the approaches that for-profit hospitals, schools, colleges, nursing homes, and rehabilitation centers are taking to attract community support. For-profit hospitals can be found to be offering free office space to doctors, selling certain services including financial and public relations to smaller hospitals, using sophisticated advertising. For-profit schools and universities will be found to be offering classes in specific job-related areas instructed by faculty drawn from business and industry. For-profit rehabilitation programs will be found using sophisticated video-tape training in job-seeking skills such as employment interviews. For-profit nursing homes may have menus rivaling those of fine restaurants—complete with candlelight, wine, and other amenities.

Each nonprofit should research and maintain a file on what the competing for-profits are doing to enhance their business. Studying the allocations of for-profit resources, even though these resources may far exceed those available to the nonprofit, indicates areas of priority and concern that should be evaluated by the nonprofit. The same study can discover an area that is being downgraded because it is not attracting community support, while another is being upgraded in response to community interest evidenced in media reports and surveys. Competition can be healthy if its lessons are known, understood, and used to the advantage of the nonprofit.

The nonprofit should be equally abreast of developments of all major competitors in its field of interest. In addition to the for-profits, there are other nonprofits, both private and public (government). What are these organizations doing that can be evaluated and used either to improve existing services and introduce new services, or eliminate duplication?

Competition is healthy for the nonprofit that is aware, informed, and open to ideas and change. Thinking and acting competitively can help the nonprofit accomplish its goals more efficiently and effectively.

POSITIONING YOUR ALLIES

Every nonprofit has its allies in the community. These allies are a valuable resource in positioning the nonprofit as a community leader. Allies are there to be developed, and the effective nonprofit will respond to its allies for mutual benefit. Allies want something in return for their assistance and cooperation. Their wants may be as simple to satisfy as invitations to nonprofit events. The most frequent requirement of nonprofit allies seems to be the positive public relations that the nonprofit can generate for them. Allies are found in every social sector, including business, public and private nonprofits, individuals. Recognizing them and meeting their needs is important to the nonprofit's positioning.

Examples of related allies include:

MUSEUMS: Department stores, antique dealers, book shops, art students, art schools, artists, crafts people, public libraries and patrons, art galleries and patrons, historic houses and patrons, advertising agencies, corporate headquarters, business and professional associations, restaurants that display artworks, government.

HOSPITALS: Service organizations, self-help groups, charitable organizations interested in health-related areas, doctors, nursing schools and students, medical schools and students, book stores, public libraries and patrons, volunteer organizations, youth groups, recreation and exercise programs.

UNIVERSITIES: High schools and students, senior citizen centers, public libraries and patrons, government, book shops, department stores, shopping malls, job-training programs, employment offices, corporations, business and professional associations.

Allies can be identified through questioning and constituent referral. Don't limit your knowledge of allies to the staff and users of the organization but reach out through other constituents to seek suggestions and ideas on natural allies. The nonprofit can generate allies by participating in city-wide observations and celebrations that may not be directly related to the purpose of the nonprofit but that are useful in introducing new contact and allies. Allies, like constituents, want to be wanted, and two-way communications and benefits are essential. Seeking assistance also means seeking recommendations and absorbing them into the ongoing programs of the nonprofit.

COOPERATING FOR MUTUAL BENEFIT

University presidents delivering commencement speeches at private and public high schools are developing new allies among the graduating students and their parents as well as among the faculties of the high schools and nongraduating students and parents. The university president is emphasizing the important contribution of the university to the community while the high school is gaining recognition for its efforts in education.

The same cooperative spirit extends to hospital directors addressing organizations of senior citizens or at nonprofit health groups. Or to the director of a museum addressing a graduating class of nurses or a group of volunteers at a volunteer clearinghouse. These are examples of mutually beneficial appearances emphasizing the community of concern among the nonprofit leadership.

This same spirit should extend to exchanging articles between nonprofits for publication; speakers for television programs; guests for radio interviews; editorials in others' newsletters. Nonprofits are a distinct entity making unique contributions to their communities, and their own cooperation heightens the visibility and reinforces the value of their contributions.

Those nonprofits with buildings (universities, colleges, schools, hospitals, historic houses) should be encouraging other nonprofits to use their facilities for conferences, meetings, seminars, social and special events. The nonprofit facility should also be offered to allies for similar functions, related to the goal of the nonprofit.

The property-owning nonprofit has a valuable community asset in its physical space . . . valuable for the potential profitable operation it offers the nonprofit, which provides catering, technical equipment rental, etc. Valuable, too, for the community identification of the space when it is used by other nonprofits and allies. Physical space can be a source of funds as well as a benefit to the position of the nonprofit.

CONSORTIUMS: ALLYING WITH OTHERS
WITH SIMILAR INTERESTS AND NEEDS

Consortiums of universities, hospitals, human service delivery organizations can perform many tasks that the individual nonprofit could not perform successfully. In addition to training, cooperative purchasing, cooperative financial and legal assistance, consortiums offer marketing and public relations capabilities that may otherwise not be affordable. A group of human service delivery nonprofits can, through a consortium, produce public service campaigns emphasizing the need for human services in the community and the response that the community is making through its human service agencies. The United Way is one such consortium, and it can offer a nonprofit many advantages in addition to its well-known fundraising abilities.

SUSTAINING THE NONPROFIT'S POSITION

Continuity is crucial. Continuity of events, services, quality, effort on behalf of the community, and visibility affect the nonprofit's position in the community. After the identification of constituencies, natural allies, and other interested community supporters, the nonprofit maintains its relationship to these important groups through continuity. One way of providing continuity is through a calendar (Figures 9–2 and 9–3).

Visible continuity is maintained by regularly scheduled events as well as by institutional development in marketing and advertising. As an example, the importance of education to the job seeker can be underscored by university consortium public service advertising which emphasizes the value of education by highlighting specific individuals who have enriched their lives or job opportunities through education. Additionally, individual universities can augment this group public service advertising by paid advertising of their own specific offerings to target groups. Target groups in this case could include elderly people, industrial workers in need of retraining, women returning to the job market, men and women concerned with growth and job change, recent students needing additional skills for the changing job market.

Calendar

MONACO·MONTE·CARLO

DATED MATERIAL

The Detroit Institute of Arts ———————— October 1982

FIGURE 9–2. Courtesy of the Detroit Institute of Arts. Lithograph *Monaco—Monte-Carlo* by Alphonse Mucha, gift of Mr. and Mrs. Bernard F. Walker, the Detroit Institute of Arts, 5200 Woodward Avenue, Detroit, Michigan 48202.

An illustration of this kind of dual approach is the publicity that Harvard and Stanford have attracted to their programs for recycling doctoral graduates into careers in business. News stories and editorials take the message to the community, while specific direct mail marketing can be addressed to doctoral graduates who may be interested in the program to enhance their job potential.

THE ADVERTISING COUNCIL CAMPAIGNS

Founded in the early years of World War II by the advertising industry, the Advertising Council is the industry's pro-bono arm and produces national advertising campaigns for nonprofit and government organizations. The Advertising Council campaigns average two or more years in duration and receive millions of dollars in donated public service time and space from the media throughout the country. Among the campaigns that the Advertising Council produces each year are those on broad generic topics that have included elderly Americans, child abuse, nutrition and health, pollution, economics, religion, education. Specific campaigns contribute to the success of major national nonprofits such as the Red Cross and United Way. The Advertising Council has rigid and specific standards applying to all campaigns which it accepts and agrees to handle.

The criteria that the Advertising Council applies to its applicants are useful to nonprofits when considering any public service campaign.

THE ADVERTISING COUNCIL CRITERIA

1. That the project be non-commercial, non-denominational, non-partisan political, and not designed to influence legislation.
2. That the purpose of the project be such that the advertising methodology can help achieve its objectives.
3. That, if the organization is a fundraising one, the Advertising Council will take into consideration whether or not it currently meets the standards of public and private accreditation organizations such as the National Information Bureau.
4. That the project be national in scope, or sufficiently national so that it is relevant to media audiences in communities throughout the nation.
5. That the appeal for support shall be one properly made to Americans generally whether delivered by national or local media. The project will not be rejected because it is in the interest of one group if the action messages have wide appeal, national significance, and local applicability.
6. That the project be of sufficient seriousness and public importance to warrant donations of space or time by national and local media."[3]

Because many of the Advertising Council campaigns deal with broad concerns, they are, in fact, the institutional advertising for numerous nonprofit organizations. It is important that the nonprofit be abreast of the current campaigns of the Advertising Council so that it can tie in with these campaigns in its own advertising and marketing programs. It is an additional opportunity for visibility

---

[3]*Public Service Advertising BULLETIN*, the Advertising Council Inc., 825 Third Avenue, New York, NY 10002. September–October 1979.

and position in the nonprofit's community. For example, if an Advertising Council campaign is focusing on the problem of pollution, environmental nonprofits can urge local media to use the campaign while producing information about the nonprofit's efforts to curb pollution at the same time. These campaigns benefit those not in the position to have their own public service advertising campaigns as well as those with advertising budgets. It is another consortium concept that can be used to the nonprofit's advantage through tie-ins and association.

CHANGE AS AGENT PROVOCATEUR

Positioning is awareness of, and response to, change. But change can also be an agent provocateur leading to crisis, criticism, and confusion about the purpose and quality of an organization. St. Paul's Episcopal Church in Washington, D.C., found that responding to the well-publicized need to feed and nurture "street people" was not a manageable task. Beginning with a small, limited purpose of feeding the "street people" in the neighborhood immediately surrounding the church, this grew in a few short months to unmanageable proportions, with people from the entire city showing up for free meals. The church stopped its food program and went back to the drawing board to find another way to assist its neighborhood hungry and needy. The demand overwhelmed the resources.[4]

Was this caused by lack of planning and foresight, or was it caused by not assessing what was already available in the community and what useful role a group with limited resources could play? Or was it that the church had chosen to play a role for which it and its members were not equipped? The church's membership supported the feeding program and also stood behind the decision to end the program. If anything, the church strengthened its ties with its own members while evincing support for community problems.

Responding to publicized needs and demands for change requires an evaluation of what an organization can provide. Art museums with lavish endowments are criticized by their communities for not using these endowments to help meet the needs of unemployed people. Universities are criticized for not admitting students who are culturally deprived and who do not meet the university's standards. Hospitals are criticized for refusing admission to indigents.

These are demands for change, and many of these demands originate from the nonprofit's constituencies. Hiding from these demands by pleading ignorance will damage the authority and leadership of the nonprofit. Capitulating to the demands may bring about ruin. Each nonprofit has the responsibility for acknowledging demands for change, regardless of the impertinence or impossibility of the demands, and for addressing these demands with factual, nonemotional presentations and affirmation of what the nonprofit is and what it can and cannot do. Uninformed resistance to change will damage the position of the nonprofit more surely, possibly, than misadventures in trying to meet demands without available resources and knowledge.

Change is important to the continuity and future of the nonprofit. The ability to adapt to change and demands is indicative of the nonprofit's position in the community and illustrative of its leadership and responsiveness.

4"The Wages of Charity," Beverly A. Reece, the *Washington Post*, September 19, 1982.

POSITIONING: DYNAMIC NONPROFIT EXAMPLES

Adopt and adapt the lessons learned from the following case studies. How do they relate to the needs of your nonprofit; how can you learn from them? What examples can you find in your own city or town that you can adopt and adapt? Build a file of case studies for reference, for reinforcement of your own ideas, for concepts.

Brown University: Prospering by Responding to Consumers.

Brown University in Providence, Rhode Island, received the most applications of any school in the Ivy League for its fall 1983 class. Brown received 13,250 for a class of 1,375, up 13 percent over last year. Brown is one of the most popular schools on the East Coast and has shed its image as a haven for students who could not get into more prestigious institutions.

Howard R. Swearer, president of Brown, cites the university's unusual open curriculum, its relaxed atmosphere, and the pride in the school as three of the factors relating to today's popularity, a popularity which comes at a time when many schools are faced with severe drops in applications from a much smaller pool of high school graduates. Brown's flexible curriculum dates from 1969 when it was instituted in response to student activism. Brown has retained this flexible curriculum, unlike many other schools, and students are encouraged to create their own liberal arts education. Students are also encouraged to take courses they might otherwise be afraid of as fewer courses are required for graduation. This gives students the freedom to experiment and fail. Brown's students and faculty praise the school for diversity and freedom and friendliness. Students and faculty regularly meet informally at coffee parties and other occasions.

Brown officials also point out that of 1982 graduates, more than 90 percent of those who applied to law or medical schools were accepted, along with all of those who applied to business schools.[5]

Cooperating to Achieve a Mutual Need.

Four small Washington, D.C., nonprofit organizations specializing in low-income housing formed a new nonprofit "Manna." Manna combines the organizations' resources in locating, rehabilitating, and selling homes to low-income families. The rehabilitation of the housing is done by community-based workers, Manna's own construction experts, and the labor of prospective occupants, if feasible. The developer who directs the rehabilitation of the houses receives a small profit, as does Manna, which uses its profit to purchase additional properties. Equity-sharing is sometimes offered to low-income purchasers. Equity-sharing is an investor providing most of the downpayment and closing costs and realizing the tax advantages. At the end of a fixed period of time, the low-income family can buy out the investor at a price fixed at the time of the original sale. The creation of Manna by the four small nonprofits offered the opportunity to undertake projects that none of the four may have been able to undertake on its own.[6]

---

[5]"Brown Outpacing Rivals in Ivy League Popularity," Fox Butterfield, the *New York Times*, March 20, 1983.

[6]"Nonprofit Group Helps Create New Homeowners," Ann Mariano, the *Washington Post*, January 1, 1983.

Cooperating for Profit.

The Hospital Council of the National Capitol Area is a nonprofit organization with a membership drawn from all health care facilities in the Capitol area: hospitals, HMOs, nursing homes, hospices, clinics.

The Hospital Council estimates that it saved its 74-member organizations $2 million through its group purchase plan in 1981 alone. The Council also offers a newsletter, seminars, training workshops, and related services to its members.[7]

Innovating to Retain Position.

The University of Pennsylvania's Wharton School of Finance and Economics is generally considered to be among the top three business schools in the United States. Wharton is now aiming to be "Number One" in the world by establishing ties with 20 universities throughout the world and by forming a new institute for international management studies. Students in the institute will receive training in business as well as in the languages and cultures of selected regions of the world. Wharton is responding to the internationalization of American corporations. Wharton is also diversifying beyond the traditional management disciplines into areas of interest to nonprofit managers, including health care, public policy, the arts, and transportation.[8]

Attracting Students by Responding to Major Social Issues.

Taylor University in Upland, Indiana, attracted 24 students for the 1983 spring semester by introducing tuition waivers for the unemployed. It waived tuition for some students whose parents were out of work and for some jobless students. The imaginative responsiveness to high unemployment attracted the attention of, among others, the *Wall Street Journal*.[9]

Attracting Friends with a Purpose.

The nonprofit Alexandria (Virginia) Hospital has a friends group that celebrated its fiftieth anniversary in 1983. The group, called "The Twig," has 128 members who raise money for the hospital, provide volunteer support, and are active in the community on behalf of the hospital and its needs. Some friends go on to the hospital's board of trustees. The group has raised hundreds of thousands of dollars for the hospital, and its fundraising activities are important community social events.[10]

---

[7]Unpublished student study.

[8]"Wharton's Quest to Be Best: School Has a New Dean, a New Home, a New Goal," David A. Vise, the *Washington Post*, March 27, 1983.

[9]"Unemployment May Help Some Get Admitted to Taylor University," Carolyn Phillips, the *Wall Street Journal*, January 24, 1983.

[10]Program, "The Twig 50th Anniversary Gala," March 5, 1983.

FIGURE 9–3.　Copyright 1983. Alexandria Hospital, Health Promotion
　　　　　　Department, 4320 Seminary Road, Alexandria, Virginia 22304.

You Can Choose a Better Lifestyle

Dr. John W. Farquhar, the preventive medicine expert at Stanford Medical School, tells of a 38-year-old salesman who had a profound influence on the physician's life. The man was assigned as a heart attack patient to Dr. Farquhar during his final year in medical school. Throughout a difficult recovery and until the patient's death four years later, the doctor discovered there was relatively little the health care system could do for this individual. The damage had been too extensive. He could only share the man's anquish for lost health that had been taken so long for granted. He could only grieve with the family over the disability and eventual loss of a loved one. And, he came to realize that a heart attack or stroke is not "a nice, clean way to go!"

This story illustrates that while most of us live as though our day-to-day habits don't matter, our behavior patterns can have dramatic results. Although the product of our behavior may not be seen today, our actions combine like bricks laid one upon another. If our habits are healthy ones, they can act as a buttress against disease. Yet, if we string countless unhealthy actions together, we may find ourselves separated from well-being and longer life.

The touchstone of good health likes in attacking disease at its roots. We must prevent its growth and thus stop illness from flourishing. In other words, we should each create a lifestyle that enhances good health rather than depletes it. For many of us, this means changing several of the life patterns that we have consciously, or unconsciously chosen for ourselves. Choosing a better lifestyle is a way to do this.

(Excerpted from *Lifeguide,* a quarterly newsletter available to members of the Wellness Circle.)

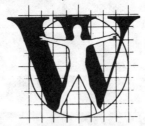

Classes marked with this symbol *(W)* are offered to Wellness Circle Members at a (10%) discount. For more information regarding the Wellness Circle please call 370-WELL.

Jacqueline Baird
Director, Health Promotion

Kim Teachout
Health Promotion Assistant

Lithographics
Printing Department

FIGURE 9–3 *(continued).*

Look What's New . . .

"How to Make the Best of Prime Time"
Develop Critical T.V. Viewing Skills

August 10, 1983; 7:00 p.m.
Leader: Carolyn Rapp, accredited Television Awareness Training
Leader, member of Watch.

Statistics tell us that American children watch an average of 27 hours of TV each week and that the average TV-watching child sees more than 22,000 commercials a year. Whether or not your child is a heavy viewer, the information picked up from television impacts on both his mental and physical health. By exploring some of the issues of children and television — commercials, violence, stereotyping and health related issues — you can learn how to help your child derive maximum benefit from his TV viewing. With television viewing being the number one American pastime, this course will provide parents with home activities to help children limit TV viewing time, choose programs intelligently, and understand the messages that come off the screen. For additional information please call Health Promotion at 370-WELL or 379-3494. Preregistration required. Fee: $5.00 per person/$7.00 per couple. Children free. Discount to employees. *(W)*
Location: Alexandria Hospital, HEC conference room

Endometriosis and Infertility

August 24, 1983; 7:00 p.m.
Presenter: Dr. Darryl Barnes, OB/GYN, Alexandria Hospital

Endometriosis, the growth of the tissue normally found inside the uterus in abnormal locations, is a major cause of chronic pelvic pain and infertility. It is found in more than 20% of all women, and is a factor in almost 50% of women with infertility. Come and learn about this important gynecologic problem as Dr. Barnes of the Alexandria Hospital's Department of Gynecology and Obstetrics discusses endometriosis and its role in infertility. For registration and information, please call 370-WELL or 379-3494. Fee: $3.00; discount to employees. *(W)*
Location: Alexandria Hospital, HEC conference room.

Saving Your Skin

August 17, 1983; 7:00 - 9:00 p.m.
Presenters: Dr. John Gibson, Dermatologist, Alexandria Hospital;
Stacy Barrentine, Licensed Esthetician

Do you know why the skin ages and wrinkles? Are you aware of seasonal changes in your skin? Do you know how to combat common

continued next page

1

FIGURE 9–3 *(continued)*.

skin problems such as acne, eczema, excessive oiliness or dryness, and warts? Dr. Gibson will discuss these topics and other important aspects of skin care. Following Dr. Gibson, Stacy Barrentine will address the subject of facials and hair removal. Make up hints for all skin types will be given during a make up application demonstration on a member of the audience. Registration requested. For more information call 370-WELL or 379-3494. Fee: $5.00 community; discount to employees.*(W)*

Location: Alexandria Hospital, HEC conference room.

Alcohol Awareness Program

August 15, 1983; 7:00 - 9:00 p.m.
Panel: Andrew Molchon, M.D., Edullfo Gonzales, M.D., Brenda Destro, M.S.W., Wayne K.
Facilitator: Larry Fabian, M.S.W., Alexandria Hospital

This program is designed to disseminate information to the public about alcohol use and abuse. The presentation will offer a general overview of alcoholism and the problems frequently associated with drinking. A panel of experts will address current alcohol treatment practices, medical management of alcoholic patients, and alcohol's place in society. Discussion will also focus on Alcoholism as a disease. This program is the first in a series of Alcohol Awareness programs that will be offered on a continuing basis. For additional information, please call 370-WELL or 379-3494. Reservations requested. No charge.

Location: Alexandria Hospital, HEC conference room.

Shouldn't You Know CPR?
(cardiopulmonary resuscitation)

August 1 & 3; 9 & 11; 16 & 18, 1983; 6:30 - 10:30 p.m.
Instructors: Emergency Department Personnel, Alexandria Hospital

A unique and challenging opportunity to perform a valuable public service and to gain an important skill . . . LEARN CPR. CPR saves lives! Almost 700,000 Americans die each year from heart attacks. The "attacks" are cardiac arrests caused by a number of events; electrical shock, industrial accidents, disease, or other causes. At least half of them occur to someone you know in the home, worksite, or in an area where immediate medical help is unavailable. When bystanders do not know CPR, the victim dies needlessly and sometimes painfully.

Become Red Cross Certified in CPR and Obstructed Airway Methods for the adult, infant, and child. Fee: $12.00; discount for employees. Call 379-3073 for registration. *(W)*

Location: Alexandria Hospital, Physical Therapy Department.

2

FIGURE 9–3 *(continued).*

Babysitting Course

Monday & Wednesday, August 29 & 31, 1983; 4:30 - 8:30 p.m. (2-part series)
Instructor: Certified American Red Cross Instructor
For young people, babysitting is one of the first opportunities to earn money and to learn job responsibilities. Students participating in the babysitting course will learn how to supervise children, prevent accidents, give first aid, care for and feed infants and children. Additionally, they will benefit from information about characteristics of different age groups, group play, and socialization, discipline, nutrition and baby care skills. Students must be age 11 years or older to participate and will be American Red Cross certified upon completion of the course. Great way to *earn some summer funds!* Fee: $7.00. *(W)*
Location: Alexandria Hospital School of Nursing, classroom #3. For registration and information call the Health Promotion Department at 370-WELL or 379-3494.

Special Interest & Support Groups

One Day Weight Loss Workshop: How to Reduce Emotion-Based Eating

August 20, 1983; 9:00 a.m. - 5:00 p.m.
Instructor: Lucille G. Shandloff, Ph. D.
Overeating and overweight are caused by underlying emotional triggers that result in excessive appetite, binges, and cravings for particular foods, such as sweets. By dealing with these causes you can rehabilitate your body's natural ''appestat'', stop overeating, lose weight, and keep it off. Call 921-9444 for enrollment information. Fee: $75. Class materials $15.00. *(W)*
Location: Alexandria Hospital, School of Nursing, Classroom #1.

Smoke Stoppers Graduate Seminar

August 8, 1983; 7:30 - 9:00 p.m.
Leader: Evelyn Runyon, R.N., Smoke Stoppers Lecturer
Guest: Kim Teachout, B.S., certified Aerobic Fitness Instructor
Now that you are a non-smoker, aerobic activity will increase your cardiovascular endurance and your lungs vital air capacity. This month's seminar will address ''aerobic'' activities and their role in our total physical and mental well-being. Come learn how to identify your

continued next page

3

FIGURE 9–3 *(continued)*.

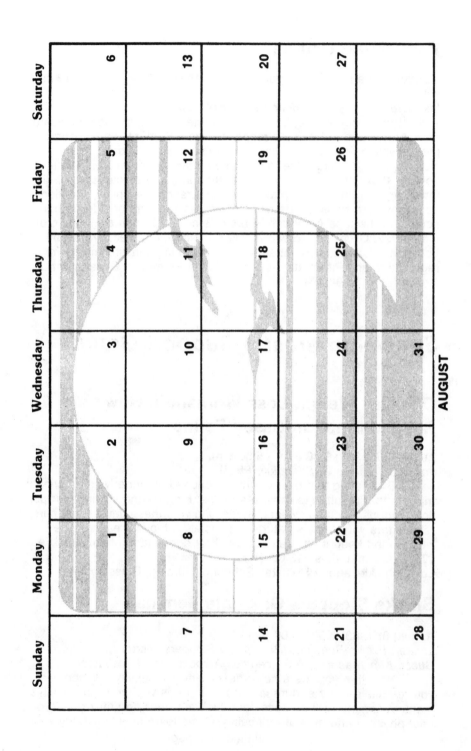

4

FIGURE 9–3 *(continued)*.

target zone, pulse, & resting heart rate. Refreshments served. For information and registration, call 370-WELL or 379-3494. No charge. Location: Alexandria Hospital, School of Nursing, classroom #3.

Chronic Pain Outreach of Northern Va.

August 2, 1983; 7:30 - 9:30 p.m.
Co-Chairmen: Dianna Michael & Ruth Hunt

Chronic Pain Outreach (CPO) is a self-help group offering emotional support to individuals & families who are trying to cope with a chronic pain situation including a debilitating disease process & physical/hidden handicaps. CPO provides a vehicle through which self-motivation is achieved by 1) giving/receiving support, 2) providing an outlet for frustration, anger, or fear, 3)working towards practical solutions to life-threatening situations. CPO works to stimulate positive attitudinal changes, promote family understanding, & help professional people become more aware of the emotional needs of the individual in a chronic pain situation. No charge. For more information call 971-0420, or 255-2120.
Location: Alexandria Hospital, 4th Floor Conference Room.

Diabetes Rap Session

August 17, 1983; 8:00 p.m.
Facilitators: Mary Little and Audrey Gassie, Northern Va. Diabetes Group

This informal rap session is open to individuals who would like to learn more about diabetes. Programs help diabetics, families, and friends understand and manage diabetes. All interested individuals welcome. For more information call 998-6511 or 256-5972.
Location: Alexandria Hospital, 4th Floor Conference Room.

Support Group for Amputees

Fridays, August 5, 12, 19, 26, 1983; 9:45 a.m. - 10:45 a.m.
Coordinator: Lynda Rogers-Seeley, B.S.W.

Support group established to assist the amputee adjust to the loss of a limb. The group is open to any amputee. For registration please call 379-3580. No charge.
Location: Alexandria Hospital Unit C Conference Room.

Aerobic Fitness Interest Group

August 16, 1983; 7:00 p.m.
Leader: Kim Teachout, B.S., Aerobic Fitness Instructor
Guest: Dr. Eric Lauf, Foot Surgery & Podiatric Medicine

Are you a weekend athlete? Do you know how to choose the proper footwear for your sport? Knowledge of these areas will help reduce your chance of injury and discomfort. Dr. Eric Lauf will ad-

continued next page

5

FIGURE 9–3 *(continued).*

dress common athletic foot problems, as well as basic prevention & treatment techniques for both the novice and serious athlete. Discussion will also cover stretching, strengthening, and sports related injuries. Guests and friends welcome. No charge. Registration requested. For more information and registration, call the Health Promotion Department at 370-WELL or 379-3494.
Location Alexandria Hospital, School of Nursing classroom #1.

Prosthetic Conference

August 5, 1983; 11:00 a.m. - 12:00 noon
Multidisciplinary team approach to the care of individuals with amputations. Family and client are included in the planning of treatment, type of prosthesis, and rehabilitation program. For appointment, call 379-3535. Fee: $25.00.
Location: Alexandria Hospital, Physical Medicine

Herpes Support Group

August 18, 1983; 7:30 - 9:00 p.m.
Facilitator: Gloria Davis, R.N.
Herpes Support Group is for a networking of those persons who believe they have or are confirmed as having Herpes. We will discuss the ramifications, both physical and psychological, in being diagnosed as having Herpes. This meeting is also open to those who would like more information about Herpes. For more information call Health Promotion at 370-WELL. No registration necessary.
Location: Alexandria Hospital. School of Nursing classroom #1.

"Our New Baby" Sibling Class

Saturday, August 6, 27, 1983; 9:00 - 10:00 a.m.
Sunday, August 14, 1983; 10:30-12:00 noon
Class is designed for "expectant" brothers and sisters between the ages of 2½ and 6. Recommended for children one month prior to arrival of newborn. Open to all families. To register call 379-3029 between 10:00 a.m. - 2:00 p.m. Fee: $5.00 1st child. $3.00 each additional child. *(W)*

"Thinking Of Having A Baby . . .?"

Thursday, August 25, 1983: 7:00 - 10:00 p.m.
Instructor: Leith Mullaly, R.N.
Class is designed for those considering parenthood. The one session class will include topics such as; Is parenthood for us?; Prepregnancy health status; Pregnancy after age 30; Infertility; Financial aspects of childbearing; Working mothers and child care options; Environmental factors impacting on pregnancy; and How to select a

continued next page

6

FIGURE 9–3 *(continued).*

hospital and physician. Open to all. To register call 379-3029 between 10:00 a.m. - 2:00 p.m. Fee: $3.00 per couple.*(W)*
Location: Alexandria Hospital, Visitor's Entrance Lobby.

We're Pregnant - Now What?

Tuesday, August 9 & 16, 1983; 7:30 - 9:30 p.m.
This 2 session class will provide information to expectant parents in making a healthy adjustment to pregnancy. Topics include: physical changes and relief of minor discomfort; nutrition; fetal growth and development; body mechanics and exercise; emotional changes in pregnancy, etc. To register call 379-3029 between 10:00 a.m. - 2:00 p.m. Fee: $10.00 per couple. *(W)*
Location: Alexandria Hospital, Visitor's Entrance Lobby.

Obstetrical Tours

August 3, 7, 14, 21, 28, 1983; 2:00 - 3:00 p.m.
August 1, 16, 1983; 8:00 - 9:00 p.m.
Tour of labor area, recovery room, nursery and post partum unit. To register call 379-3029 between 10:00 a.m. - 2:00 p.m. One week prior registration requested No Charge.
Location: Alexandria Hospital, Patient Ent. Lobby

Short Stay Delivery Class

Monday, August 22, 1983; 7:30 - 9:30 p.m.
Instructor: Leith Mullaly, R.N.
This one night class is especially designed for families who plan to leave the hospital within the first 24 hours after birth. The focus will be on care of mother and baby in the first days after delivery. A discussion of potential complications and warning signs as well as infant resuscitation will be included. (Couples will want to discuss the option of a Short Stay with their doctors.) To register call 379-3029 between 10:00 a.m. - 2:00 p.m. Fee: $5.00. *(W)*
Location: Alexandria Hospital, Education & Training classrooms.

Alcoholics Anonymous/Al-Anon/Alateen

August 1-31, 1983; 8:30 p.m. - 9:30 p.m.
For further information call Dr. Bill Drohan at 642-4898 or 425-5468.
Location Alexandria Hospital. Saturday thru Thursday - cafeteria & staff development classroom. Friday - auditorium. Alateen: Saturday evenings 4th floor conference room.

7

FIGURE 9–3 *(continued)*.

Health-Line Tape

First At An Auto Accident

While driving along the road, you see a car accident ahead. Your first impulse is to stop and help since the ambulance has not yet arrived. But you wonder, will an untrained person be able to help the injured victims? Yes!

Alexandria Hospital presents "First At An Auto Accident," tape number 1400, Health-Line's tape of the month. The health message stresses that your head, hands, and the air in your lungs can mean life or death for an injured person before the ambulance arrives.

The tape explains the proper actions to take at the scene of an accident including instructions for clearing air passageways, mouth-to-mouth resuscitation for non-breathing babies and adults, stopping bleeding, and splinting a fracture.

Residents who wish to hear this message should dial 370-8287.

A Health-Line brochure listing the 252 health topics and more information is available by calling the public relations department at 379-3196.

8

FIGURE 9–3 *(continued)*.

Definitions for Health & Wellness

Wellness: Involves self-directed behavioral change and is a lifelong learning process (in which) happiness and fulfillment combine with health as equally important outcomes. (Adamson, et al 1979)

Health Promotion: Begins with people who are basically healthy and seek the development of community and individual measures which can help them to develop lifestyles that can maintain and enhance the state of well-being. (HEW, Healthy People, 1979)

To call for information, class registration, or to be added to the calendar mailing list, please call Health Promotion at 370-WELL, between the hours of 8:30 a.m. - 5:00 p.m. Please note registration form below.

Make checks payable to **Alexandria Hospital.**

────────────── — **CUT HERE** — ──────────────

Please use this form to pre-register for Health Promotion Activity class or to be added to the Calendar mailing list.

Name _____

Address _____

City _____ Zip _____ Phone # _____

☐ Add to mailing list.

☐ Registration: Class _____

HEALTH PROMOTION   Activity Date _____
DEPARTMENT
Alexandria Hospital   ☐ Fee $ _____ enclosed
4320 Seminary Road
Alexandria, Virginia 22304   ☐ Fee not applicable

FIGURE 9–3 *(continued)*.

The Library Is for Reading.

For years public libraries have offered reading programs for children. The Peninsula Public Library in Lawrence, New York, offers free weekly seminars in the classics for adults ranging from 35 to 70 years of age. The classes, taught by a volunteer, are positioning the library as a valuable educational resource for tax-paying, voting, mature adults. The classical series began at the request of community members following a guest appearance by the volunteer classics teacher.[11]

Attracting Tomorrow's Audience.

The John F. Kennedy Center in Washington, D.C., is also known as the National Center for the Performing Arts. To build its national reputation as well as to generate future audiences, the Center's Educational Office annually sponsors the American College Theater Festival which selected seven productions in 1983 out of 400 applicants. The Festival attracts broad national attention and has become a major college theater event in the United States. The Center is building future audiences while strengthening its role as a national performing arts resource.[12]

Girl Scouts of the U.S.A.: Preparing Tomorrow's Woman.

The Girl Scouts have met change. The impact of women returning to work has profoundly affected the programs, activities, and directions that the Girl Scouts are taking. Girl Scouts still camp out and still sell cookies ($1.25 a box in 1982 for a gross of $219 million), but today's Girl Scout badges are as likely to be awarded for "aerospace," "business-wise," "computer fun," and "Ms. Fix-it," as for cooking skills. The emphasis is on woman's changed social role, and the Girl Scouts organization prepares young women to be self-reliant, self-aware, and ready for the world of competitive work. The Girl Scouts' 1981 membership of 2.8 million (including adults) showed a 1.6 percent increase over 1980, the first membership increase in 12 years. Among the new members of the Girl Scouts are minority-group girls, economically disadvantaged girls, and expectant mothers. Controversial issues like sexuality and venereal disease are addressed in seminars on issues affecting today's girls. Girl Scout officials have prepared for these dramatic changes in the organization by taking management seminars on strategic planning, feasibility testing, and the setting of operating objectives. The organization has recruited major corporate participation on its board of trustees and as fundraising leaders. The change in the Girl Scouts is comprehensive, from the top down as well as from the bottom up.[13]

---

[11] " 'College' in a Library on L.I.: A Free Classical Education," Barry Abramson, the *New York Times*, August 22, 1982.

[12] "Gallaudet College's Original Script Is Festival Winner," the *Articulator*, the National Committee Arts for the Handicapped, March 1983.

[13] " 'Be Prepared'—the Girl Scouts Make Many Changes to Stay Viable in the 1980s," Maria Shao, the *Wall Street Journal*, July 15, 1982.

A Nonprofit That Monitors the Quality of Other Nonprofit Services.

The Citizens' Committee for Children of New York, Inc., of New York City is a nonprofit watchdog agency that monitors services for children in the areas of physical and mental health, housing, education, social services, and juvenile justice. Since 1961, the organization has offered an orientation course in community leadership to develop new leaders and volunteers for programs and services to children. Participants in the one-day-a-week, ten-week course observe existing services on field trips. Some of the participants have gone on to start nonprofit organizations to correct injustices or to fill gaps in program services. The watchdog group issues reports and studies on its findings to rectify deficiencies and assist government and other nonprofit groups to provide better services.[14]

The New York Junior League: Attracting Volunteers.

The Junior League is a national service organization dedicated to volunteer activities through its chapters in their respective communities. A new League member must pledge a certain number of active volunteer hours per week. Traditionally the League has helped children and the elderly, sent food and clothing to the poor and the sick, and provided guides for museums. The League raises funds from membership dues and social events. Changes in the New York Junior League began about ten years ago when the members insisted on taking public stands on such issues as ERA and abortion. The New York Junior League leadership recognized the importance of responding to major social issues affecting the membership in volunteer work as well as through public statements. Today's New York member may be conducting workshops at prisons on writing job resumés, shopping with food stamps, dressing for interviews, taking advantage of free events in New York City, learning the subway system, or self-examination for breast cancer. League members also staff projects for victims of rape and incest and answer questions on venereal disease on a telephone "hotline." They visit jails to educate prisoners on alcoholism and its linkage to crime. The group finances posters and other public information materials on issues of concern to women. The League's public stance on issues and the issue-oriented volunteer opportunities are a response to the membership. Of today's 1900 members, 81 percent work at least on a part-time basis. The members are professionals who want to use their volunteer time effectively in programs that have meaning and that are socially oriented and topical. The New York Junior League continues to be a viable organization because it has responded to its members' interests as well as to their changed role in society.[15]

Positioning

Positioning, then, is accepting change, adapting it, demonstrating leadership, ingenuity, and a willingness to take risks. Positioning is strengthening membership through responsiveness and through timely, topical programs. Po-

---

[14]"Volunteers Visit Juvenile Centers," Ron Alexander, the *New York Times*, March 20, 1983.
[15]"The Junior League Takes Off White Gloves," Nan Robertson, the *New York Times*, January 16, 1983.

sitioning is based on questioning and the involvement of members, users, volunteers, staff; cooperation; knowledge of the competition; and staying abreast of developments both in society and within the organization.

CHAPTER **10**

Building a Topflight
Public Relations Team

Building a team for community leadership requires a nonprofit to identify and attract professional public relations skills and to match these skills with people and resources. A first-rate team requires careful assembly dependent on the resources of the organization. The success of many nonprofits will depend on attracting a director/president/administrator with professional public relations skills. For larger and more affluent nonprofits, the public relations manager will be a key assistant to the director. This is the team leader.

The team's success will depend on the acceptance of professional public relations as an integral management technique crucial to the well-being of the entire organization. Successful public relations cannot exist in isolation. Its effectiveness depends on the entire organization being supporters.

START AT THE TOP

The board of trustees must make the commitment to public relations through the plan. The board and the director will then cooperatively allocate resources, assign specific job functions, and position the team and its leader to allow the fulfillment of the plan. For those nonprofits where the director is not the leader of the public relations team, the position of leader must be positioned to report directly to the chief executive. This position reinforces the chief executive's commitment to professional public relations.

Commitment from the top does not disappear when the plan and the team are set in motion. Board members and management officials must be in the vanguard of community leadership through fundraising efforts, public and media appearances. The team leader will supply the guidance and counsel to make this relationship an effective and responsible one.

EFFECTIVE PUBLIC RELATIONS IS A TWO-WAY STREET

To insure the participation of the board, staff, volunteers and service users, the leadership team must build and maintain open two-way communications. Effective informal communications include telephone calls and personal visits. These informal communications should be supplemented, depending on the organization's size, by meetings, newsletters, training programs, counseling on effective public outreach efforts, project evaluations, and involvement in community development projects.

A board of trustees may elect to have a subcommittee specifically responsible for community and public relations programming. Members of this subcommittee should represent professions including advertising, journalism, broadcast, marketing, management, fundraising, public relations. This subcommittee, or the full board, must be involved in recommending on approaches and needs, and must also be kept informed on programs, materials, and approaches being developed to meet specific goals and objectives.

Both formal and informal methods are needed for effective, ongoing two-way communications.

RESISTANCE TO PUBLIC RELATIONS

The effective professional is aware of, and sensitive to, internal resistance to public relations techniques. Public relations techniques may be thought to be limited to publicity alone or considered to be misleading and unworthy of the nonprofit. They may be seen as an unnecessary luxury. This criticism can be well grounded if a nonprofit is pursuing public relations as a narrow, isolated function rather than as the management technique that it has become. The production of publicity through press releases is only as integral to the management technique as the processing of travel monies through vouchers is to financial management.

An astute team leader will begin by identifying the understanding of public relations through questioning and assessing the opinions of staff, board members, volunteers and consumers. This assessment can be the basis for building recognition of the analytical, positioning and forecasting skills of professional public relations, and deciding how these skills will benefit the entire organization.

One outcome of this assessment of the understanding of public relations as a management technique may be to designate the technique in terms that best meet the objectives of the nonprofit. A wide range of terms are already in use by nonprofits. These terms include external affairs, public affairs, public education, public information, marketing, communications, development, community affairs, community relations.

The designation of this management technique that best suits the nonprofit's constituents while safeguarding clarity is a way to respond to reservations and resistance.

NONPROFIT PUBLIC RELATIONS IS DISTINCT AND DIFFERENT

It is distinct in that it must meet the standards of public trust at all times. It is different in that it must be accountable to the public at all times.

Its success depends on its effective contributions to the community and to the media, for it relies heavily on the cooperation of the community and the media for its visibility.

It frequently emphasizes intangibles such as "quality," "contribution," "dignity." Its only "product" may be intangible—the "contributions" of its consumers, members, users. Dealing effectively with these intangibles is very different than dealing with a commercial product or a new law or regulation.

Today's successful nonprofit leadership position is additionally based on competitiveness and aggressiveness, attributes that depart from tradition. There is a new willingness to compete for public recognition and support. There is a new willingness to be aggressive about the needs of the nonprofit and its consumers.

Today's nonprofit is aggressive in identifying needs, competitive in its services to the community. Its leadership is based on knowledge, cost-effectiveness, accountability, and confidence. It cannot rest on past triumphs or pretend to be able to provide a service that it cannot. It understands its audiences and responds with ability and confidence. It makes its views publicly known, even if its views are unpopular.

Unpopular viewpoints may be the nonprofit's distinct contribution to the community, however unwilling the community seems to be. Nonprofit organizations today are not passive. They are active in espousing society's vanguard views and in addressing serious social, economic, and political issues. They may be taking this lead on behalf of all people or for a particular group of professionals or members. The nonprofit's willingness to take the lead is its distinction. It is this that makes the nonprofit the driving force that it is, or could be.

This leadership role may find the nonprofit dealing with either a subject that is unpopular, or a problem that has been unnoticed. Both of these present unique challenges to the nonprofit in reaching audiences and building community support. Persistence in developing allies in the community and in presenting the point of view will build the nonprofit's case.

The nonprofit's unique characteristics are a fresh and valuable attraction in recruiting for both staff and volunteer positions. The nonprofit can offer a young professional a scope and depth of responsibility that few for-profit firms can match. These attractive dimensions are the nonprofit's edge in recruiting.

QUALITIES OF A TEAM LEADER

What makes an effective manager? This question provokes many answers. Corporate leaders are divided over the merits of the MBA in providing effective managers. Academics are divided over how best to prepare a public relations manager. Many colleges offer public relations through journalism schools, others through schools of public communications.

Universities should consider offering graduate public relations programs in Colleges of Business Administration.

The following checklist is a guide to the attributes of a professional public relations manager. These attributes can be altered to suit the nonprofit's plan, its resources, its goals, its audiences, its ability to pay.

<u>Checklist of Characteristics</u>
- Leadership qualities
- Community contacts
- Organizational skills
- Writing skills
- Speaking skills
- Education
- Experience in public relations
  —Nonprofit
    —private
    —public
  —For-profit
- Research skills
- Marketing experience
- Advertising skills
- Financial, budgeting experience
- Understanding of cost benefit analysis
- Fundraising experience
- Experience with nonprofits
  —as a student
  —as a volunteer
  —as staff
  —as consumer
- Knowledge of nonprofit's purpose
- Commitment to nonprofit   .
- Publication experience
- Journalism/broadcast experience
- Media contacts
- Public speaking experience

The selection of a professional team leader is particularly crucial to a low-budget nonprofit which may have its community leadership based on the selection of a creative and innovative person. To attract the right person, or to develop that person from among present staff, volunteers, members, or consumers, the nonprofit will have to offer incentives through responsibility, flexibility, support and salary. The particular incentive to be stressed will depend on the resources available to the nonprofit. The mix of incentives remains the same for all nonprofits as, for example, the promise of a high salary with low responsibility will not produce the leadership the organization seeks.

BUILDING SUPPORT AT THE START

These characteristics lend themselves to a questionnaire format, perhaps with a scale of "less to most desirable." This questionnaire can be shared with the board, volunteers, staff and consumers—or a sampling of each group—to help determine how these groups feel about the skills most needed for a manager. Seeking this advice will enhance the visibility and importance of the team leader's role.

THE REST OF THE TEAM

The characteristics of all team members will be determined by the specific functions needed to accomplish the planned tasks. There are specific skills, background, and experience that are helpful to all functions on the team. Members should be recruited for their abilities in research, membership development, publications, fundraising, special events. The greater the number of skills, the greater the potential for growth. Nonprofits prosper on well-grounded and well-rounded team members.

Fund-Raiser.	Depth and breadth in community contacts.
	Speaking and writing skills.
	Creative thinker and problem solver.
	Iniative in originating ideas and following through.
	Fearlessness.
	An understanding of appropriateness.
	A sense of humor.
	Familiarity with tax laws.
	Knowledge of fundraising technicalities in the advantages to the donor.
	Ability to write grants.
	Foundation familiarity.
	Government grant experience.
	Familiarity with legislation affecting nonprofit.
	Identification with nonprofit's cause.
	Track record—even if it's door-to-door in school.
Writer/Editor.	Ability to write in the "active" voice.
	Intimate knowledge of grammar and punctuation.
	Love of pressure and deadlines.
	Knowledge of printing techniques.
	Cost consciousness.
	Advertising and marketing skills.
	Ability to attract good articles from others.
	Ability to write a wide range of materials, including annual reports, speeches, etc.
	Judgment.
	Ability to produce final copy.
	A writing, editing, and publishing track record.
Events.	Ability to handle details.
	Unflappable.
	Ability to predict all that could go wrong.
	Problem-solving skills.
	Ability to meet deadlines.
	Skill in identifying issues.
	Ability to delegate.
	A track record in organizing time, people, and events.

Production.   Professional standards.
                   Sense of timing and proportions.
                   Cost consciousness.
                   Advertising experience.
                   Radio/television/publication experience.
                   Ability to work with technical materials and technicians.

ASSESSING YOUR TEAM

The characteristics of team members can be assessed. So too can their performances. For some nonprofits, "track records" may mean high school or college experience, such as fundraising for youth groups or writing for a school paper. For other nonprofits, editors of famous magazines may be competing for an opening. Assessing characteristics and performance depends on the dimension of the tasks and the level at which the jobs were filled.

Some nonprofits will benefit by pooling their resources with other nonprofits to build a mutually beneficial team. Still others will use professional contractors and consultants to perform many of the team functions.

All nonprofits will benefit from keeping abreast of the competition by maintaining a file on competing products and by evaluating materials against the competition. This is also a means of identifying potential team members.

Many nonprofits will identify the basic skills among volunteers. Volunteers already have an interest in the organization, knowledge of its services, and contacts of varying strengths within the community. Volunteers can be developed through training and experience into valuable team members.

Consumers and members are additional sources of strength in building community support and in raising public awareness and funds. Service recipients from low social and economic backgrounds can gain in self-confidence as they participate in community programs for the organization. Identification, development, and training are supporters in developing consumer team members.

There is no limit to the contributions that volunteers and consumers can make, if asked, encouraged, and given the means. Both groups are frequently untapped resources.

MANY DO'S AND A FEW DON'TS

DO assemble a team that will provide planning and program assistance to
   the entire organization.
DO remember that the nonprofit's first obligation is to provide the best possible service to the community.
DO remember that the public always comes first.
DO recruit from specific, written job descriptions.
DO clarify in writing the exact duties and responsibilities of the team member and management's support.
DO have written ethics and standards of integrity to avoid any misunderstanding of the nonprofit's role.
DO provide professional respect to your team, including a professional work setting.

DON'T over-recruit for positions with no growth.

DO pay competitively.

DO use professional consultants and contractors as needed.

DO keep up with other nonprofits for ideas on materials, programs, contractors, potential staff.

DO encourage two-way communications and a clear, simple, chain of command.

DO identify potential employees who have a commitment to the organization and who fit the "style" of the nonprofit.

DO expect a lot, and demand a lot, from creative, talented people.

DO listen carefully to your team's ideas and recommendations and incorporate them, unless the reasons against these are sound and well-explained.

DO keep trustees informed and involved in the work of the team.

DO demand accountability from the team.

DO insist on cost-effective materials.

DON'T hesitate to end programs that are not meeting planned goals or that are not cost effective.

DO compliment the team frequently, as talented, creative people enjoy reinforcement.

DO establish and insist on deadlines.

DO criticize the team for its mistakes.

DON'T attack the team for mistakes that are not its own.

DON'T be afraid of controversy or criticism.

DO speak out on issues of concern to the nonprofit.

DO cooperate with other nonprofits on programs to reach larger audiences or to raise larger issues.

DO use frequent performance reviews with the team to insure that goals are clearly understood and are being met.

DON'T overlook the importance of consumer/members and volunteers in all community programs.

DO use training and development to enhance the skills and knowledge of the team, all staff, volunteers and users.

DON'T overlook the potential of existing resources whose jobs or lives could be enhanced by being members of the team.

"GOOD PUBLIC PERCEPTIONS WILL COME FROM THE ACADEMIC SUBSTANCE OF THE UNIVERSITY, NOT THE SHADOWS OR IMAGES"[1]

"The first thing I want to do is lower expectations about what P.R. (public relations) can do. . ." Barry Jagoda reportedly said when he was named director of the George Washington University Office of News and Public Affairs in March 1983.[2] (Prior to March 1983, the Office of News and Public Affairs was known as the "office of public relations.")

---

[1] "Jagoda named head of public affairs," by Virginia Kirk, the *GW Hatchet*, George Washington University, Washington, D.C., March 24, 1983.

[2] Ibid.

Interviewed by the George Washington University student newspaper, the *GW Hatchet,* on his appointment, Mr. Jagoda went on to say that public relations ". . . is the responsibility of the entire administration, faculty and members of the student body."[3]

The student newspaper ran an accompanying editorial drawing from Mr. Jagoda's interview and commenting on the significance of the appointment:

"The Office (Office of News and Public Affairs) needs to be informed on the issues in order to disseminate the news quickly and give the stuents and public some warning on what's coming up. Too many times students don't find out ahead of time that construction will take up half the Quad for two years or that tuition and housing costs will take a large jump.

"An open communications policy between the administration and the public affairs office, and then with the rest of the University, is a start in creating feelings of trust on the inside."

The editorial went on to identify Mr. Jagoda's responsibilities to the University: ". . . Jagoda is correct when he says the main problem to be worked on is academic substance. But that's improving every day and the public affairs office should be among the first to know about such activities and get the word out."[4]

This editorial recognizes that the change in today's nonprofit public relations is more than a change in the title of an office. The new prominence of the management technique of public relations is evidenced by the University's willingness to hire a person of Mr. Jagoda's calibre and experience. (He is a former media advisor to President Carter, CBS News producer, contributing editor to *Texas Monthly,* and writer and editor at NBC News.)

The editorial urges that the University's trustees and president contact the Office of News and Public Affairs so that the Office "shouldn't endeavor only to promote the University . . ." but to play a much broader role in informing "the campus" and in uniting "the entire community."[5]

QUALITY BEGETS QUALITY

Quality is the highest criteria for the nonprofit to use in assembling its team. The same high quality that the nonprofit demands of its services to its publics is integral to its public relations programs.

The leadership team can be built by hiring new people, by developing existing staff, volunteers, consumers, or by contracting specific programs out to professionals in the community.

The leadership team is based on quality and professional standards.

---

[3]Ibid.
[4]Editorial, the *GW Hatchet,* March 24, 1983.
[5]Ibid.

CHAPTER 11

Making Your Organization a Dominant Force in the Community

Being Number One demands leadership . . . leadership in providing quality services, information, contribution to the community, research, ideas, innovations, programs, and problem identification.
broad coalition of tax-exempt organizations. Distinction between "lobbying" and "advocacy" can be subtle, and confusion can reign as to what activities constitute

GOVERNMENT RELATIONS

The Internal Revenue Service determines the tax-exempt status of nonprofit organizations and identifies those organizations eligible to receive tax-deductible contributions.[1] The Internal Revenue Service establishes the rules and regulations governing tax-exempt organizations under the Internal Revenue Code of 1954, mandated by the United States Congress.[2]

An organization must abide by the Internal Revenue Service rules and regulations to maintain its privileged tax-exempt status. Likewise, those tax-exempt organizations in Section 501 (c) of the IRS Code that are also eligible for tax-deductible contributions must adhere to the rules applying to the organization's government relations. Private nonprofits that have tax-exempt status under Section 501 (c) 3 and that have the right to solicit tax-deductible donations are prohibited from endorsing and funding candidates and from lobbying to influence legislation.

---

[1]*Exempt Organizations Handbook.* Internal Revenue Service. Attention: TX:D:P:RR. 1111 Constitution Avenue, N.W., Washington, D.C. 20224

[2]"Tax-Exempt Status for Your Organization." Publication 557 (Rev. Jan. 1982), Department of the Treasury, Internal Revenue Service, Washington, D.C. 20224.

While lobbying is generally recognized as the influencing of legislation and the support of candidates for office, it is a hazy area. There are federal government agencies in addition to the IRS which regulate lobbying activities by nonprofit organizations. These agencies include the Office of Management and Budget, the Defense Department, and the General Services Administration. Their concerns are with grants and contracts. Nonprofits must be fully informed on exactly what they can and cannot do if they are receiving federal grants or contracts. In spring 1983, the Office of Management and Budget issued proposed revisions in its regulations affecting lobbying use of government dollars to nonprofit organizations. These rules were set aside after extensive efforts by a broad coalition of tax-exempt organizations. Distinction between "lobbying" and "advocacy" can be subtle, and confusion can reign as to what activities constitute "lobbying" as opposed to "advocacy." It is a paramount issue for tax-exempt organizations. Rules and regulations must be understood by the nonprofit manager who must also keep abreast of proposed and actual changes in these regulations and rules.

IRS regulations can also be controversial and may be taken to the courts for clarification. Veterans' groups that are designated as 501 (c) (19) organizations by the IRS, and that are tax-exempt as well as eligible to receive tax-deductible contributions are allowed to "lobby." This exception was upheld by the U.S. Supreme Court in 1983.

There are many variables. An association of citizens with a common goal may be eligible for tax-exempt status under IRS Section 501 (c) (4) and allowed some lobbying activity directly related to its goal, but denied tax-deductible contributions. There are lobbying restrictions based on a determination of the percentage of income spent for this purpose.

For trade and labor tax-exempt organizations, lobbying is allowed through a separate entity called a Political Action Committee (PAC). The Political Action Committee raises funds that are distinct from the tax-exempt organization and that are specifically for the influencing of legislation and the support of candidates. A PAC can protect the parent organization's tax-exempt status while fulfilling a lobbying function.

The complexity of the lobbying and advocacy issue as it affects the tax-exempt nonprofit organization mandates that the nonprofit have effective government relations, expert legal and tax advice, and ethical standards. As governments are responsible for establishing and determining the complex rules governing the tax-exempt organization, governments can be a major source of timely and reliable information about what the nonprofit can and cannot do in this area. Additionally, 501 (c) (3) lobbying prohibitions must not foster nonprofit passivity or inaction. Handled carefully, government relations are essential to the impact and leadership of the tax-exempt organization eligible for tax-deductible contributions. contributions.

Rather than being intimidated, the knowledgeable 501 (c) (3) nonprofit will find that the Internal Revenue Service allows considerable leeway for government relations (Figure 11–1).

Understanding the scope provided the nonprofit may, at first reading, be difficult to anyone but a tax specialist. The nonprofit manager must be intimately familiar with the IRS rules and regulations that affect the nonprofit and must

". . . the term influencing legislation <u>does not include</u> the following activities:

1) Making available the results of nonpartisan analysis, study or research;

2) Providing technical advice or assistance (where such advice would otherwise constitute the influencing of legislation) to a government body, or to a committee or other subdivision thereof, in response to a written request by such body or subdivision;

3) Appearing before, or communicating with, any legislative body with respect to a possible decision of that body which might affect the existence of the organization, its powers and duties, its tax-exempt status, or the deduction of contributions to the organization;

4) Communicating with a government official or employee, other than—

    a) A communication with a member or employee of a legislative body (when such communication would otherwise constitute the influencing of legislation), or

    b) A communication with the principal purpose of influencing legislation.

Also excluded (<u>not</u> lobbying activities) are communications between an organization and its bona fide members with respect to legislation or proposed legislation of direct interest to the organization and such members, unless these communications directly encourage the members to influence legislation or directly encourage the members to urge nonmembers to influence legislation.[3]

    FIGURE 11–1. **"Tax-Exempt Status for Your Organization," Publication 557 (Rev. Jan. 1982), Department of the Treasury, Internal Revenue Service, Washington, D.C., p. 30.**

keep abreast of the changes affecting these rules and regulations. Fully understanding the limitations, and being aware of the possibilities, is the foundation of effective government relations.

    A succinct example of the range of permissible government relations for a 501 (c) (3) organization is the following report from the Epilepsy Foundation of America:

> *Government Liaison.* EFA (Epilepsy Foundation of America) provides information to Congress and federal government agencies on the needs and concerns of people with epilepsy, as well as measures necessary to accomplish the prevention and control of the condition.
>
> It also educates members of the epilepsy movement regarding relevant federal programs and how to work effectively with all levels of government. A government affairs newsletter, "Capitol Observes," has a monthly circulation of approximately 1,900. During 1982, EFA testified, provided written statements for the record, or wrote to Members of Congress regarding such issues as medical research, employment training, block grants, and appropriations for the Departments of Health and Human Services, Education, and Labor.[4]

---

[3]Ibid, p. 30.

[4]*National Spokesman,* April 1983, Epilepsy Foundation of America, 4351 Garden City Drive, Landover, Maryland 20785.

None of these activities are "lobbying." Note the emphasis on effective contacts at all levels of government. National nonprofits such as the Epilepsy Foundation of America work cooperatively with affiliates throughout the United States. The support for a national program comes from these affiliates, and to succeed requires the support of all levels of government—local, state, and federal.

Conversely, the locally based nonprofit can also develop support at all levels of government. Governments, at all levels, have an important contribution to make to nonprofits, whether the nonprofit is national or local.

One of the permissible activities is being called upon for technical advice or assistance by a government body. This body will frequently be a legislative one. Being called upon is more than a flattering coincidence. It requires that the nonprofit be well known, and respected by legislators and other government officials.

GETTING TO KNOW YOUR GOVERNMENT

The nonprofit maintains two government relations lists: the peripheral and the crucial. These two may interchange occasionally but there is a reason for these separate lists.

The Peripheral.

This list would include the President, the Governor, the Mayor, Members of Council, Senators, and Congressional representatives . . . The highest elected offices, the most visible, the most politically sensitive. This group, depending on the organization's scope, would be contacted by letter (all elected officials are saluted as "The Honorable"), invited to specific functions, asked to speak to particular audiences, honored for specific contributions.

The Crucial.

This list would include those government officials responsible for funding, legislation, programs of direct concern to the nonprofit. This list would be informed of the organization's problems, needs and progress, and invited to the activities offered to the Peripherals. The Crucials are the people who are directly responsible for the well-being of the organization and who have direct access to the Peripherals. The Crucials can be exposed to far more information about the nonprofit as they are more directly concerned, interested, and in need of information.

Government relations encompasses more than sharing information. It includes identifying problems, substantiating the need for government assistance to supplement private resources, suggesting ways that legislation can meet specific nonprofit community needs.

Governments are a major source of direct and indirect funding for nonprofits. By the application of these resources, governments determine future directions and develop the emphases that have a significant impact on the nonprofit's growth.

Examples of this impact abound at all levels of government. One example is the tax incentives offered to private employers to hire and train specific categories of people. Many of these people come out of nonprofit training programs, and nonprofits are using government relations to encourage tax incentives to find jobs for their people. Another example is the tax incentives in restoring historic properties and in designating historic areas in cities and towns. Again the non-profits working in historic preservation are vitally interested in encouraging these examples. A third example is the public concern for safeguarding America's leadership in science and technology. In May 1983, the Nuclear Science Advisory Committee (which reports to the U.S. Department of Energy and the National Science Foundation), competitively awarded a $140 million national center for physics research to a group of 22 private and public nonprofit universities in a preliminary decision. The center, if funded, promises to provide leadership in physics as well as a contribution to the research programs, prestige, position, and funding of the 22 cooperating universities.[5]

These developments don't just happen. They require the leadership of the nonprofits concerned with the particular issue to use effective government relations to further their goals. Cooperating with other nonprofits is an effective way of increasing the identification of the need and the potential solutions.

PLANNING EFFECTIVE GOVERNMENT RELATIONS

Plan in advance exactly what the nonprofit offers, what it needs, what information substantiates the needs, and precisely outline suggested solutions. The nonprofit is ready to initiate government relations.

- Initiate the visit.
- Make an appointment in advance stating the purpose of the visit. This may be done by phone or in writing.
- Take to the appointment a written outline of the points the nonprofit wants to make. This serves as a guide as well as a statement to leave with the government official.
- Highlight, in writing, the accomplishments of the nonprofit, its expertise, information resources, position, and contributions to the community.
- Present problems that are pertinent to the official and indicate specific suggestions for solving or alleviating these problems.
- Leave a "Roladex" card with names(s), addresses and telephone number of the nonprofit for the official's phone index. Use the nonprofit's issue category as the subject, i.e., "Historic Preservation," "Medical," "Adult Education."
- Ask for specific action. This can include a commitment from the official to attend a function, speak at a seminar.
- As the nonprofit is requesting an involvement from the official, the organization must also offer something in return. A two-way relationship is the essence of a continuing relationship.

---

[5]"College Consortium Wins Lab Support," Philip J. Hilts. The *Washington Post*, Sunday, May 8, 1983.

- Nonprofit staff are not the only effective people to visit government officials. Volunteers, consumers, community leaders allied with the nonprofit are among the excellent choices available to the nonprofit. All should be equally well prepared and armed with precise information and materials.
- Establish common ground, a mutual interest, a shared concern.
- Cooperate with others in presenting a united front to government officials. Identify mutual concerns and attract allies to these concerns for impact.

A group of private nonprofit cultural organizations in the nation's capital worked together to reach national political leaders to emphasize the particular demands and unique functions of nonprofit private cultural groups in the capital.

Assessing their shared concerns, these private nonprofits determined that they all provided services to audiences coming to the capital city from throughout the country. These organizations also realized that much of the cultural competition in Washington, D.C., comes from public nonprofits with substantial government funding. Based on these cogent and urgent points, the private nonprofit cultural groups approached the city's major funder, the government. They sought government funds to service consumers from throughout the country and to compete effectively with the public nonprofits. This private collection of cultural agencies found listeners in the U.S. Congress and legislation has been introduced to provide them with a special fund.[6]

This is an example of cooperation for mutual benefit. The private organizations in this case had to present cogent reasoning to support their views. Their approach is basic to government relations. Shared concerns, mutual benefit. This is also basic to fundraising.

FINDING YOUR FUNDING SOURCES

Nonprofit leadership takes money. Finding money can take a disproportionate amount of energy, time, and resources. For these reasons, funding must be approached on a planned basis and the most likely sources are the first to be approached. The most likely sources of funds are those individuals and organizations to which the nonprofit contributes. This contribution may be either tangible or intangible. It can range from providing a for-free service to giving a feeling of self-worth. It requires assessment and planning before funders are approached so that the two-way benefit is out in front of the request for funding.

Everybody wants something, and this "everybody" includes the major sources of funding the nonprofit—governments, corporations, foundations, individuals. The three inanimates are staffed by people, people with individual as well as collective concerns. The nonprofit that approaches a corporation with the knowledge that it is approaching human beings will have accomplished a major first step in finding funding sources. (See Figure 11–2.)

Corporations.

Corporate giving to nonprofit organizations is not restricted to the financial. Corporations are contributing through urban investments, the loaning of person-

---

[6]"Special Fund Endorsed for D.C. Arts Groups," Phil McCombs. The *Washington Post*, Friday, May 6, 1983.

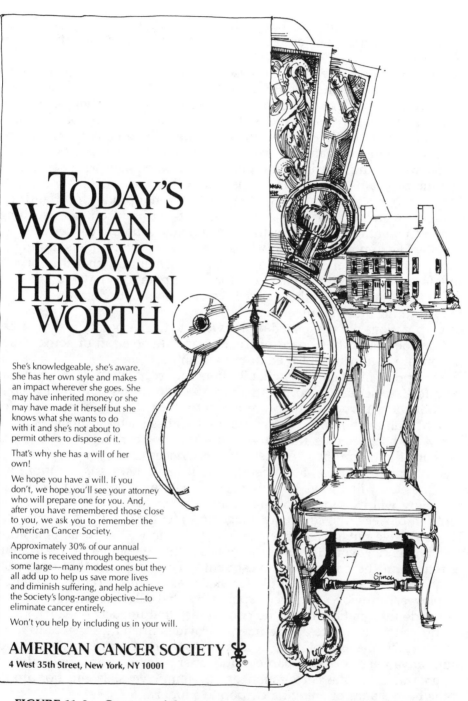

TODAY'S WOMAN KNOWS HER OWN WORTH

She's knowledgeable, she's aware. She has her own style and makes an impact wherever she goes. She may have inherited money or she may have made it herself but she knows what she wants to do with it and she's not about to permit others to dispose of it.

That's why she has a will of her own!

We hope you have a will. If you don't, we hope you'll see your attorney who will prepare one for you. And, after you have remembered those close to you, we ask you to remember the American Cancer Society.

Approximately 30% of our annual income is received through bequests—some large—many modest ones but they all add up to help us save more lives and diminish suffering, and help achieve the Society's long-range objective—to eliminate cancer entirely.

Won't you help by including us in your will.

AMERICAN CANCER SOCIETY
4 West 35th Street, New York, NY 10001

FIGURE 11–2. Courtesy of the American Cancer Society, 4 West 35th Street, New York, New York 10001. Emery Advertising Corporation of Baltimore created the ad and the copywriter was its Executive Vice President, Miss Mary Busch.

nel to both public and private nonprofit organizations, training of the unemployed, corporate support of employee volunteer programs, donations of materials and space.

The nonprofit organizations representing business, the U.S. Chamber of Commerce and the National Association of Manufacturers, urge their members to play active roles in developing their communities by identifying and assisting nonprofit organizations. Corporations, however, see the major contribution they make is generating wealth and jobs and then the individual corporate employee can make contributions financially as well as in volunteer work.

Corporate "caring" for its community is shared equally with corporate concern that the programs it funds and assists are valid, accountable, and cost effective. Many corporate leaders know little about the nonprofit world and its specific needs and problems. It is the obligation of the nonprofit approaching the corporation to identify and answer these legitimate corporate concerns.

An effective approach to a corporation begins with an understanding of the corporation's functions and products and an assessment of what the corporation has done for nonprofits in the past. Most large corporations have offices devoted to community relations, and these offices can supply the background on the corporation's funding and volunteer activities.

As corporations are composed of individuals, the corporation should be represented on the nonprofit's board of trustees and involved in ongoing programs if a relationship is to be established and maintained.

The nonprofit must analyze what it offers the corporation. Can the nonprofit provide a for-free service to corporate employees? Can the nonprofit utilize corporate products or corporate space, and what return can the nonprofit offer the corporation? Can the nonprofit use corporate facilities such as cafeterias for meals for elderly, or board rooms for loaned art works, or corporate publications for articles about the nonprofit's services? What services could the corporation provide the nonprofit: financial, advertising, public relations, transportation?

The question will always be, what return will the corporation receive for its support? How will its support of the nonprofit benefit the community, the corporation's employees, the corporate image and identity?

The extensive publicity in the past few years about the social obligations of the corporation can work for those nonprofits that demonstrate their ability to offer a return on the corporate "investment." The nonprofit that demonstrates that it can upgrade corporate employee skills, assist the corporation with troubled employees, provide volunteer experiences that relate to the employee's job goals, provide information about the community that impacts on corporate planning, improve the corporate environment, provide enriching services to the community in which the corporation is located, use the corporation's products to maximum advantage for both parties, and offer satisfying and rewarding community programs for the corporation and its employees, is the nonprofit that stands the best chance of enjoying corporate support.

A. Bartlett Giamatti, the president of Yale University, addressed this issue of commonality between the university and the corporation:

> It is essential that our friends from the corporate world, who may find the university quirky and mystifying, at least recognize what is at issue. . . . Without some awareness of how a university is put together, and how it is man-

aged, the conversations with the corporate world cannot really move ahead. . . . What does this all mean for the management of a university? It means the management of the institution must be conducted in a spirit and manner that do not run counter to the essential purpose of the place: to remain independent and to use this precious asset to promote teaching, scholarship and the dissemination of knowledge. . . . As these two "worlds" (corporations and universities) move closer, not for the first time and in fits and starts, it is necessary to map out the common ground.[7]

Foundations.

While governments announce the availability of grants, foundations generally do not. The 25,000 nonprofit, tax-exempt foundations in the United States are a source of funding on about the same level yearly as that of the corporation. The nonprofit seeking a grant from a foundation has a richness of resources available to it. Nonprofit organizations that specifically advise and counsel on seeking grants include the Foundation Center, the Grantsmanship Center, the National Society of Fund-Raising Executives, and the American Association of Fund-Raising Counsel. These and other organizations collectively offer a wealth of resources and knowledge about foundations, grant writing, and proposals.

This is a well-explored area and the nonprofit does not have to start from scratch. The same ground rules apply to foundations as to corporations. The approach to foundations should be carefully planned and assessed before initiating the approach. After identifying those foundations that have financed nonprofits in similar areas of concern or that have a general funding record in allied areas of concern, take the same steps that you would to approach a government official or a corporate official. Do your homework; be prepared; try to arrange a personal visit by a representative of the nonprofit. Cooperate with the foundation on designing a grant proposal that meets both the foundation's interests as well as the organization's capabilities. Again, the nonprofit must initiate and follow through on its foundation contacts.

For novices, writing a grant proposal can be an overwhelming experience. Review successful proposals from other nonprofits, using the expertise of the nonprofit organizations in the area. Don't be afraid and don't write unnecessarily. Foundation grant reviewers are human too and they don't want to read poorly organized, poorly thought-out, or poorly written documents. Keep your writing clear and direct. Always remember that short declarative sentences, the "active" rather than the "passive" voice, lucidity, humor, and positive presentations are the most persuasive messages.

Other Nonprofit Funders.

Nonprofits other than foundations also give grants. The grants can be for a wide variety of specialized subjects. Again, use available resources to identify those organizations that give grant monies and determine how your nonprofit

---

[7]"Universities and Corporations: Mapping Out Common Ground," A. Bartlett Giamatti. The *Washington Post*, Tuesday, April 5, 1983.

could benefit these organizations. Major health-issue organizations, for example, frequently give grants for medical research and other related issues.

The same rules apply. Research, assess, prepare. The National Multiple Sclerosis Society is an example of a 501 (c) 3 nonprofit that also awards grants. The Society extends about $6 million a year through grants for special projects. It received 150 applications in 1982, about 30% of which were funded. The Society offers the following tips on what it is seeking when reviewing grant applications:

Some Questions Considered in Evaluating a Grant:

- Is this work of great importance?
- Is it a solid proposal?
- Are the ideas well developed?
- Is the project feasible?
- Are there good facilities for doing this research?
- Are the research methods appropriate?
- Does the applicant know how to use those methods?
- Has he or she published findings supporting this research?
- Is he or she asking too much money?
- Are all the goals embodied in the grant truly valid? Can some be cut?
- Is the approach too global? Does it try to do too much at once?
- Is this work strictly related to multiple sclerosis?[8]

The successful grant is analyzed and developed from both the grantee's as well as the grantor's perspectives. A grant, like any funding, is a two-way street, and successful ones satisfy the requirements of the grantee and the grantor. Whether a grant-giving nonprofit is offering a formal grant or is seeking informal assistance from other nonprofits, the same care must be taken to accomplish the result. An example is nonprofit human service providing agencies which are attracting funding from tax-exempt religious organizations. This is a rich market for funding basic human services as religious organizations may not have the capability of delivering a needed service but do have the interest and the money to fund it through another organization. Nonprofit providers offering emergency housing, food programs, shelters for runaways, drug and alcohol rehabilitation programs are receiving support from religious groups.

Individuals.

What does the nonprofit offer the donating individual? How does the nonprofit alert individuals to the many ways that these individuals can be supportive of it? Individual support is too important to be left to chance. The nonprofit must be specific in seeking funds, offer a variety of ways of contributing, and continually remind individuals of the importance of their support as well as the numerous ways by which they can expand that support.

The approach to the individual should be personalized, identifying the benefits to the individual, and establishing the two-way street of giving and receiving.

---

[8]*Inside MS*, winter 1983. National Multiple Sclerosis Society, 205 East 42nd Street, New York, NY 10017.

Many organizations collaborate on seeking money from individuals. The United Way and the United Black Fund are two major national nonprofits composed of affiliated nonprofit organizations which provide yearly campaigns and comprehensive information to prospective donors. These campaigns are known as "annual" campaigns and their purpose is to provide operating money to affiliated nonprofits. Another form of campaign is the "special" which the individual nonprofit organizes for a specific purpose other than for operating costs. "Special" campaigns are in addition to "annual" ones. These special campaigns seek building funds, endowments, new equipment, expansion. To keep a campaign special, it must have a beginning and ending time frame, a specific financial goal, and a specific objective. A special campaign is not open ended. It complements the annual campaign and succeeds by reaching new donors and by encouraging "depth" contribution from ongoing donors.

Both annual and special campaigns, while based on individuals, also foster the corporate donor and highlight the participation of cooperating corporations.

A major inducement to the donor is the tax benefit. This benefit varies according to the individual's wealth and the nature of the contribution. Professional fundraisers are resources in developing individual contributions and offer many innovative ways to attract donations. For there are many ways for an individual to contribute, including bequests, gifts in honor of another, memorial gifts, donations to organizations by request of the family of a deceased person, gifts of cash and personal property, life insurance gifts, life income gifts, matching fund gifts, deferred payment annuities, charitable remainder trusts, charitable gift annuities, pooled income funds, gifts of real estate.

The ways to give are nearly as numerous as the ways to ask for gifts. Major, national nonprofit organizations produce detailed information for prospective donors. Reminders keep the concept of a major gift in the potential donor's mind. Giving has long and deep roots in the human consciousness and the successful nonprofit offers a wide range of possibilities to meet this human need.

Established nonprofits, particularly those with permanency and those addressing such major generic concerns as education or health, are sources of information on donations. Other information resources include lawyers and bankers who specialize in donations. Individuals are the resource on which a nonprofit builds. Start-up funding frequently depends on a supportive, donating board of trustees. Many corporate and foundation funders are hesitant to provide start-up monies. The successful nonprofit will begin with a solid base of individual supporters, supplementing this base with government, foundation and corporate grants, but always maintaining a large individual support network.

The wisdom of a solid base of individual supporters is testified to by the upheavals in the nonprofit world recently when the governments at all levels reduced funding to nonprofits because of Proposition 13s and changing philosophies and reallocation of resources. Hundreds of nonprofits whose base was the government, and not individuals, found their funding severely reduced, and found themselves unprepared to successfully compete for other sources of funds. Some of these nonprofits may fail, and society will be the loser. Others will merge. Still others will reach out for individual support and succeed on a much stronger, broader-based footing.

Barbara Bode, president of the Children's Foundation in Washington, D.C., was quoted in the *New York Times Magazine* on Sunday, January 2, 1983 about this reduction of government funding:

> . . . we're merely being realistic. Now we're funded through foundations, churches and private donations, but in two to three years, we plan to be self-sufficient, not dependent on grants. We're starting a number of income-producing projects—for instance, selling medical and life insurance to day-care associations, publishing a cookbook for family day-care providers. And we're trying to show providers around the country how they can get along without subsidies should Federal support of family daycare be cut; how to act as businesses, taking tax deductions. . . .

The *New York Times Magazine* describes the Children's Foundation as "a nonprofit national advocacy center for child nutrition and home-based child-care programs, once . . . funded by the now-defunct Federal Community Services Administration."[9]

All tax-exempt organizations thrive on individuals as members, consumers, supporters, donors. Individuals are the basis of the nonprofit. (See Figures 11–3 and 11–4.)

National Symphony Orchestra

John F. Kennedy Center for the Performing Arts, Washington, D.C. 20566

Dear Friend—

On behalf of Music Director Mstislav Rostropovich, the President and Board of Directors of the National Symphony Orchestra, may I extend a personal invitation to you?

May I send you two complimentary tickets to a full rehearsal of the National Symphony Orchestra at the Concert Hall of the John F. Kennedy Center for the Performing Arts?

The choice of dates is yours. Three <u>dress</u> rehearsals are available to you— Tuesday, February 1st, at 10:00 a.m.; Tuesday, March 29th, at 10:00 a.m.; or Tuesday, May 3rd, at 10:00 a.m.

This invitation is made with "no strings attached." The tickets are yours, with my compliments, simply by returning the enclosed "Acceptance Card" with your choice of dates indicated.

The complimentary tickets will be sent to you by return mail.

But, because I'm able to extend this invitation only to a limited number of individuals, your invitation is <u>not</u> transferable.

FIGURE 11–3.   1983 Membership Appeal Letter. National Symphony Orchestra Association, John F. Kennedy Center for the Performing Arts, Washington, D.C. 20037.

[9]The *New York Times Magazine*, Sunday, January 2, 1983, p. 23.

You may ask yourself, "Why am I being invited—and why to a <u>full</u> dress rehearsal of the National Symphony Orchestra (not normally open to the public)?"

The answer is quite simple.

Over the past 52 years, the National Symphony Orchestra has grown from a small, fledgling orchestra that presented 24 concerts a year into a world-class musical institution that delights audiences throughout the world with more than 200 concerts a year.

Under the inspired leadership of Maestro Mstislav Rostropovich . . . a conductor of international prominence, as well as one of the greatest cellists ever . . . the Orchestra now ranks among the finest musical organizations in the world.

Musical giants like Leonard Bernstein, Aaron Copland, Isaac Stern and others have performed with the Orchestra as guest artists.

And critics on every continent have praised the National Symphony as one of the world's premier orchestras.

Yet, <u>too few Washingtonians are aware of the world-stature of their orchestra,</u> or of the <u>musical</u> excellence available to them in the Concert Hall of the John F. Kennedy Center.

And, even fewer have any idea how an orchestra works . . . what rehearsals are like, who the musicians and conductors are, how the National Symphony's guest artists are selected and what it's like to see them work with the Orchestra.

This is why I'm extending this invitation to you . . .

. . . to allow you to see, first-hand, why the National Symphony Orchestra is so outstanding . . . why you, as a Washingtonian, can be proud to have such an internationally-acclaimed orchestra right here in our nation's capital.

But, I'm also extending this invitation for another reason.

As I'm sure you can imagine, the costs of operating a world-class orchestra such as the National Symphony are staggering.

During the 1982–1983 concert season, it will cost more than $10.4 million to keep the Orchestra operating. <u>Yet ticket sales will cover less than half of this cost.</u>

(And this, despite the fact that Orchestra attendance is excellent, with many performances "standing room only.")

From where does the rest of the income come?

Quite simply, from <u>you</u> . . . and other Washingtonians . . . who are proud to have the National Symphony Orchestra as part of the Washington cultural scene.

Through the <u>National Symphony Orchestra Association</u>, interested individuals have contributed hundreds of thousands of dollars to keep the Orchestra's outstanding quality and reputation an effective cultural force in Washington.

And, in exchange, a special package of benefits and privileges has been arranged for Association members.

Members . . . whose contributions range from $25 to more than $1,000 . . . may enjoy:

- priority ticket-buying opportunities
- invitations to selected "dress rehearsals"

FIGURE 11–3 *(continued).*

- invitations to receptions and special events during concert intermissions and after performances

- a complimentary subscription to the "National Symphony Orchestra NEWS", an insider's look at the Orchestra and its operations

Plus, members enjoy the satisfaction of supporting a world-class orchestra . . . an orchestra that brings to the Washington area musical excellence equaled by few other orchestras in the world!

Let me give you an example of just <u>how</u> outstanding this group of musicians truly is.

During February of last year, the National Symphony Orchestra performed on tour in 16 major cities of Europe. They performed in the great concert halls of Germany, Austria, France, and other nations.

And, wherever they went, the critics raved!

"Such perfection, when compared with our day-to-day musical experience, makes us turn pale with envy."

Mannheim, Germany

"Never has so much symphonic joy taken place at a concert by a visiting symphony . . ."

Berlin

"It took only ten minutes to convince us that the National Symphony Orchestra sparkled . . ."

Paris

Won't you consider how <u>you</u> can be part of Washington's . . . and our entire nation's . . . <u>National</u> Symphony Orchestra?

Accept my "no strings attached" invitation to attend one of the limited-admittance rehearsals, as my guest, to see and hear <u>your</u> orchestra at work.

And, consider how your membership contribution of $25, $50, $100 or more will help continue the Washington tradition of musical excellence we now enjoy through the National Symphony Orchestra.

When you accept this invitation—to attend the rehearsal <u>and</u> to join the National Symphony Orchestra Association—you will become a member of the select group of Washingtonians actively committed to musical excellence in our nation's capital . . . and throughout the world.

I look forward to hearing from you . . . and to meeting you at one of the Orchestra's performances.

Most sincerely yours,

Henry Fogel
Executive Director

P.S. I am able to make only a <u>limited number</u> of seats available for these special limited-attendance rehearsals. May I hear from you as quickly as possible, so I may send your tickets?

FIGURE 11-3 *(continued).*

FIGURE 11–4. Courtesy of the Folger Theatre, 201 East Capitol Street S.E.,
Washington, D.C. 20003. Design by Kevin Osborn of the
Writers' Center.

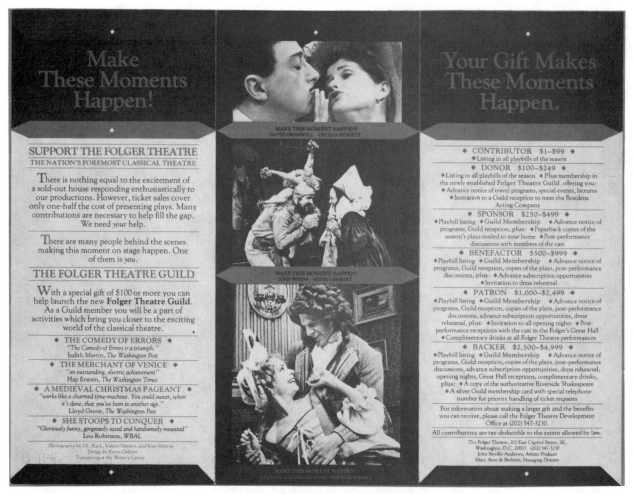

FIGURE 11–4 *(continued)*.

Volunteers.

This group provides significant individual participants in the nonprofit and a basis for funding. Volunteer board members often provide start-up and bail-out monies. Volunteers make effective fundraisers and are crucial to the nonprofit's relationships with government, corporations, foundations, and other funding nonprofits.

Volunteers are involved for many reasons, reasons as complex as human nature. They are not necessarily permanent fixtures of any one nonprofit. There is no guaranteed way to keep a volunteer committed to a specific nonprofit or to the nonprofit world in general. There are, however, methods to maintain the existing volunteer and to encourage new ones. The first step is to understand the volunteer and the reasons why the volunteer is involved in your organization. This understanding will lead to programs that will attract the uninvolved volunteer as well as give the agency the opportunity to be a leader in attracting and keeping volunteers. Leadership in recruiting and maintaining volunteer commitment requires planning and careful execution. The object of planning is to provide both the agency and the volunteer with a beneficial relationship. The following ten steps are helpful in establishing a volunteer program.

1. *Hired Volunteer Coordinator.* This coordinator may be drawn from existing volunteers or hired for expertise in managing volunteers. Management of volunteers is essential. Relying on an unpaid volunteer to coordinate otherers is less likely to be successful than having a paid staff person backed by management in this crucial role.

2. *Recruitment.* New volunteers can be identified by community outreach programs, including the use of media to advertise for volunteers with specific skills (pertinent to the agency's needs), informal word-of-mouth networking through existing volunteers, church and school bulletins, supermarket bulletin boards, speakers' bureaus, high school and college recruitment drives.

3. *Orientation.* A responding prospective volunteer should be given an orientation program about the agency and about volunteer job possibilities. This orientation encourages a two-way dialogue and is an effort to match the job opening with the individual's interests and skills.

4. *Job Descriptions.* The volunteer function must have a specific written job description. This written job description alerts the volunteer to requirements and obligations and affords the volunteer coordinator the opportunity to review regularly the performance of the volunteer. This performance review should be shared with the volunteer and the agency management. Volunteering is a real job and needs to be treated as such. Volunteers not meeting requirements should be warned and/or terminated. The nonproductive volunteer is a morale problem for other volunteers as well as a drag on the efficiency of the agency.

5. *Growth Opportunities.* The volunteer should have the opportunity to progress through a variety of jobs. This progression can depend on the volunteer's interest and motivation. A volunteer ladder encourages people to move in directions of their own interests, skills, and career goals. A ladder should be formalized. Volunteers can be offered high school or college credits with the cooperation of local schools and universities. Obtaining credits is a responsibility of the volunteer coordinator. Organizations that treat such credit opportunities lightly are going to attract volunteers with little or no commitment.

6. *Benefits.* The organization should reimburse volunteers for out-of-pocket expenses such as lunches, parking fees, bus fares, babysitters.

7. *Recognition.* Publicly honoring and awarding volunteers at agency-sponsored community events. This is an inducement for volunteers to tackle more difficult assignments and to make better use of the volunteer ladder.

8. *Perks.* Nonprofit cultural organizations can provide complimentary tickets, back-stage visits, invitations to previews and receptions. Other organizations can provide professional training and lectures by professionals about the nonprofit's area of concern. If the nonprofit is presenting programs of interest to children, volunteers' children can be included in invitations.

9. *Job Development.* A significant contribution of volunteer work is the ability to express the growth in duties and responsibilities on a resumé when applying for a paid job. Volunteer coordinators can assist volunteers in making the transition to a paid job through formal job skill programs and through contacts in the community. This is an added inducement to the serious volunteer.

10. *Cooperating with Others.* Many voluntary organizations now depend on "volunteer clearing houses" to recruit volunteers. Clearinghouses can offer a wider range of volunteer jobs than individual nonprofits and can screen and orient the potential volunteer for the sponsor agency. Other forms of community cooperation can be the design of volunteer program opportunities for elderly people, disabled people, juvenile delinquents, and others on probation and/or parole. The requirements of these special programs will depend on the nature, specific needs, and interests of the potential volunteer.

Understanding the Volunteer.

According to a report issued by the President's Task Force on Private Sector Initiatives, a Gallup study found that over 80 million Americans volunteered between March 1980 and March 1981. Included among these volunteers are young people (7.7 million aged 14–17) and employed people (55 percent of full-time employed people, both men and women, are volunteers). These volunteers contributed over $64 billion in services a year.[10]

The same report quoted a 1981 survey conducted by the nonprofit American Association of Retired Persons which showed that 30 percent of Americans over 55 were serving as volunteers. Of those not volunteering, 20 percent said they were interested in doing so. The report found that at present older Americans are volunteering in numbers far less than those of other age groups. It pointed out that many older Americans are not volunteering because they are not asked. The report found older Americans ". . . if they can be reached and encouraged, a potential source of more volunteers."[11]

Some 400 corporations were found to have formal volunteer programs. These programs:

Make information about community volunteer opportunities available to employees via in-house publications, bulletin board notices, flyers, and clearing-

---

[10]"Volunteers: a Valuable Resource. Prepared for Policy Makers." The President's Task Force on Private Sector Initiatives, Washington, D.C., December 1982.

[11]Ibid.

houses within the company which match individual employees with community volunteer jobs.

Allow nonprofit groups to recruit employees on company premises, as at volunteer fairs.

Grant forms of released time to employees who wish to volunteer during regular working hours.

Give recognition to employees who volunteer.[12]

The report underscores the significant contributions that volunteers are making to the nation and to the nonprofit organization. The Red Cross, for example, maintains its national leadership in support and services through 1.4 million volunteers from coast to coast.

Understanding the volunteer is based on the awareness of the individual's motivation. This motivation changes, and there are indicators that signal these changes and their role in the nonprofit's recruiting and maintenance volunteer programs. Some indicators depend on age, others on social position, education, professional interests. Factors such as altruism and idealism can be significant. The factors frequently overlap, but can be divided into professional, family, personal, social. Understanding these factors assists the nonprofit in motivating and using volunteers to mutual advantage. They can help the organization in targeting and marketing volunteers.

Professional

- The student looking for career experiences and specific training.
- The politically ambitious.
- The salesperson building sales contacts.
- The store owner building community awareness and goodwill.
- The person seeking a paid job with the nonprofit.
- The corporate employee building a reputation within the corporation.
- The adult wanting to use a skill that is unused in paid employment.
- The mother wishing to enter or return to the job market.
- The motivated seeking community leadership.
- The person thinking of changing paid jobs.

Family

Using as an example middle-class parents from the time of the first child's birth, their interests will include the following: pre-natal, birth defects, family planning, children's television, preschool, nursery school, Boy and Girl Scouts, camping, sports groups (Little League, soccer, tennis), PTA, drama, dance, art organizations, church and synagogue, drug and alcohol abuse programs, juvenile delinquency prevention, safe driving campaigns, universities, sororities, fraternities, and alumni organizations.

Personal

"Save the Whale," "Ban the Bomb," United Nations organizations, literary, artistic and cultural organizations, battered women's shelters, animal protec-

---

[12]Ibid.

tion, prison reform, environmental groups, handicapped organizations, self-help groups, minority groups, cause organizations.

Social

Community civic associations, singles groups, social clubs, cultural organizations, leading national nonprofits (the Red Cross, United Way, Easter Seal), historic groups, old house groups, preservation groups.

Obviously, the individual volunteer's motivation may embrace all of these indicators. Taken as a whole they are only one factor that an organization can use to attract and maintain volunteers. They are signficant groupings, however, for a nonprofit to use in motivating volunteers.

Successful volunteer programs require questioning and sampling present and potential volunteers to discover the factors most important to the attraction and maintenance of volunteers. Untapped volunteer resources and the growing numbers of full-time employed volunteers demand structured and relevant volunteer programs.

The volunteer, developed and treated as an integral part of the nonprofit, can help to produce the community support that the nonprofit needs to survive and prosper.

Volunteers as "Members."

One means of structuring volunteer programs is through membership obligation. A membership program, with accompanying yearly dues, can offer volunteers more opportunities and perks than the organization may otherwise be able to extend. Members' fee can cover, or assist in covering, these additional offerings. The category of the membership can determine the amount of yearly fees, and several categories can make membership possible for most volunteers. Member scholarships can be offered to those who cannot pay member fees but who are motivated volunteers.

Using a volunteer member fee basis can allow a nonprofit to offer such inducements as discounts in cafeterias, restaurants, bookstores and shops, free admission to events, and free tickets to special theater or film programs. Fees can pay for a regular volunteer/member newsletter profiling the accomplishments of volunteer/members, listing upcoming events, and presenting news designed to further volunteer involvement.

Being Number One in your community requires leadership and money. The two are directly related. The nonprofit organization that demonstrates its leadership in the community will be building a strong network of support throughout the community. The best base is a broad base. The successful nonprofit will build its base through government relations, funding sources, and volunteers.

CHAPTER **12**

Putting "Profit" into the Nonprofit Organization

"Dreams depend on money," said Ardis Krainik, general manager of the nonprofit Lyric Opera of Chicago, in an interview in the *Wall Street Journal*.[1]

Producing a profit for the nonprofit can require more than effective government relations, productive fundraising, and successful community leadership. The benefits of profitability can be increased quality and quantity of services, heightened contributions to the community, greater satisfaction for service recipients, staff, volunteers, and members.

Profitability can also mean breaking with tradition, alienating important volunteers, attracting critical public attention. The profit may be based on user fees, sales of property, products and information, a variety of profit-making activities that could appear to be the antithesis of the nonprofit.

FACING THE NEED FOR PROFITABILITY

Making profitable decisions can be painful. The successful nonprofit manager recognizes this by soliciting the backing of the board of trustees and taking the lead in facing the responsibility for the need to be profitable. An editorial by the International President of Alpha Phi, a nonprofit organization of women, tackles the issue directly in the organization's magazine:

> Alpha Phi is a sisterhood—but it is also a business. Behind the sisterhood is a corporation. Your Fraternity leaders must address themselves to business concerns, or we could lose the sisterhood we all wish to perpetuate. . . .
>
> The fact that Alpha Phi International Fraternity is a corporation with international, district and local executives may seem to be unorthodox in a sisterhood; however, using this concept should help members of Alpha Phi understand why decisions made by these executives need to be based on sound business practices. In other words, we have to let the purse rule instead of the heart, even if sometimes the heart must weep.[2]

---

[1] "Scaling Back: Under a New Manager, Chicago's Lyric Opera Thrives on a Shoestring," by Meg Cox, the *Wall Street Journal*, June 3, 1983.

[2] *Alpha Phi Quarterly*, Spring 1983.

The nonprofit manager's willingness to face the issue of profitability squarely and openly can help to overcome resistance and to build support for management decisions taken to meet financial challenges.

PROFITABILITY CAN BE COST EFFECTIVE

Making decisions based on profitability can assist the nonprofit in putting its own house in order. The accountable, cost-effective nonprofit is a basis for achieving profitability and efficiency.

When Ardis Krainik was appointed the general manager of the Lyric Opera of Chicago in 1981, the company was sharing the severe financial problems of many opera companies in the United States. All department heads were required to submit a budget, for the first time, and then each department head was asked to reduce the submitted budget by 10 percent. In 1982, the Lyric Opera produced a season that

> . . . was 98 percent sold-out. Lyric has $1.1 million in the bank. Benefactors are pleased, and critics sometimes are, too. And Lyric owes it all to cost-cutting, computers and Ardis Krainik, its new general manager.[3]

The Lyric Opera uses computers to track the multitude of expenses that go into producing a season of opera, and Miss Krainik holds "what she calls 'budget responsibility meetings,' "[4] where each department's budget is scrutinized against actual expenditures. Department heads are charged with bringing their part of a production in at, or under, budget. This careful scrutiny of every budget item has been accompanied by the cancellation of productions considered too expensive, the mounting of productions for which costumes and scenery were already owned by the company, and the search for cheaper alternatives for every item purchased. Some staff reductions and dual use of scheduled rehearsals have brought additional savings. Miss Krainik has practiced cost effectiveness and "started flying economy class,"[5] and finding prviate donors to fund the Lyric Opera's parties.

Management leadership and efficient, cost-effective organization are the basis for profitability in the nonprofit.

EXAMPLES OF NONPROFITS SEEKING PROFITABILITY

1. Sending a Show on the Road.

The Lyric Opera of Chicago is negotiating a Broadway run for its production of *The Mikado*.[6] The Houston Opera has had great success with road shows of *Porgy and Bess* and *Showboat*. The cooperating producer assumes the risks and costs.

---

[3]"Scaling Back: Under a New Manager, Chicago's Lyric Opera Thrives on a Shoestring," by Meg Cox, the *Wall Street Journal,* June 3, 1983.
[4]Ibid.
[5]Ibid.
[6]Ibid.

2. Meeting Competitors' Prices.

Two Ohio hospitals cut the basic emergency room charge to meet the competition for for-profit "urgent-care" medical centers. One Ohio nonprofit plans to open its own "urgent-care" center.[7]

3. Licensing Names.

The University of California at Los Angeles began licensing its name in 1973 to manufacturers of clothing and other items. During a recent fiscal year, UCLA received between 7½ and 10 percent of wholesale volume on some $5 million in domestic sales. Overseas sales are booming for licensed college and university names, and UCLA merchandise attracted $30 million in sales in Japan in 1979.[8]

4. Serving Two Purposes.

Georgetown University cooperated with the Folger Theatre in Washington, D.C., and offered a course on the process of staging a Shakespearean play. The play studied was *All's Well That Ends Well*, and the course accompanied the play's scheduled rehearsals prior to its opening at the Folger.

5. Collecting Delinquent Student Loans to Provide Scholarship Funds.

Harvard University has a $500,000 computer system that "flags late payments on a daily basis"[9] and a staff of 15 people in the collection office. "The balance due from delinquent graduates of Harvard's medical and dental schools fell to $216,000 as of December 31, 1982, a delinquency rate of 7 percent compared with $536,000 on June 30, 1981, a 19 percent rate.[10]

6. Involving Members in Purchases.

The Hunter Museum of Art in Chattanooga, Tennessee, formed a "Collectors Group" of donors who contribute a minimum of $500 to an acquisition fund. "A few people contributed more than $10,000 each to the museum."[11] This Collectors Group traveled to New York City (at the individual member's own expense) and, armed with the acquisition fund, purchased new artworks for the museum. On returning to Chattanooga one of the Collectors Group commented that "everyone wants to do it again next year. We should up the ante."[12] According to the director of the Hunter Museum of Art, "I've been involved in the community for 25 years and I've never had more fun."[13]

---

[7]USA TODAY, June 3, 1983.

[8]Ibid.

[9]"Colleges' Student-Loan Collection Efforts Getting Tougher as Federal Pressure Grows," by Burt Schorr, the *Wall Street Journal*, February 7, 1983.

[10]Ibid.

[11]"A Group Shopping Spree Stocks a Museum with Art," by Carol Lawson, the *New York Times*, June 20, 1982.

[12]Ibid.

[13]Ibid.

7. Members Writing and Selling Cookbooks.

The Wolf Trap Associates, a 3,000-member volunteer group associated with the Wolf Trap Foundation in Virginia, has been averaging $9,000 a year for the past several years selling a member-produced picnic cookbook.[14] The Alexandria Hospital volunteer group, The Twig, sells a cookbook based on favorite city recipes. Each cookbook is tailored to the interests of the nonprofit audience.

8. Syndications for Low-Income Housing.

A pool of funds from individual investors who receive tax write-offs for real estate investments. A faster depreciation of real estate due to tax law changes in 1981 made syndications attractive to investors. Nonprofits have become developers maintaining control of the project while turning over ownership shares to private investors. Two Massachusetts examples are Villa Victoria in Boston and the Riverside-Cambridgeport Community Corporation.[15]

9. Advertising for Space.

The American Leprosy Missions of Bloomfield, New Jersey, took an advertisment in the *Wall Street Journal* seeking the donation of a 10-to-12-thousand square-foot building suitable for its headquarters.[16]

10. Producing Programs That Are Topical and of Interest to Business.

The National Foreign Trade Council Foundation advertised in the *Wall Street Journal* a one-day conference on U.S.-Saudi Arabia economic interests for a $150 per-person fee.[17]

11. Sales of Research Rights to Corporations.

Yale University signed an agreement in October 1982 giving Bristol-Myers Company the rights to license and sell any cancer drugs that Yale develops. In return, Bristol-Myers will give Yale $600,000 annually for five years. This is Yale's second corporate-sponsored research agreement. Its first, in February 1982, gave the Celanese Corporation of New York exclusive rights to results of research into the structure and function of enzymes. Celanese gave Yale a $1.1 million three-year grant.[18]

12. Sales of Urban Property.

"A spokesman for the National Council of Churches says that 'almost any church in a downtown urban area is a possible target for development, and with

---

[14]"Recipes for Rebuilding: Cookbook Sales to Help Wolf Trap Rise Again," by Sarah Fritschner, the *Washington Post*, 1982.

[15]"Nonprofits Put Syndications to New Use," by Sandra Evans Teeley, the *Washington Post*, August 7, 1982.

[16]The *Wall Street Journal*, January 20, 1983.

[17]The *Wall Street Journal*, January 10, 1983.

[18]The *Washington Post*, October 20, 1982.

the recession, churches are more likely to sell.' "[19] A New York Seventh Day Adventist church sold its building, which was difficult and expensive to maintain, and made a $2 million profit on the building. It had owned the building for about five years. After buying a new church, "the congregation established a scholarship fund for member children and donated money to other, less fortunate churches."[20]

13. Leasing Back Property from Investors.

Bennington College in Vermont plans to lease its 650-acre campus to a group of private investors, including alumni, for upfront cash. Bennington would then lease the campus back and pay the investors at low interest rates for a period of 20 years. "This college has always been in the vanguard of things since its founding, and it is in this venture that we are undertaking these things," the chairman of Bennington's trustees said in approving the lease-back agreement.[21] The lease-back arrangement was permitted by the changes in the tax laws in 1981. Bennington's president said that the lease arrangement was "a way to allow nonprofit institutions to convert their capital equity to cash, as homeowners do who refinance their mortgages."[22] (In 1983, Congress was examining the various 1981 tax law changes with the intent to limit or eliminate some of the investor arrangements.)[23]

14. Commercial Ventures.

The nonprofit Federation Employment and Guidance Services, "the largest nonprofit employment and training undertaking in New York,"[24] responded to reductions in federal government support by offering commercial services to private employers that range from setting up rehabilitation programs for alcoholics to running a pre-retirement counseling service, to assessing promotion and career potential of employees. The executive director of the Federation said that the Federation "has already obtained contracts totaling $150,000. It now has a score of clients for the commerical ventures in the metropolitan (New York) area—including hospitals, utilities, a university, insurance companies and three major industrial concerns—and it has prospects of $3 million a year."[25]

15. Low-Interest Student Loans Financed by Tax-Exempt Bonds.

Dartmouth College sold $29 million in tax-exempt bonds through state agencies in June 1982.[26] The money is used for student loans and repaid by students at a higher interest rate than that paid to purchasers of the bonds. A number of

---

[19]"More Urban Churches Sell Their Property, Making a Large Profit but Upsetting Some," by Luis Ubinas, the *Wall Street Journal*, September 27, 1982.

[20]Ibid.

[21]The *Washington Post*, April 20, 1983.

[22]"Administration Backs Effort To Change Tax Leasing Law," by Thomas W. Lippman, the *Washington Post*, June 9, 1983.

[23]Ibid.

[24]"Nonprofit Group Goes into Business," by Kathleen Teltsch, the *New York Times*, March 6, 1983.

[25]Ibid.

[26]"Campus Crunch: Declining Federal Aid, Soaring Tuitions Test Ingenuity of Colleges," by Anne Mackay-Smith, the *Wall Street Journal*, September 24, 1982.

private nonprofit schools are considering similar actions; among them are Boston College, Boston University, Harvard, and Northwestern.[27]

16. The Barter System.

Students at Warren Wilson College in Tennessee can barter their labor in exchange for room and board. The college's students can also work for the college in the summer for tuition credit.[28] Bartered work includes clerical and maintenance functions that the college would otherwise have to contract out or hire staff to perform.

17. Prepayment of Tuition.

The University of Southern California and Washington University in St. Louis offer a prepayment of tuition for a degree in advance, thus avoiding any tuition increases.[29]

18. Lowering Tuition for Night and Weekend Classes.

Westbrook College in Maine competes for students by lowering tuition charges for night and weekend courses, which require fewer staff, extracurricular activities, and course offerings.[30]

19. Selling Air Rights.

The Museum of Modern Art in New York sold the air rights over the museum to developers for construction of a highrise condominium apartment building which now rises above the museum. The museum, in addition to the upfront cash payment, will continue to receive yearly income from the condominium owners.

20. Selling Excess Property for Development.

The New York Historical Society is exploring the development of part of its property as an apartment building. The Historical Society's building is a New York City landmark. The excess property lies behind the main building.[31]

21. Raffling Property.

The St. Francis of Assisi Church in Triangle, Virginia, has raffled two single-family detached houses valued at $100,000 for $100 a ticket. The tickets were tax deductible.

---

[27]Ibid.
[28]Ibid.
[29]Ibid.
[30]Ibid.
[31]"Group Planning a New Building at West 76th St.," by David W. Dunlap, the *New York Times*, March 18, 1983.

22. Attracting Equipment Donations.

The 1981 tax law increased a manufacturer's deductible allowable for the donation of new scientific equipment to colleges and universities for research purposes. Boston's Northeastern University estimates that donations of computers or software account for about ten percent of all gifts received.[32]

23. Raising Prices for Staff.

The AFL-CIO doubled the traditionally low price of the soup-and-sandwich lunch in its headquarters cafeteria and raised the interest rate on loans to members through the credit union. Field representatives were issued smaller cars than in the past to save fuel costs.[33]

24. Advertising for Trustees.

Embry-Riddle Aeronautical University in Florida advertised in the *Wall Street Journal* for trustees willing to invest a minimum of $1 million for financial assistance to students. The ad offered tax-exemption for the investment.[34]

25. Paid Commercial Advertising on Public Television.

A 14-month experiment of running paid advertising on nonprofit public television was found in an interim study by the National Association of Public Television Stations to be accepted by most viewers as a "fact of public-television life in an age of federal budget cuts."[35]

26. Expanding Services for Members.

The American Trucking Association increased its offerings of workshops, seminars, and continuing education for members as a source of revenue. The executive director of the association's sales and marketing council commented that "you can get some good money out of that sort of thing."[36]

27. Improving Members' Job Prospects.

The American Speech-Language-Hearing Association finds that its certification of audiologists and speech therapists enhances members' chances in a tight job market. Providing a job bank for members entering the job market and for those who are changing jobs is another member inducement.[37]

---

[32]The *Wall Street Journal*, December 23, 1982.
[33]"Recession Forces Organized Labor to Cut Staff and Some Programs," by Robert S. Greenberger, the *Wall Street Journal*, December 23, 1982.
[34]"School Advertises for New Trustees," the *New York Times*, June 13, 1982.
[35]"Putting Ads on Public TV Angers Few," by Jane Mayer, the *Wall Street Journal*, March 24, 1983.
[36]"Associations Helped and Hurt by Recession," by Thomas B. Edsall, the *Washington Post*, March 28, 1983.
[37]Ibid.

28. Using Adversity to Promote Membership.

The National Association of Social Workers attributes its slight increase in membership to "the sense that now there is a greater need to support the association."[38]

29. Offering Group Insurance Plans.

Many professional and trade associations offer a variety of insurance plans to their members on a lower cost group basis. The associations gain a percentage of policy sales. Insurance plans include accident, death, health, liability.

30. Quality Management.

The Minneapolis-based Dayton-Hudson Corporation, one of the country's major retailers, has a "comprehensive arts support program"[39] which annually reviews the major recipients of the corporations' donations for "artistic performance, the quality of their management, their financial well-being and the ability of their programs to reach the community."[40]

31. Corporate Cooperation.

The University of Bridgeport in Connecticut took a full-page advertisement in the *New York Times* to offer prospective students "real jobs, real pay ($10,000 to $24,000), in the real world, through optional, alternative semester co-operative education programs with major corporations such as GE, Xerox, Sikorsky."[41]

32. Matching Mature Students with Colleges.

Elderhostel, Inc., of Boston is a nonprofit corporation that offers people 60 or over study programs at colleges throughout the United States and abroad. Most of the programs are offered in the summer when the colleges have unused facilities available. The colleges provide faculty, select the course offerings, and set fees for room, board and tuition. All expenses are paid by the mature participants. The 1983 program matched 78,000 students with 634 institutions, while thousands more were turned away because of lack of facilities.[42]

33. Joint Ventures.

Duke University in North Carolina leased campus land to a developer in exchange for athletic and social facilities for faculty, students, and staff without having to provide capital. Park College in Missouri agreed to let a private cor-

---

[38]Ibid.

[39]"Big Business Tightens Its Arts Budget," by Sandra Salmans, the *New York Times*, February 20, 1983.

[40]Ibid.

[41]The *New York Times*, April 19, 1983.

[42]"The Senior Class: More and More Students Aged 60 and Up Take One-Week Courses at Colleges Here and Abroad," by Ray Vicker, the *Wall Street Journal*, April 12, 1983.

poration quarry and mine limestone on the college property. In exchange, the sale of the limestone will provide revenue for the college. In North Carolina, St. Andrews Presbyterian College is converting 200 of its 820 acres to development of a shopping center, private housing, a hospital and offices.[43]

34. Cooperating with Other Nonprofits.

Fifteen of the nation's leading art museums offer reciprocal member privileges in each others' museum. While this category of membership is relatively expensive, it is attractive to corporate and business people and others who travel. Art lovers will frequently visit another city to see a particular exhibit or simply to visit another museum. This reciprocal membership permits free admission to all museums, free admission to some special exhibits and members' previews at all museums, discount on most purchases from all museum shops, as well as discounts on concert and lecture series offered by the various museums. The museums participating in reciprocal membership are Corcoran Gallery of Art; Dallas Museum of Fine Arts; Denver Art Museum; the Detroit Institute of Arts; Indianapolis Museum of Art; Los Angeles County Museum of Art; the Metropolitan Museum of Art; the Minneapolis Institute of Arts; Museum of Art, Carnegie Institute; Museum of Fine Arts, Boston; Philadelphia Museum of Art; the Seattle Art Museum; the Toledo Museum of Art; the Virginia Museum; and Wadsworth Atheneum, Hartford.

35. Joint Ventures for Donations.

New York's Memorial Sloan-Kettering Cancer Center receives watches from a private business which appraises the watches for donors who in turn can take the appraised value off their income taxes. Sloan-Kettering plans to auction the most valuable watches and sell the others through its thrift and gift shops. The private firm hopes to sell new watches to donors.[44]

36. Attracting Technology for Special Uses.

George Washington University in Washington, D.C., attracted a grant from Xerox to purchase a reading machine for visually impaired students.[45]

37. Dealing with Low Nonprofit Salaries through Encouraging Consulting as a Supplement.

Faculty salaries at universities have dropped an estimated 20 percent in the past ten years. To keep faculty, many universities encourage consulting jobs outside of the university and frequently reserve Fridays as consulting days for faculty by scheduling no classes. Consulting varies with the professor's specialty,

---

[43]"What Colleges Will Do to Pay the Rent," by Carol P. Halstead, the *New York Times*, April 24, 1983.
[44]"New York City Store Finds a Way to Make a Watch Tax-Deductible," by Ron Winslow, the *Wall Street Journal*, April 11, 1983.
[45]"GW acquires reading machine for the blind," by Cheryl Miller, the *GW Hatchet*, April 4, 1983.

but serving as expert witnesses in trials is a lucrative source of outside income for many faculty members.[46]

38. Selling Tickets.

The Cultural Alliance of Greater Washington, D.C., established a central ticket booth modeled after the one in New York City. The central ticket booth offers same-day, half-price tickets to theater and other events. The Washington, D.C., ticket booth did $750,000 in business in a year.[47]

39. Setting Up a Consumer-Run Credit Union.

Georgetown University is establishing a student-run credit union to help meet student financial needs. The credit union has obtained a federal charter which will permit the student-run credit union to accept insured deposits from nonmembers such as corporations.[48]

40. Investing in the Future.

Trinity College in Connecticut matches students with individual corporate scholarship providers. The individual matching gives the corporate sponsor a personal involvement with the campus as well as with the individual student(s) it is sponsoring. The corporate donor also may identify the scholarship recipient as a future employee.[49]

41. Auctioning Desirable Dorm Rooms.

George Washington University holds an auction in the spring where students bid on their choice of dormitory accommodation for the following academic year. The money raised is used for scholarships for students in need of housing aid.[50]

42. A For-Profit Business.

A humane society in Michigan runs a low-priced veterinary service as a for-profit business.[51]

43. Saving Dollars on Publications.

The American Society of Association Executives purchased high tech type-setting equipment to produce its own type for publications and to reduce pro-

---

[46]"Academia's Experts: Professors Are Taking More Consulting Jobs, with College Approval," by Virginia Inman, the *Wall Street Journal*, March 31, 1983.

[47]"Jablow to Resign as Chief of Cultural Alliance," by Carla Hall, the *Washington Post*, March 24, 1983.

[48]"College to Open Credit Union," by John Dougherty, the *Washington Post*, February 21, 1983.

[49]"College Puts Businesses to Work for Students," the *New York Times*, February 20, 1983.

[50]"Auction aims for $15,000 for housing scholarships," the *GW Hatchet*, January 27, 1983.

[51]The *Wall Street Journal*, March 16, 1983.

duction and duplication costs. The society can be a proving ground for high tech as an additional service to its members.[52]

44. Attracting New "Chair" Donors.

Museums are joining universities and hospitals in attracting endowments for salaries of department chairmen and adding the donor's name to the chairmen's titles. The Metropolitan Museum of Art has introduced new titles for endowed chairs in the Departments of American and Primitive Art.[53]

45. Mail Order.

Catalogues are big business. Brown University in Rhode Island offered its alumni a special gift catalogue of items ranging in price from $10 to $10,000.[54]

46. Attracting Corporate Support by Bucking the Tide.

The Nature Conservancy, a nonprofit environmental group founded in 1950, avoids the political and legal activity and corporate animosity that is often associated with environmental organizations. A result of its well-managed, carefully planned and marketed strategy is its success in finding corporate cash and property for its conservation program. The Conservancy enlists individual corporate supporters who take an active part in finding additional corporate support. As federal funding of land acquisition diminishes, the Conservancy has increased its acquisitions through corporate sponsorship.[55]

47. Public Universities' Cooperation on Shared Programming.

The Western Interstate Commission for Higher Education (WICHE) located in Denver is a broker of higher education programs between 13 Rocky Mountain and Pacific states. In 1983, WICHE arranged interstate exchanges for 1,409 students enrolled in 140 graduate and professional programs at 50 universities in the 13 states. This cooperative arrangement allows a medical student from a state without a medical school to attend one in another state, with the home state subsidizing the tuition. In return for the tuition assistance, the student (depending on the state) agrees to return to the home state to work for a specified amount of time or to repay some or all of the tuition assistance. An assistant dean at Colorado State's veterinary college speaks highly of this cooperative plan: "By selling so many seats a year, we can have one really good veterinary medicine program in the region and at less expense than if other states tried to provide the same training."[56]

---

[52]"ASAE Saves Money with New Typesetting Technology," the *Washington Association Executive*, November 9, 1982.

[53]"Endowments for Met Museum," by Grace Glueck, the *New York Times*, March 15, 1983.

[54]"Some Colleges Adopt Money-Making Schemes," the *GW Hatchet*, February 10, 1983.

[55]"Unlikely Alliance: In Distinct Departure, Environmental Group Woos Big Business," by Ken Wells, the *Wall Street Journal*, February 7, 1983.

[56]"Education Agreement in West Lets Colleges, Specialize, Excel," by Eugene Carlson, the *Wall Street Journal*, April 12, 1983.

48. University's Offer of a Public School Supplement.

Fordham University in New York founded the Center School to keep promising students in a declining public school system and to offer both seasoned and student teachers the opportunity to "explore new concepts of teaching."[57] These innovations are shared with the public schools in the area, and the Center School's support comes from the school district, Fordham University, and other private and public funders. The Center School uses volunteers from the community as both teachers and role models for a wide variety of jobs and talents.[58]

49. Surplus Schools.

Nonprofit organizations are obtaining long-term, low-cost leases from communities across the United States, allowing a variety of services to be performed in surplus school buildings. Services include programs for elderly persons, day care, battered women, recreation. These programs are supported by the communities surrounding the surplus school properties. One community is planning to convert a surplus school into housing for elderly people.[59]

50. Libraries and Colleges Combining to Provide Alternative Educational Centers.

Videocassette courses available through the Chicago public library system enable students to finish high school work with a G.E.D., or to take college-level courses in a wide variety of subjects. Credit is available through the City Colleges of Chicago for certain courses and the City Colleges provide the libraries with videocassette equipment. Courses are less expensive than if taken on a campus. An estimated 1,700 people are taking courses through the Chicago libraries each year.[60]

51. Colleges Cooperating to Attract Funding for Student Loans.

Nine colleges and universities located in the District of Columbia have joined forces to provide an alternative student loan program through private underwriting.[61]

52. Historic and Old Property Renovation.

The 1981 tax-law changes allowed additional tax breaks for investors involved in the rehabilitation of historic and old properties. The Torpedo Factory Art Center in Alexandria, Virginia, is an example of an old building rehabilitated by city-backed public bonds and loans and then sold to investors at a higher price

---

[57]"A School to Keep Them in Public School," by Anne M. Mancuso, the *New York Times*, April 24, 1983.
[58]Ibid.
[59]"Fairfax County Plans to Transform Surplus School to House the Elderly," by Wendy Swallow, the *Washington Post*, May 7, 1983.
[60]"Libraries on the Way to Universityhood," by Ronald Gross, the *New York Times*, April 24, 1983.
[61]"Consortium loan program in place, 2nd set for fall," by Terri Sorensen, the *GW Hatchet*, February 10, 1983.

on a lease-back arrangement. The investors will enjoy an additional tax break allowable on the refurbishing of the old building.[62]

53. Publishing Wish Lists.

Lake Forest, Illinois, a Chicago suburb, published a wish list entitled "the Lake Forest Handbook—a Tradition of Excellence through Giving."[63] The "Handbook," distributed to Lake Forest residents, offers donors a variety of inexpensive-to-expensive tax-deductible gifts to provide the community. The Junior League of Colorado Springs, Colorado, is leading that community's drive to improve its parks.[64] The involvement of the private, nonprofit Junior League in improving its public nonprofit community's services for all citizens is an example of cooperation which can benefit both organization and community.

54. Cooperation between a University and Its Town.

Yale University announced the establishment of an endowment to improve the public schools in Yale's community, New Haven, Connecticut. Both Yale and New Haven are pledged to raising money for the endowment and in cooperating on using these funds. The National Endowment for the Humanities provided a grant to launch the cooperative endowment program. The program includes Yale professors giving seminars to middle and high school teachers. The endowment will provide professors' salaries and honoraria to the participating public school teachers.[65]

55. Cooperation between Nonprofit and the Federal Government.

The Department of Housing and Urban Development announced in 1982 a number of contracts to nonprofit associations involved with housing matters to conduct a variety of programs which the government agency would have otherwise had to staff and produce on its own. According to a report in the *Washington Post*, "the idea is to encourage voluntary cooperation, particularly the inexpensive kind."[66]

56. Responding to Women in the Workforce.

The nonprofit Day Care Fund of New York has introduced a Blue-Cross-type plan through which employers can provide day care benefits to employees. The plan responds to soaring demand for day care as more mothers enter the work force.[67]

---

[62]"Financing of Art Center Is Somewhat Convoluted," by Michel Marriott, the *Washington Post*, April 3, 1983.

[63]"Some Cities Print Catalogs to Lure Gifts," by Harlan S. Byrne, the *Wall Street Journal*, September 15, 1982.

[64]Ibid.

[65]"Yale Gets Grant to Help Raise Level of Public Schools," by Irvin Molotsky, the *New York Times*, September 26, 1982.

[66]The *Washington Association Executive*, January 4, 1983.

[67]"NYC employers' latest benefit for working parents: Day care," by Richard Benedetto, *USA TODAY*, June 16, 1983.

LEADERSHIP, THE FUNDAMENTAL FOR PROFITABILITY

Each of these examples indicates the breadth of leadership the nonprofit organization is offering to its community. The successful nonprofit will plan how it can achieve profitability on its own, in cooperation with other nonprofits (both public and private), and in seizing advantages offered it by government regulations and funding. In order to fully realize profitability, the nonprofit must have a firm plan, expert advice on legal and tax matters, strong community contacts, a leadership team willing to take bold action. It must know its strengths, the strengths that are a basis for building leadership in profitability.

CHAPTER 13

Planning for Growth and Prosperity

The 1980s have introduced sweeping changes to a probing, restless America. Technology is creating new jobs while wiping out old ones. The population is on the move from east to west, from north to south. Manufacturing techniques have been found obsolete. International competition for American markets is keen. Job security, even for the government, seems to be a thing of the past.

While many nonprofit organizations have been "the only game in town," the only organization dealing with a specific cause, professional interest, service, this unique position is no longer a guarantee of secure position and community support.

Major urban art museums, once secure in their position as the only museum within hundreds of miles, are now being challenged by suburban and small town museums and nonprofit artist organizations such as the Torpedo Factory in Alexandria, Virginia. The Torpedo Factory, for example, offers a group of working artists in their studios creating the art that can be enjoyed, purchased, and "lived"—all under one roof. While the Torpedo Factory will not draw tourists away from the nearby world-famous National Gallery in Washington, D.C., it will compete effectively for local support and local loyalties. Urban art museums in cities that are not major tourist attractions will find that competition from new collections and new approaches to art will be formidable.

Labor unions, professional associations, and trade associations are finding their once-secure uniqueness challenged by changing jobs, changing interests, changing priorities, and a demand for member participation.

DEMOGRAPHICS: OPPORTUNITY FOR GROWTH

Nonprofits are not resting on their laurels. Many have become alert to demographic changes and are realizing the benefits these changes offer them. The nonprofit Joffrey Ballet moved to Los Angeles where it established a new "home base" for six months of the year, maintaining its old base in New York for the other six months. In making this move, the Joffrey has captured a new audience, a new support base, a means of growing and prospering by meeting the needs of a second home town.

The National Geographic Society responded to demographics by introducing a new edition of its magazine *National Geographic* for a highly selective market, readers in 36 wealthy metropolitan areas. These readers represent a higher average income than the readers of the major edition of the magazine, and lower advertising rates are an added inducement to advertisers for the new edition. The Society plans to introduce other editions of its magazine aimed at specific demographic groups.[1]

Demographic changes are producing a variety of responses from nonprofits. Many nonprofits, because of property and investments, will not be able to establish "second homes" or to tailor publications to more affluent customers. Many will fight it out on their home fronts. The Cultural Assistance Center of New York City published a report[2] that "makes it clear that any marked falling-off in the quality of New York's cultural institutions would have a catastrophic effect upon the economy of the city."[3]

The report found that "the arts have a $5.6 billion impact on the New York City and New York-New Jersey metropolitan economy, and that more than $2 billion in personal income and over 117,000 jobs are generated by the arts in the metropolitan area."[4]

John Russell, writing in the *New York Times*, used the report to argue against threatened removal of property tax exemption for museums because these institutions do not seem to fit the New York State property-tax law exemption for "educational institutions." Mr. Russell, specifically addressing the New York law, but speaking for the tax-exempt status of museums and other cultural and historical organizations throughout the country which either are, or may be, facing similar situations as jurisdictions search for tax revenues, said: "The truth about the tax-exempt status of museums is not that they rob the economy of its rightful dues in the interests of a privileged few. It is that they generate both income and employment for the city as a whole. By any rational accounting, they bring in more than they take out. It can also be said of the 'arts industry' that unlike so many other forms of industry it has become progressively more buoyant, more inventive and more highly prized during the period since World War II."[5]

FIGHTING BACK

The passive nonprofit is not going to retain community leadership. Fighting back can be best accomplished by facts such as those found in the Cultural Assistance Center's report and by important allies such as Mr. Russell. The City of Boston is fighting back. It is fighting the demographic battle by attracting new high tech industries as well as by supporting existing employers.

[1]"Geographic's Troubled World," by Philip Shenon, the *New York Times*, December 19, 1982.
[2]"Should Museums Be Exempt from Taxes?", by John Russell, the *New York Times*, March 20, 1983.
[3]Ibid.
[4]Ibid.
[5]Ibid.

The Boston Redevelopment Authority found that "service employment is expanding by about 7% a year in Greater Boston, compared with 1.8% nationally."[6] Two particularly important nonprofit employers in the Boston area are the health industry and universities. "The health industry provides more jobs than any other industry and is projected to account for about 20% of the job growth through the 1980s," while "area universities provide 90,000 jobs for people who serve 250,000 students."[7] These universities "also spawn new businesses and themselves bring in money. For example, the Pentagon's naval research detachment is overseeing 1,100 contracts valued at $150 million for basic research at area colleges."[8]

Boston's nonprofits are fighting back with facts and seeking growth and prosperity through the federal government's current big spender, the Department of Defense.

Demographics are providing growth opportunities for associations that represent senior citizens as the population ages.[9] Trade associations of electronics and computer firms are also strong.[10]

Alertness to the opportunities offered by demographic changes is important to the nonprofit. The *Wall Street Journal* reported that a 1983 follow-up to the 1980 Census found that the nation's population had increased by 2.9% in the time interval, while areas of Texas, Florida, California, Nevada, Colorado, Utah, and Wyoming were experiencing growth rates at 7%.[11]

CONSUMERS CHANGING WITH DEMOGRAPHICS

Along with the changes in demographics are the changes in the American people. "The marketplace of 1990 won't be dominated by the middle-class, family-oriented 'belongers' who are mostly motivated by their desire to fit in with their peers. Instead, the most influential group is likely to be the 'inner-directed' consumers who are more self-reliant and less status-conscious. This new mass market, however, will be tougher than 'belongers' for marketers to reach. The 'inner-directed' group wants high-quality products, exhibits less brand loyalty and is more willing to experiment."[12] This forecast, reported in the *Wall Street Journal*, is directed at manufacturers and producers of consumer products. It has direct bearing, however, on the nonprofit's approach to its publics. For if the public is changing as dramatically as this report indicates, the nonprofit organization will have to redirect its services and community relations programs to meet the expectations of the new consumer.

[6]"High-Tech, Service Businesses Keep Boston Economy Robust," by Johnnie L. Roberts, the *Wall Street Journal*, January 11, 1983.
[7]Ibid.
[8]Ibid.
[9]"Trade Associations Are Shrinking with Economy," by Sandra Evans Teeley, the *Washington Post*, January 31, 1983.
[10]Ibid.
[11]"Parking Violators . . . Changes in Population . . . State Worries," by Eugene Carlson, the *Wall Street Journal*, June 14, 1983.
[12]" 'Inner-Directed' Consumers . . . Pay-TV Ads . . . Erasable Pens," the *Wall Street Journal*, May 5, 1983.

Public response to major issues in the United States is already producing new consumers. An example is the growing awareness of toxic wastes and the response to this waste and its disposal. The *Wall Street Journal* reports that this is "creating a new grass-roots environmental movement. People in many of these protest groups belonged to the so-called silent majority during the 1960s and 1970s. They are farmers, blue-collar workers and small-business owners whose civic involvement used to start and stop at the voting booth. Now they tote picket signs, write letters to congressmen and make speeches for the first time in their lives."[13]

An awareness of issues, a mistrust of "big" government and "big" business, offers new opportunities for the nonprofit. The protection of animal movement in the United States is demonstrating that it offers active leadership in fighting cruelty to animals. Some recent actions of animal welfare advocates included the investigation of a laboratory using research monkeys and a challenge to a corporation that imports goose liver pâté. The Humane Society of America bought stock and appeared before a stockholders' meeting of the corporation to testify against the importation of the pâté because of the cruelty to pâté geese. Raising these issues publically has increased public awareness of the animal welfare movement and gives new vigor to the movement. According to the *Washington Post*, the Humane Society has 200,000 members and seven regional offices with an additional 1,500 independent humane societies throughout the country.[14]

Another way of being a leader is by responding to consumer concerns. The American Automobile Association introduced a program to teach kindergarten through third grade students about the perils of drunk driving.[15] The Association's leadership in producing this program coincides with the rising consumer/public concern evidenced by the vigorous growth of organizations like Mothers Against Drunk Driving (MADD) and Students Against Drunk Driving (SADD).

REFLECTIONS ON EXCELLENCE

The achievement of excellence is a goal of the 1980s nonprofit manager. An informed and intelligent use of professional management techniques is integral to this goal. Both outdated techniques and outmoded shibboleths must be discarded. Public relations based on press releases is replaced by professional community relations research, planning, and programming. The concept that an elite organization is not contributing to the public is replaced by a factual and accountable realization of the direct and indirect contributions of the organization to its community.

America is a land of contradictions. Great wealth and poverty . . . concern and apathy . . . new immigrants posing health and welfare problems on the one hand while offering strong family unity and a quest for accomplishment on the

[13]"Amateur Ecologists: Local Citizen Groups Take a Growing Role Fighting Toxic Dumps," by Ronald Alsop, the *Wall Street Journal*, April 18, 1983.
[14]"Humane Society Raises Unappetizing Questions About Pâté," by Johanna Steinmetz, the *Washington Post*, May 11, 1983.
[15]"AAA Program Teaches Youngsters Perils of Drunken Driving," the *Washington Association Executive*, November 23, 1982.

other . . . the growing realization that "hand outs" need to be replaced by incentives and "hands up," not only to foster individual development and dignity but also to benefit the economics of society.

Universities are responding to reduced incoming freshmen classes by reducing class sizes to insure that standards will not be lowered to attract more students; by recruiting out-of-work adults as students, by offering restructured short courses for senior citizens and other target populations.

Hospitals are responding to high health care costs and reduced patient loads by opening unused facilities to hospice and nursing care providers.

Professional associations are responding to a difficult job market by improving career planning, by offering job banks and networks of potential employers.

Trade associations are developing new markets and new incentives for their members.

Museums are responding to demands for public service by cooperating with local governments in providing low-cost public transportation access, by cooperative programs with schools and institutions, by providing new outlets for cultural programs through films and television.

The nonprofit is not alone. Governments, at all levels, depend on nonprofits for urgent services and information. These governments are supporting nonprofits through legislation, tax exemptions, grants and contracts. Additional support is being found through sharing government property and personnel.

(And more support is on the way through funds available through new legislation such as the 1983 Jobs Training and Partnership Act.)

Corporations are also supportive of the nonprofit, and this support will grow as corporate earnings improve. Firms like Control Data Corporation of Minnesota provide their own innovative social and economic development programs.

Foundations are showing bold leadership by awarding no-strings-attached stipends to promote scholarly activity and to fund research in pressing problem areas.

The executive director of the National Neurofibromatosis Foundation commented on the nonprofit in the 1980s in an editorial in the Foundation's newsletter:

> The 1980s may well become a decade of collaboration. I can clearly envision many nonprofits combining resources (both human and financial) to keep pace with the changing times and with growth . . . the challenges we face in the nonprofit world, in the profit world and in all other segments of society are not very different from each other.[16]

The nonprofit manager is meeting the 1980s. The success of this meeting will be enhanced by the use of professional management in community and public relations. The nation looks to the nonprofit for excellence and leadership. The 1980s nonprofit manager will insure that both are there.

---

[16]The National Neurofibromatosis Foundation, Inc, *Newsletter*, Volume 5, No. 3, fall 1982.

Appendix: Nonprofits as Resources

NONPROFITS OFFER RICH RESOURCES

Nonprofit organizations themselves are frequently rich resources. The following sample of nonprofit organizations is an indication of the depth and breadth of expertise available through nonprofit organizations.

Nonprofit leadership is not limited to the organizations listed here. There are nonprofit resources in member development, fundraising, programming available in every community. New ideas abound in the nonprofit world, and the skillful manager is abreast of these ideas and uses them to build for a future of growth and prosperity.

THE ADVERTISING COUNCIL INC
825 Third Avenue
New York NY 10022

This nonprofit organization represents the world of commercial advertising and draws on the talents of this world to assist nonprofit and government organizations in national public service campaigns. The Council handles both the creation and distribution of public service campaigns. It has specific criteria for eligibility and primarily services large and affluent nonprofits. While its services are beyond the reach of most nonprofits, its generic campaigns offer tie-in possibilities for nonprofits with allied interests.

Publications: *Public Service Advertising Bulletin*

Offices: New York NY; Washington DC; Los Angeles CA.

AMERICAN ASSOCIATION OF FUND-RAISING COUNSEL INC
25 West 43rd Street
New York NY 10036

Members of this Association are firms which are exclusively or primarily organized to provide fundraising counseling services, feasibility studies, campaign management, and related public relations, to nonprofit institutions and agencies seeking philanthropic support.

AMERICAN ASSOCIATION OF MUSEUMS
1055 Thomas Jefferson Street NW
Washington DC 20007

A professional association of people affiliated with museums. The Association has a public relations committee, meetings and publications.

AMERICAN ASSOCIATION FOR PUBLIC OPINION RESEARCH
PO Box 17
Princeton NJ 08540

The Association is a professional society of individuals engaged in public opinion and social research. Its membership includes persons from every sector of the research community—those who work in academic institutions, in commercial organizations, or in other profit-making or nonprofit organizations.

Publications: An annual listing of organizations represented in its membership which is a source of agencies involved in various types of survey research for potential clients.

AMERICAN INSTITUTE OF GRAPHIC ARTS
1059 Third Avenue
New York NY 10021

The Institute is a national organization of graphic design and graphic arts professionals. The Institute answers hundreds of requests for information and references related to graphic design. Publications: a national list of graphic design organizations; an international list of periodicals related to graphic design; "Graphic Design for Non-Profit Organizations," a manual designed to help institutions improve their communications and minimize expenditures without sacrificing diversity.

AMERICAN SOCIETY OF ASSOCIATION EXECUTIVES
1575 Eye Street NW
Washington DC 20005

A professional association of executives and staff specialists on nonprofit voluntary membership organizations such as trade associations, professional societies, civic, fraternal, and philanthropic organizations and foundations. Offerings include professional development and education, professional certification, contacts, government affairs, awards, program evaluation and job referral services. Meetings.

Publications: *Association Management Magazine.* Many other books, cassette tapes, publications.

AMERICAN SOCIETY FOR HOSPITAL PUBLIC RELATIONS of the
AMERICAN HOSPITAL ASSOCIATION
840 North Lake Shore Drive
Chicago IL 60611

A personal membership society affiliated with the American Hospital Association. Members encompass a broad spectrum of hospital public relations practitioners—from beginner to seasoned professional. Goals include: educational programs at both national and regional levels; exchange of ideas, information and expertise among members; information on critical issues; professional standards.

Publications: *Hospital Public Relations* newsletter.

CHAMBER OF COMMERCE OF THE UNITED STATES
1615 H Street NW
Washington DC 20062

The Chamber's Center for Leadership Development conducts the Institutes for Organization Management, a comprehensive continuing education program designed for association and other voluntary organization executives. The Institutes offer a six-year sequential program consisting of one full week of study per year. Institutes are held at a variety of universities throughout the United States at different times each year.

COMMON CAUSE
2030 M Street NW
Washington DC 20036

An organization encouraging responsible government. Publication: *Citizen's Action Guide* offers tips on government relations.

COUNCIL FOR THE ADVANCEMENT AND SUPPORT OF EDUCATION
Suite 400, 11 DuPont Circle NW
Washington DC 20036

Offers seminars and training programs in locations throughout the United States on staff productivity, publications, fundraising, alumni and community development. Publications: *CASE Currents, CASE Creative Communications Newsletter*.

THE FOUNDATION CENTER
888 Seventh Avenue
New York NY 10019

The Foundation Center is a national service organization supported primarily by foundations. It provides a single authoritative source of factual information on philanthropic giving and helps in finding out where to apply most appropriately for funding. Publications: varied. National Libraries: New York and Washington DC. Field Offices: San Francisco, CA and Cleveland OH.

THE GRANTSMANSHIP CENTER
1031 South Grand Avenue
Los Angeles CA 90015

The Center describes itself as the "nonprofit world's largest training institution." Founded in 1972, the Center has trained more than 18,000 staff of
public and private agencies in grantsmanship, program management, and
fundraising. The Center offers a variety of training programs and seminars
in locations throughout the country. Publications: *The Grantsmanship Center
News*.

INDEPENDENT SECTOR
1828 L Street NW
Washington DC 20036

A nonprofit organization created to preserve and enhance the national tradition of giving, volunteering, and not-for-profit initiative. Voting members
are organizations with national interests and impact in philanthropy, voluntary action and other activity related to the independent pursuit of the
educational, scientific, health, welfare, cultural and religious life of the nation. Specific program areas cover public education, communication within
the nonprofit sector, research, encouragement of effective nonprofit operation and management, government relations, and increasing giving and volunteering to nonprofits. Publications: subjects include research findings,
lobbying, fundraising through tax provisions, volunteering and giving
studies.

INTERNATIONAL ASSOCIATION OF BUSINESS COMMUNICATORS
870 Market Street, Suite 940
San Francisco CA 94102

An association of for-profit, nonprofit and government public relations
professionals. Chapters throughout the U.S., Canada, United Kingdom and
the Phillippines with members in 41 other countries. Member services include: publications; a member directory; research; a bank of resources on
communications ideas and problems; seminars; awards; a jobline; professional accreditation; and an annual conference.

NATIONAL ASSOCIATION OF GOVERNMENT COMMUNICATORS
80 South Early Street
Alexandria VA 22304

A nonprofit association dedicated to the advancement of communicators as
an essential professional resource at every level of national, state and local
government. Publications: newsletter. Annual training conference.

NATIONAL SOCIETY OF FUND RAISING EXECUTIVES
1511 K Street NW
Washington DC 20005

A professional organization of fund raising executives operating a strong, local chapter framework where persons of a variety of fund raising backgrounds meet together monthly in the interests of the professional. Services to members include: annual conference; professional certification; legislative and program information; training programs; job information. Publications: *NSFRE NEWS, NSFRE Journal, Sightlines, Legislative Alerts.*

PUBLIC RELATIONS SOCIETY OF AMERICA
845 Third Avenue
New York NY 10022

A professional organization of public relations professionals from the for-profit, nonprofit and government sectors. The Society has special sections concerned with social services, health and education. Chapters are located throughout the U.S. and the local chapters provide public service to non-profit organizations through public service councils. Member services include professional accreditation and job information. Publications: *Public Relations Journal,* many others. Training programs are provided through:

> The New York University/Public Relations Society of America Program
> THE NEW YORK UNIVERSITY
> School of Continuing Education
> Business and Management Programs, Room 1412
> 310 Madison Avenue
> New York NY 10017

> This program offers seminars and workshops in locations throughout the U.S. on subjects including financial management, employee/internal communications, public relations and public affairs planning and management, advertising, market research, writing, editing, and media relations.

THE PROFESSIONAL DEVELOPMENT INSTITUTE
University College
PACE UNIVERSITY
331 Madison Avenue, Room 603
New York NY 10017

This program offers seminars throughout the country on subjects including: planning and managing government public affairs and public information programs; speech writing; computers in public relations; financial management; internal publications layout and design; issues management; newsletter writing and production; marketing strategies and publicity techniques. Publication: *Public Relations Resources.*

UNITED WAY OF AMERICA
United Way Plaza
Alexandria VA 22314

A nonprofit membership association which provides fund-raising, budgeting, management, planning and allocations and communications support to members on the national, regional and local levels. Produces a wide variety of films and publications and training materials. Administers staff and volunteer leadership development training through the National Academy for Voluntarism.

VOLUNTEER: The National Center for Citizen Involvement
1111 North 19th Street, Suite 500
Arlington VA 22209

A national nonprofit organization promoting voluntary activity through a network of Voluntary Action Centers and Volunteer Bureaus. Engages in research and training and publishes a variety of materials. Holds an annual conference on developing strategies, techniques and skills in recruiting and maintaining volunteers. Figure A–1 shows the schedule of the 1983 National Conference of VOLUNTEER, indicating the wealth of information nonprofits offer each year.

The 1983 National Conference on
Citizen Involvement

Creative
Involvement for
Productive
Communities

June 26-30, 1983

Stanford University
Palo Alto,
California

sponsored by:

VOLUNTEER:
The National
Center for
Citizen Involvement

FIGURE A–1.   Reprinted with permission of VOLUNTEER: The National
Center for Citizen Involvement, 1111 North Nineteenth Street,
Suite 500, Arlington, Virginia 22209. The heart logo is the
registered trademark of VOLUNTEER.

CONFERENCE SCHEDULE

Sunday, June 26

10:00 am–6:00 pm   REGISTRATION

2:00–5:00 pm   NATIONAL VAC MEETING

5:00–6:30 pm   DINNER

7:00–8:30 pm   PLENARY:
HAZEL HENDERSON
"Creative Involvement for Productive Communities: Shaping the Future"

8:30–10:00 pm   GET ACQUAINTED RECEPTION

Monday, June 27

7:00–8:30 am   BREAKFAST

8:00–9:00 am   REGISTRATION

8:30–10:00 am   PLENARY:
PETER E. HAAS
"Creative Corporate Involvement"

10:30 am–NOON   WORKSHOP SESSION I
a. Creative Resource Raising from Corporations
b. Getting the Most Out of Being a Volunteer
c. Personal Public Relations: Tooting Your Horn with Class
d. Effective Recruitment of Volunteers
e. Getting VAC Funding from United Way
f. Perspectives on International Volunteering
g. Creating Community Partnerships
h. Volunteers for State Government: Loaned Executive Programs
i. Meet the Speaker

NOON–1:30 pm   LUNCH
Program Profile Roundtables

1:30–3:00 pm   PLENARY:
JOHN McKNIGHT
"Citizen Action in a Professional World"

3:30–5:00 pm   WORKSHOP SESSION II
a. Corporate Retiree Involvement Programs
b. Preventing Volunteer Burnout
c. Utilizing Cable TV
d. Dealing with Staff Resistance to Volunteers
e. Impact of Computers on VAC Operations
f. Community Organizing
g. Working with Youth Volunteers
h. Volunteer Programs for Local Government
i. Meet the Speaker

5:00–6:30 pm   DINNER

7:00–8:30 pm   SPECIAL GROUP MEETINGS

Tuesday, June 28

7:00–8:30 am   BREAKFAST

8:00–9:00 am   REGISTRATION

8:30–10:00 am   WORKSHOP SESSION III
a. Creating Recruitment Networks Inside Corporations
b. Legal Liability of Volunteer Programs
c. Transitioning from Volunteering to Paid Work
d. Screening and Interviewing Volunteers
e. Charging Fees for VAC Services
f. Recruiting the Young Professional
g. Working with Senior Volunteers
h. Setting Up a Volunteer Skillsbank
i. Proposal Writing from the Funders' Viewpoint

10:30 am–NOON   WORKSHOP SESSION IV
a. Setting Up a Corporate Volunteer Skillsbank
b. Volunteers in the Arts and Humanities
c. Sources of Technical Assistance
d. How to Fire a Volunteer
e. Recruiting Families as Volunteers
f. Church/Labor Partnerships
g. Alternate Sentencing Programs
h. How to Run a Special Event
i. Fundraising for People Who Hate Fundraising

NOON–1:30 pm   LUNCH
Program Profile Roundtables

1:30–3:00 pm   PLENARY:
EVA SCHINDLER-RAINMAN
"The Multi-Cultural Volunteer Community: Working with Diversity"

3:30–5:00 pm   WORKSHOP SESSION V
a. Models for VAC/Corporate Partnerships
b. Insurance for Volunteer Programs
c. Accounting for Non-Accountants
d. Effective Recruitment of Volunteers
e. Improving Board/Staff Relations
f. Volunteer Legislation in the 98th Congress
g. The Handicapped as Volunteers
h. Introduction to Community Computers
i. Meet the Speaker

5:00–6:30 pm   DINNER

7:00–11:00 pm   SAN FRANCISCO BY NIGHT (Optional Tour)

7:30–10:00 pm   FILM FESTIVAL

FIGURE A–1 *(continued).*

7:00–8:30 am   BREAKFAST

8:00–9:00 am   REGISTRATION

8:30–10:00am   WORKSHOP SESSION VI
a. How to Tap Organized Labor
b. Calculating the True Value of Volunteer Time
c. Ethics in Volunteer Administration
d. Dealing with Agency Resistance to Volunteers
e. Legal Liability of Volunteer Board Members
f. The Federal Government and Volunteering
g. Fund Raising from Churches
h. Volunteers for State Government: The Minnesota Project
i. Proposal Writing from the Funders' Viewpoint

10:30–NOON   PLENARY:

WALTER DAVIS
"Building the Volunteer/Labor Partnership"

NOON–1:30 pm   LUNCH
Program Profile Roundtables

1:30–3:00 pm   WORKSHOP SESSION VII

a. Linking Employee Involvement and Corporate Contributions
b. Designing Programs to Train Volunteers
c. Conflict Management
d. Designing Volunteer Jobs for Results
e. How VACs Can Be Leaders in the Community
f. The Shape of Things to Come
g. Planning
h. How Small Nonprofits Can Run Businesses
i. Meet the Speaker

3:30–5:00 pm   WORKSHOP SESSION VIII
a. Management and Technical Assistance from Corporations
b. How to Be a Consultant
c. Communication Skills
d. Designing Volunteer Jobs for Results
e. VAC/Agency Relationships
f. Volunteering and Unemployment
g. Volunteers in Educational Settings
h. Improving Volunteer/Union Relations
i. Hard-Core Fundraising

5:30–6:30 pm   RECEPTION

6:30–8:00 pm   BARBEQUE

7:00–8:30 am   BREAKFAST

9:00am–NOON   WORKSHOP SESSION IX
a. Time Management
b. How to Be a Leader
c. Community-Based Fundraising

d. Marketing
e. Creativity
f. Using the Media
g. Stress Management

NOON–1:30 pm   CLOSING LUNCH

The 1983 National Conference on Citizen Involvement is designed for you!

FIGURE A–1 (continued).

PUBLICATIONS

In addition to the publications of the nonprofit organizations listed above, the nonprofit manager has a wealth of other nonprofit and for-profit organizations to turn to for information and ideas. The value of these publications depends on the nature of the nonprofit and the needs and interests of the manager. A sampling of useful publications include the following:

ASSOCIATION TRENDS
7204 Clarendon Road
Bethesda MD 20814

A national weekly newspaper for association executives.

CHARITABLE GIFT PLANNING NEWS
c/o Associate Editor, Suite 308
901 Battery Street
San Francisco CA 94111

Monthly newsletter focusing on donations and taxes.

FOUNDATION NEWS
1828 L Street NW
Washington DC 20036

A bimonthly magazine published by the Council on Foundations, Inc. Monitors the nonprofit world and philanthropy.

LRC-W NEWSBRIEFS
Dupont Circle Building, Suite 823
1346 Connecticut Avenue NW
Washington DC 20036

Monthly newsletter published by the Lutheran Resources Commission on available grants, government funding and regulations, programs, legislation, and ideas of critical interest to nonprofits.

PR CASEBOOK
PO Box 431
Cohasset MA 02025

Monthly publication of highlights of selected public relations programs.

RAGAN REPORT
407 South Dearborn
Chicago IL 60605

Weekly newsletter for writers and editors.

US ASSOCIATION EXECUTIVE
2607-24th Street NW
Washington DC 20008

Bi-monthly publication focusing on news and programs concerning nonprofit trade and professional associations.

SELECTED SERVICES

Community and Public Relations Counseling.

RUFFNER ASSOCIATES
2306 King Street
Alexandria VA 22301

Seminars on planning and producing effective nonprofit community and public relations programs.

Cultural Programs Guides.

Theatre Development Fund
1501 Broadway
New York NY 10036

Publication: SOLD OUT, publicity and marketing guide for cultural groups in New York area.

Greater Philadelphia Cultural Alliance
1718 Locust Street
Philadelphia PA 19103

Publication: FOR IMMEDIATE RELEASE, a publicity guide for Philadelphia area cultural organizations.

Local Resources.

Major cities throughout the country offer a wealth of local resources for nonprofit organizations. In addition to the local chapters of organizations such as the Public Relations Society of America, Women in Communications, and the International Association of Business Communicators, many United Way offices produce media lists and other valuable information for nonprofits. "Publicity Clubs," associations of public relations professionals offering workshops and seminars, are located in New York City, San Diego, San Francisco, Los Angeles, Boston, and Chicago.

The Washington (D.C.) Council of Agencies represents the trend of nonprofits to join together for support and success. The Council's member organizations are 501 (c) (3) organizations located in the Washington D.C. metropolitan area. Through the Council, nonprofits can take advantage of multiple management, collective buying power and influence. The Council's services include health, dental and life insurance; tax-deferred retirement plan; casualty and liability insurance; computer service; nonprofit list rental; mailing service; phone answering, message and maildrop services; bookkeeping and computerized accounting; space sharing; furniture and equipment rental; office supply discounts; printing, typesetting and graphic services; training in management, communications and leadership; and advocacy in both the public and private sectors.

In an editorial in the *Washington Post*,[1] the collaboration of nonprofits was firmly applauded:

---

[1]*The Washington Post*, Saturday, November 19, 1983.

. . . this cooperative concept, while only recently catching on among nonprofit organizations, is not new; governments in the region are sharing resources and uniting to address all sorts of issues . . .

Absent some new generosity on the part of the federal government, the council's focus—on getting more bang for the philanthropic buck—is the most sensible, constructive response.

Washington Council of Agencies
1309 L Street NW
Washington DC 20005

Media Analysis.

The three national firms listed here provide media analysis (press clippings, television and radio monitoring). In addition, these firms provide up-dated mailing lists, mailing labels, directories of media contacts:

BACON'S PR AND MEDIA INFORMATION SYSTEMS
332 South Michigan Avenue
Chicago IL 60604

BURELLE'S PRESS SERVICES
75 East Northfield Avenue
Livingston NJ 07039

LUCE PRESS SERVICES
420 Lexington Avenue
New York NY 10017

Meetings/Conventions.

CUSTOM NEWS INC.
2607 - 24th Street NW
Washington DC 20008

Publisher of custom newspapers for large meetings and conventions. The papers are tailored to the event and available at the time of the event.

Public Service Advertising.

DOUG WYLES PRODUCTIONS INC.
49 West 76th Street
New York NY 10023

Experienced producers and distributors of television public service materials and campaigns. Publishes *PSA/the Magazine of Public Service Advertising.*

NORTH AMERICAN PRECIS SYNDICATE INC.
201 East 42nd Street
New York NY 10017

A major producer and distributor of information releases, columns and art-work to newspapers throughout the country. Produces and distributes scripts for radio and television. Publications: many on generating publicity and media attention.

PLANNED COMMUNICATION SERVICES INC.
12 East 46th Street
New York NY 10017

A leading producer-distributor of public service television (film and video-tape) and radio (tape and record) announcements. An innovative and award-winning firm with many nonprofit clients. Publication: *Public Service Communicator*.

PROFESSIONAL MEDIA SERVICES INC.
41 Varick Hill Road
Waban MA 02168

A production house specializing in public service campaigns for nonprofit organizations.

PUBLIC INTEREST ADVERTISING
935 Park Avenue
New York NY 10028

Specialists in print and television campaign creation and production for non-profits. No distribution.

PUBLIC RELATIONS AIDS INC.
330 West 34th Street
New York NY 10001

Computerized media production service with offices in cities across the country. Publication: *Publicist,* a bi-monthly.

Telemarketing.

TELEMARKETING ASSOCIATES INC.
1629 K Street NW, Suite 520
Washington DC 20006

Telephone marketing firm with experience at the national, regional, state, and local levels. Has nonprofit clients.

Index